CONFESSIONAL LUTHERAN DOGMATICS

John R. Stephenson, Editor
John A. Maxfield, Assistant Editor

XI

BAPTISM

by

David P. Scaer

Published by
The Luther Academy
Ft. Wayne, Indiana

Jennifer H. Maxfield, Technical Editor

©1999 by The Luther Academy, 6600 North Clinton St., Ft. Wayne, IN 46825
Luther Academy books are available through www.logia.org.

All rights reserved. Except where cited for the purposes of review, no part of this publication may be reproduced, stored in a retrieval system, or transmitted in any form or by any means, electronic, mechanical, photocopying, recording, or otherwise, without the prior permission of The Luther Academy.

Biblical references, except where noted, are from the Revised Standard Version of the Bible, copyrighted 1946, 1952 © 1971, 1973. Used by permission. Quotations from *The Book of Concord*, trans. and ed. Theodore G. Tappert, are used by permission of Augsburg Fortress Press. Quotations from *Luther's Works: The American Edition* are used by permission of Concordia Publishing House and Augsburg Fortress Press.

Library of Congress Catalog Number: 89-84112

ISBN: 978-0-9622791-2-6 (Volume XI, hardcover)
    978-1-935035-48-0 (Volume XI, paperback)
    978-0-9622791-0-2 (13-Volume Set)

Published in the United States of America

To those children who have been removed deliberately from the temples of their mothers' bodies. Deprived of the birth below, they are deprived of the sacrament of the birth from above. May the God who calls all children to His Son by Baptism continue graciously to take these holy innocents into His arms, ". . . for of such is the kingdom of the heavens."

CONTENTS

Preface to the General Introduction vii
General Introduction viii
Preface xi
Abbreviations xiii

Introduction: Baptism as the Foundational Sacrament 1
1. Baptism as the Remedy for Original Sin 5
2. Baptism as Divine Command 24
3. The Biblical Origins of Baptism 30
4. The Efficacy of Baptism 41
   Excursus: Ministry: An Effect of Baptism? 68
5. The Baptismal Formula: Baptism in the
   Name of the Triune God 74
6. Administration of Baptism 91
7. Baptism and the Holy Spirit 102
   Excursus: Living Water: Water and the Spirit 116
   Excursus: A Case in Pastoral Practice 119
8. Infant Baptism: An Historical Debate with
   Theological Implications 124
9. The Biblical Support for Infant Baptism 135
10. Infant Faith 147
11. Baptism's Necessity and Its Exceptions 157
12. Karl Barth on Baptism 167
13. The Ritual of Baptism 181
14. Baptism and Catechesis 194
Conclusion 200

Bibliography 203
Indices 211

PREFACE TO THE GENERAL INTRODUCTION
by Daniel Preus, President
The Luther Academy

The present volume entitled *Baptism* is the fourth to be published in the Confessional Lutheran Dogmatics series. The need for a contemporary Lutheran dogmatics has been aptly described in the General Introduction by my father, Robert Preus, who was the moving spirit behind the entire project and the General Editor for the first three volumes. Dr. Preus' death in early November 1995 and the passage of ten years from the time he wrote these observations have not in the least diminished their relevance to our present circumstances. The need for such treatises, addressing the primary articles of faith on the basis of the theology of the Lutheran Confessions, has never been more compelling than it is today. The Luther Academy, which publishes Confessional Lutheran Dogmatics, is therefore committed to completing the entire series.

A new General Editor in the person of Dr. John Stephenson has been chosen to take Dr. Preus's place. The Rev. John Maxfield meanwhile succeeds Dr. Stephenson as Assistant Editor. We are confident that under their supervision the forthcoming volumes not only will continue to find their source and foundation in Scripture and to present a thoroughly confessional point of view, but will also edify and strengthen those who read them as they faithfully address the never-ending needs of the church militant.

I welcome the issue of this treatment of the locus *De Baptismo* by a senior theologian and respected dogmatician in our circles who was closely associated with my late father for many years.

GENERAL INTRODUCTION
by
Robert D. Preus, General Editor, 1984–95
Confessional Lutheran Dogmatics

For some time now those of us in the Lutheran church who have interested ourselves in the Lutheran Confessions, taught from them, and conducted research in these great symbolic writings have recognized the need for a dogmatics resource based upon the outline and thought pattern of the Lutheran Confessions. Such a resource, heretofore available only in Leonard Hutter's little *Compendium Locorum Theologicorum*, would address theologians of our day with a truly confessional answer to the theological issues we are facing in Christianity and in our Lutheran Zion today. We were in no way interested in replacing as a textbook in our Lutheran Church—Missouri Synod Francis Pieper's monumental *Christian Dogmatics*, which has served students in our church body and others for three generations. Such an endeavor would have been unnecessary and unproductive. The authors of the various monographs in this Confessional Lutheran Dogmatics series come at their respective subjects from somewhat different vantage points and backgrounds and personal predilections as they practice dogmatics. It was decided, therefore, to issue a series of dogmatics treatises on the primary articles of faith usually taken up in traditional dogmatics since the sixteenth century—the Augsburg Confession, Philipp Melanchthon's *Loci communes*, and Martin Chemnitz's *Loci theologici*, for example.

But why the approach from the Lutheran Confessions? Are not these musty old creeds and symbols irrelevant to our day, and would not a series of monographs written from the point of view of confessional Lutheran theology be equally irrelevant to the theological issues presently confronting the church? It is because we must respond to such a question with an emphatic "no" that we presume to issue the forthcoming volumes. The Confessions, whose theology is taken directly from the Scriptures, are indeed relevant to our day, just as are the Scriptures themselves which are always "profitable for doctrine, for reproof, for correction, for instruction in righteousness" (2 Tm 3:16). There has been a real call and need for just the kind of dogmatics series here proposed, that is, a confessional Lutheran dogmatics. First of all, no dogmatics book of any kind has been published by orthodox confessional Lutheran theologians (along the lines of Elert, Pieper, Hoenecke, and Hove) within the last generation. During the same time, however, there has been a renewed interest in the Lutheran Confessions, in their function in giving form to our Lutheran presentation of doctrine, and to some extent even in norming that doctrine: note the excellent studies of Edmund Schlink, Holsten Fagerberg, Leif Grane, Peter Brunner, Wilhelm Maurer, Friedrich Mildenberger, Hermann Sasse, and others as well as the many recent books and studies written in connection with anniversary observances of the Book of Concord, the Augsburg Confession, etc. Thus, it would appear that there is need not only for a dogmatics resource in our day, but one that is strictly and consciously confessional in its presentation of doctrine and its assessment and analysis of modern theological trends throughout the Christian church. This series, of which the present volume is a part, is written to fill this need, and it is the hope and prayer of the editors that the present volume will to some extent accomplish this aim.

The volumes making up Confessional Lutheran Dogmatics are not a theology of the Lutheran Confessions; they are rather a series in dogmatics. They differ from other dogmatics books in that they are patterned strictly after the theology of the Book of Concord as they address the issues of today. They follow not only the theology of the Book of Concord, as the texts of Francis Pieper and Adolf Hoenecke and other confessional Lutheran dogmaticians have done, but, unlike these dogmaticians, the authors of the present volumes follow the actual pattern of thought (*forma et quasi typus*, ὑποτύπωσις) of the Lutheran Confessions. Such a procedure is according to the principle of the Confessions themselves; creeds and confessions are indeed a pattern and norm according to which all other books and writings are to be accepted and judged.[1] This fact will account for the agreement in both doctrine and formulation that the reader will observe within the present entire dogmatics series; the authors bind themselves not only generally to the theology of the Book of Concord, but to its content and terminology (*rebus et phrasibus*).[2]

There is another reason for the doctrinal agreement which will be apparent among the authors of the Confessional Lutheran Dogmatics. It is this: all the authors share the concept of doctrine, unity of doctrine, consensus in doctrine, and purity of doctrine consistently articulated in our Confessions. All of the Lutheran Confessions see doctrine as a singular, organic whole. Christian doctrine is like a body (*corpus doctrinae*) with parts (*partes*) or joints (*articuli*) and ligaments and members (*membra*). The plural "doctrines" is rarely used in the Confessions, as in Scripture, but rather the singular "doctrine." In the church, if one member suffers the whole body suffers; according to the organic, unitary nature

---

1. See FC SD RN.10.
2. Preface to the Book of Concord; Tappert, 13.

of Christian doctrine, if one article or member fails, the whole body of doctrine is adversely affected. Luther said, "One article is all the articles, and all articles are one."[3]

As a confessional Lutheran dogmatics, the present volume will consciously and scrupulously draw its doctrine from Scripture. All the Confessions, beginning with the creeds and concluding with the Formula of Concord, claim to be and are direct explications of Sacred Scripture. As such, their purpose is never to lead us away from Scripture, nor to summarize the Scriptures in such a way as to make their further study unnecessary. They are written to lead us *into* the Scriptures. This is exactly what their function has been in the history of the church, whether we think of the many commentaries written on the early creeds by the church fathers or the expositions of our Confessions by the reformers and their successors. The reader will therefore notice that the present work in dogmatics engages in much more direct and extensive exegesis than other works in dogmatic theology of our day, except the immense *Church Dogmatics* by Karl Barth. This is altogether proper and called for in a confessional Lutheran dogmatics text.

The present work is a kind of *loci communes*, the recapitulation of the main themes of Scripture on the basis of the confessional Lutheran outline and pattern of thought. The Lutheran Confessions themselves never claim to be the final work on the understanding and exegesis of the Scriptures; we recall Luther's statement on *oratio, meditatio, tentatio*[4] with its blasts against theological know-it-alls and how often this statement of Luther's was repeated by the post-Reformation theologians in their dogmatics works. The Confessions always lead deeper into the Scriptures, especially as new issues arise in new cultures and succeeding generations which must be faced only with theology drawn from the Scriptures and patterned after the Lutheran Confessions.

The volumes in this series are dedicated to Francis Pieper, a great confessional Lutheran dogmatician of our church, in the hope and prayer that they will help to achieve what he did so much to accomplish in his day—namely, doctrinal unity and consensus in the doctrine of the Gospel and all its articles among all Lutherans and a firm confessional Lutheran identity so sorely needed in our day.

---

3. *AE* 27:38 (*Galatians Commentary*, 1535); WA 40:II:47.32–33.
4. *Preface to the Wittenberg Edition of Luther's German Writings*, 1539; WA 50:659.4; *AE* 34:285.

PREFACE

In the fall of 1984, Dr. Robert Preus, the president of Concordia Theological Seminary in Fort Wayne, Indiana, presented his plans to some of his colleagues for a series to be called Confessional Lutheran Dogmatics. These volumes were to supplement and not replace Pieper's *Christian Dogmatics*. They were to be directed to pastors, seminary students, and all with an interest in confessional Lutheran theology. The volumes were planned more as theological essays, and not as full-scale dogmatics books. Each writer was given the freedom to develop his topic as he saw fit.

When Preus died unexpectedly on November 4, 1995, the present volume on Baptism was in the final stages of its completion as a draft, and was submitted to Dr. John Stephenson, who now continues as editor of the series. Stephenson offered valuable suggestions which further expanded the current volume's length and adjusted the discussion in certain places. Other suggestions were offered by the Reverend Daniel Preus, publisher of the series for the Luther Academy, and Dr. Martin Noland. During its evolution, the manuscript also passed through the hands of several students, among whom were Scott Stiegemeyer, Christopher Esget, Douglas Punke, and Larry Rast, who now as a colleague never allowed friendship to stifle editorial admonition. Colleagues Arthur A. Just and William C. Weinrich also reviewed the manuscript in its final stages. In November 1997 the manuscript was sent to Pastor John Maxfield, who also provided a necessary critique in calling for precision in argument and form before his wife, Jennifer, began the process of typesetting and final editorial review. Mrs. Maxfield, who offers her expertise as a technical editor of the series while tending to a family of young children, delivered their fourth child, a son, Josiah Daniel, in the midst of this process.

The various and sundry delays have all had their positive effects, among which are various additions to the sources consulted in the volume. My late friend and New Testament scholar C. S. Mann had time in retirement to take note of *Baptism in the Theology of Martin Luther* (1994) by Jonathan Trigg, another scholar of the Anglican Communion. Since this book proved to be an invaluable window into the Reformer's thought and practice, Trigg's work has been plundered lavishly, as the reader will see for himself. An article in the *Lutheran Quarterly* (Spring 1995) by still another Anglican scholar, Bryan Spinks, warned of the increasingly low esteem in which infant Baptism is held among the churches which practice it. Shortly before bringing matters to a conclusion, I had the benefit of consulting the published dissertation of a former student and now colleague, Charles Gieschen. *Angelomorphic Christology: Antecedents and Early Evidence* (1998) goes a long way toward resolving differences in the trinitarian baptismal formula in Matthew and the variety of formulas found elsewhere in the New Testament, especially in Acts.

The volume on Baptism brings to full circle my involvement in this topic, which began with a doctoral dissertation presented to Concordia Seminary, Saint Louis, in 1963. Research for "The Doctrine of Infant Baptism in the German Protestant Theology of the Nineteenth Century" first alerted me to a general inconsistency among many Lutheran theologians who had adopted the Baptist presupposition that infants could not and did not believe, yet who in most cases did not advocate discontinuing infant Baptism. Inconsistency between intellectual conviction and actual practice thankfully allowed for countless infants to be baptized. During these years my wife, Dorothy, has been with me during our pilgrimage from Münster, Germany, through Connecticut and Illinois to Fort Wayne.

After a visitor to the seminary chapel had complained about a rarely used and mostly unnoticed baptismal font at the front of the nave, it was removed. A stone baptismal font has replaced it, but now stands at (or rather, blocks) the entrance of the nave. Anyone walking through the center doors must walk around it. Already the baptismal font has served a purpose. A Christian may look at any font as the place where he or she was baptized, and hear the Triune God speaking to him or her. In the position of academic dean I had acquiesced to that request to remove the old font. Perhaps these pages may serve as partial penance for that sacramental slight. To remind us so that none of us offends against this sacrament, somewhere on or near each font Luther's words should find a place: *In baptismo sonat vox Trinitatis.*

> David P. Scaer
> Concordia Theological Seminary
> Fort Wayne, Indiana
> The Feast of the Resurrection of our Lord Jesus, 1998

ABBREVIATIONS

References to versions of the Bible:

KJV	King James (Authorized) Version
RSV	Revised Standard Version
NIV	New International Version
NKJV	New King James Version

References to the Book of Concord:

AC	Augsburg Confession
Ap.	Apology of the Augsburg Confession
SA	Smalcald Articles
Tr.	Treatise on the Power and Primacy of the Pope
SC	Small Catechism
LC	Large Catechism
FC	Formula of Concord
	Ep. Epitome of the Formula of Concord
	SD Solid Declaration of the Formula of Concord
	RN Rule and Norm of the Ep. or SD

References to the editions and translations of the Book of Concord:

BKS   *Die Bekenntnisschriften der evangelisch-lutherischen Kirche.* Edited by the Deutscher Evangelischer Kirchenausschuss. 10th ed. Göttingen: Vandenhoeck & Ruprecht, 1986.

Tappert   *The Book of Concord: The Confessions of the Evangelical Lutheran Church.* Translated and edited by Theodore G. Tappert. Philadelphia: Fortress Press, 1959.

References to the Book of Concord are to the confession, article, and paragraph number.

References to Luther's works:

WA   *D. Martin Luthers Werke. Kritische Gesamtausgabe.* 58 vols. Weimar: Hermann Böhlau und Nachfolger, 1883–1948.

WATr   *D. Martin Luthers Werke. Tischreden.* 6 vols. Weimar: Hermann Böhlaus Nachfolger, 1912–21.

AE   *Luther's Works: The American Edition.* 55 vols. Edited by Jaroslav Pelikan and Helmut T. Lehmann. St. Louis: Concordia Publishing House; Philadelphia: Fortress Press, 1958–67.

Introduction

BAPTISM AS THE FOUNDATIONAL SACRAMENT

Among Lutherans Baptism has not received the level of attention generally given to the Eucharist or to the recently renewed interest in the practice of private confession and absolution.[1] Martin Luther did not value one means of grace over another in offering forgiveness, but he did make distinctions. He viewed each sacrament as having a unique function, and one could not be substituted for another. Baptism was not simply an entrance ceremony into the Christian community, but was equated with the Christian life and established the church's boundaries. Luther claimed that papists could not call the Lutherans heretics, since they all shared the same Baptism.[2] This sacrament not only ushered the believers into the covenant, but was itself the covenant.[3] Baptism was for Luther the foundational sacrament out of which all the other sacraments took their meaning: "But baptism is the first and most important sacrament, without which the others are all nothing, as [the papists] must admit."[4] Being *in* Baptism is equivalent to being in Christ. Recent discussions on Luther's doctrines of church and ministry in the Lutheran church, especially in America, may have overlooked the more profound significance Baptism had for him. His oath as a doctor of theology provided him with the legitimacy of his Reformation, but in the face of trials his confidence was not his faith, holiness, or spiritual achievement, but rather his Baptism, which for him always remained a present reality and never simply an event of the past.

> Indeed, if I had the matter under my control, I would not want God to speak to me from heaven or to appear to me; but this I would want—and my daily prayers are directed to this end—that I might have proper respect

---

1. Jonathan D. Trigg, an Anglican Luther scholar, makes the following telling observation: "There has been a tendency in Luther scholarship for the investigation of the Reformer's sacramental theology to concentrate upon the Supper at the expense of baptism" (*Baptism in the Theology of Martin Luther* [Leiden: E. J. Brill, 1994], 8). Trigg provides a brief but useful summary of recent research on Baptism in Luther's theology.
2. *AE* 41:194–95.
3. *AE* 1:228. The Reformed use of the word covenant as a mutual agreement has limited use among Lutherans. Here again much is surrendered to the Reformed hermeneutic. Circumcision or the sacraments as covenant are arrangements of grace established by God which call for faith, but do not depend on it for their definition.
4. *AE* 41:195.

Introduction

and true appreciation for the gift of Baptism, that I have been baptized (*baptizatus sum*) . . .[5]

This Baptism required faith for justification, but Baptism and not faith provided the certainty of salvation. Some scholars have seen a contradiction between the focus in Luther's theology on justification by faith and his reliance for salvation on Baptism.[6] But faith which is *incurvatus se*, turned in on itself, is both useless and self-destructive. Such a self-reflecting faith was at the heart of the monasticism from which Luther fled and which reappeared among the Anabaptists who saw this sacrament as no more than a confession of that faith.[7] Because of man's weakness, preaching and the Eucharist were added, but Baptism remained in Luther's thought the refuge for the Christian.[8] For Luther, faith in God and in His Word meant faith in Baptism.[9]

Luther's understanding of Baptism as foundational for Christian life, together with the way this view was incorporated into the Lutheran Confessions, are presuppositions for this volume of the Confessional Lutheran Dogmatics series.[10] To be true to itself, a confessional Lutheran theology must set forth its position within the context of the Holy Scriptures. This task takes on a critical dimension among the English-speaking nations, where the forms of Christianity have Reformed rather than Lutheran roots. This we intend deliberately and unflinchingly to do. Dogmatic theology cannot be permitted to float independent of biblical theology and still claim to follow in the tradition of Luther and the Lutheran fathers. Discussion of the biblical foundation that underlies the Lutheran doctrine of Baptism is directed toward countering the influence among Lutherans of Baptist and Reformed arguments, which sometimes appear to be biblical. This Reformed and particularly Baptist influence leads many to believe that for their salvation they cannot rely on their Baptism, especially if it was administered during infancy. Modern problems with Baptism are not substantially different from those

---

5. *AE* 3:165.

6. "There is no satisfactory way of reconciling Luther's clear teaching on justification by faith alone with his views on baptismal regeneration. His contemporaries saw this chink in his armor, and so have many radicals who succeeded them" (James Atkinson, *Martin Luther and the Birth of Protestantism* [Baltimore: Penguin Books, 1968], 192).

7. *AE* 40:240.

8. *AE* 3:124.

9. Heiko Oberman, *Luther: Man Between God and the Devil*, trans. Eileen Walliser-Schwarzbart (New Haven and London: Yale University Press, 1989), 225–27.

10. So also Trigg: "But the comparative neglect of baptism is nevertheless surprising as baptismal theology raises questions which are not so immediately apparent in the context of the eucharist, especially in the areas of soteriology (the beginning of the Christian life, conversion) and ecclesiology (the nature of the church and its boundaries)" (*Baptism*, 8).

raised at the dawn of the Reformation by the Anabaptists and by Ulrich Zwingli. So, in an environment in which Baptism is often seen as unnecessary for salvation and its practice frequently limited to adults, this volume has no choice but to present the Lutheran position within its biblical framework. Dogmatic theology is intrinsically biblical theology.[11]

The depreciation of Baptism, especially infant Baptism, is not strictly a Reformation and modern phenomenon, but was already part of medieval thought, in which Penance and penitential good works became more highly regarded. Entering the monastery to do good works was the "second Baptism," which carried benefits the first and therefore subordinate Baptism did not. Baptism was administered to infants, but monastic vows took on a greater importance for salvation.[12] In comparison with Roman Catholics, the Eastern Orthodox, the Reformed, and Baptists, Lutherans have a high regard for Baptism, even if it must be noted sadly that our attention to this sacrament does not uniformly reflect this regard. In Lutheran theology, Baptism is not only the antidote to original sin and prior actual sins, but remains the refuge for the sinner throughout life, a point which even Rome cannot accept. For Rome, the grace of Baptism must be supplemented by the grace of Con-

---

11. The distinctions between biblical and dogmatic theology were not recognized until two or three centuries ago. Claims that Luther was an Old Testament scholar and hence not a dogmatic theologian are less than fully informed regarding both his career and his classroom lectures, which were as much dogmatical treatises as they were detailed exegesis of the biblical texts. He certainly did not follow a precise exegetical method in laying out grammatically the structure of each word and phrase as most modern commentators do. Though he learned Greek from his co-reformer Philipp Melanchthon, he lectured from the Latin of the Vulgate. Both Luther and Melanchthon were biblical scholars; however, both wrote dogmatical treatises, some of which became our Lutheran Confessions. Making a distinction between the disciplines of exegesis and dogmatics, as the discipline of theology does today, was implicitly present in German Pietism and reached a fuller development in the Enlightenment. Against the prevailing orthodoxy, Spener, the father of Pietism, appealed to the Bible for spiritual nourishment (Gerhard Ebeling, *Word and Faith*, trans. James W. Leitch [Philadelphia: Fortress Press, 1963], 84). Pietism offered a *theologica biblica* in distinction to the prevailing *theologia scholastica*. The Rationalism of the Enlightenment extracted any number of theologies from the Bible to correct the older orthodoxy (D. A. Carson, "Current Issues in Biblical Theology: A New Testament Perspective," *Bulletin for Biblical Research* 5 [1995]: 18–21).

My concern is that the doctrine of Baptism be set forth within the widest possible biblical perspective. On that account my theological discussion enters here and there into a detailed exegesis. If dogmatic theology must be exegetical, especially if it is to be confessional Lutheran, exegesis must overcome its Enlightenment inheritance to become a truly *theological* (dogmatical) discipline. Happily a few voices have been raised calling for a theological exegesis. In our time Karl Barth has revived a biblical theology in which the exegetical and dogmatical disciplines were combined. See David S. Yeago, "The New Testament and the Nicene Dogma: A Contribution to the Recovery of Theological Exegesis," *Pro Ecclesia* 3 (Spring 1994): 152–64 and Brevard S. Childs, "Toward Recovering Theological Exegesis," *Pro Ecclesia* 6 (Winter 1997): 16–26.

12. Oberman, *Luther*, 231.

firmation. Baptismal grace can be lost, at which time Penance becomes the sacrament to which the believer is directed.[13] In contrast to Rome, Eastern Orthodoxy sees the continued, lifelong efficacy of Baptism as a place of return for Christians, but its doctrine of human depravity is not stated with the absolute harshness of the Lutheran doctrine of original sin from which even the youngest infant needs redemption.[14] The Reformed denominations, including the Baptists, consistently find no salvific activity or divine presence in the rite itself. Their theology considers Baptism only in an ancillary, and for all practical purposes unnecessary, role. This volume serves to present the Lutheran view that Baptism is first the foundation of the Christian life, and then also its perpetual content.

---

13. While Roman Catholicism holds to the necessity of Baptism, it sees the Eucharist as the source of Christian life (*Catechism of the Catholic Church* [Mahwah, NJ: Paulist Press, 1994], para. 1324). Where Luther sees Baptism as the foundation for all other rites and sacraments, Roman Catholicism sees the totality of the Christian life summed up in the Eucharist. Baptismal grace is lost by committing grave sin and is restored not in Baptism, but in the Sacrament of Penance. Lutherans certainly hold that the Eucharist is the focus and goal of the Christian (sacramental) life, but see in Baptism the foundation of that life.

14. A fuller discussion of original sin, especially as it is articulated by the Eastern Orthodox, is more appropriately left for another volume in this series. John Meyendorff says that "the patristic doctrine of salvation is based, not on the idea of guilt inherited from Adam and from which man is relieved in Christ, but on a more existential understanding of both 'fallen' and 'redeemed' humanity" (*Byzantine Theology* [New York: Fordam University Press, 1987], 193).

1

BAPTISM AS THE REMEDY FOR ORIGINAL SIN

The doctrine of Baptism in the Lutheran Confessions was formulated in response to the Anabaptists' denial of Baptism's salvific effectiveness, especially concerning children. Their denial of Baptism to infants ignited the first division among those Christians who were opposed to the papacy.[1] This doctrine is the subject of separate articles in the Augsburg Confession (IX), the Apology (IX), Luther's Small and Large Catechisms (IV), and his Smalcald Articles (III, V). In spite of their differences, even on Baptism, the Lutherans were allied with the Roman Catholics in the understanding that this sacrament is necessary for salvation and that it is a real means of grace.

This catholic consensus sharply divided them from the Anabaptists, who understood Baptism not as a real means of grace necessary for salvation, but rather as the believer's pledge to God, a position also held by Ulrich Zwingli. John Calvin saw Baptism as an accompanying sign of God's working in the believer, but still did not view Baptism as the means through which salvation was given.[2] Even though Reformed churches, who maintained infant Baptism, attempted to distance themselves from the Anabaptists, they agreed with them in understanding Baptism primarily as a symbol and not as a means of grace.

For the Anabaptists, Baptism symbolized the confession made by the believer. With this the Reformed agreed, but they held that it also symbolized a prior act of grace. Thus, the principle that Baptism is a symbol is basic to both Anabaptist and Reformed (including Arminian) traditions.[3] This common basis was also recognized by Johann Gerhard,

---

1. Luther had suspected after the start of the Reformation a controversy would arise over Baptism from the papist side. By 1521 he had to encounter the Anaptists and then Carlstadt and Zwingli, who in spite of their differences were united in denying the sacramental quality of Baptism. In 1524 Luther had to face Zwingli's erroneous views on the Lord's Supper. If Baptism and the Lord's Supper provided the certainty for Christian faith, they were also the first and still unresolved reasons for division among the opponents of the papacy. For an overview of the importance of these sacraments at the dawn of the Reformation, see Oberman, *Luther*, 226–45.

2. *The Institutes of the Christian Religion*, trans. Henry Beveridge, 4 vols. in 2 (Grand Rapids, MI: William B. Eerdmans, 1994), IV.XV.1–5. This translation is made from the 1559 edition; all subsequent citations are to this edition unless otherwise noted.

3. In holding that the human is the cause of salvation, Arminians, which include the Methodists and the various holiness bodies, differ from the Reformed with regard to their doctrine of double predestination; but with regard to the sacraments both groups are in basic agreement. Joseph Arminius, Hugo Grotius, and other prominent theologians

who ranks in importance for Lutheran theology only after Luther and Melanchthon. He pointed out that although the Reformed theologians with whom he tangled differed among themselves on the sacraments, including Baptism, they were agreed that as mere signs they did not confer grace.[4] This was as true for the Calvinists and Arminians who baptized infants as it was for the Baptists who did not.[5] Exceptions among these groups may be found, but this does not alter the fundamental doctrinal heritage which has its roots with Zwingli and received its classical and less stringent formation by Calvin. For the Reformed as well as the Baptists, Baptism, the value of which is chiefly symbolic of God's pledge to the believer or the believer's pledge to God, has its most significant meaning in adulthood. For Luther, in sharp contrast, every Baptism, including those of adults, is in a sense an infant Baptism.[6]

When the Augsburg Confession and the Apology were written (1530 and 1530–31, respectively), what would later be recognized as the Reformed position had not fully surfaced in its classical form.[7] Thus the Anabaptists' denial of the sacramental character of Baptism and their refusal to baptize infants provided the context for the Lutheran position. Melanchthon notes in Apology IX that his Roman opponents had accepted what the Lutherans said about Baptism in the Augsburg Confession, and he reiterates the Lutheran opposition to the Anabaptists' refusal to baptize infants.[8] In this controversy the Lutherans had church

---

are often recognized as part of the Reformed tradition, though they differed sharply with classical Calvinism on the issue of the free will. See for example William Stacy Johnson and John Leith, eds., *Reformed Reader: A Sourcebook in Christian Theology*, 2 vols. (Louisville, KY: Westminster Press/John Knox Press, 1993), 1:xvi–xvii.

4. Johann Gerhard, arguably the most significant Lutheran theologian of the seventeenth century, has extensive discussions on Old and New Testament sacraments, including circumcision as a precursor of Baptism (a relationship which the Reformed used to show that neither rite conferred grace). See volume 4 of his *Loci Theologici* (ed. Eduard Preuss [1770; reprint, 9 vols. in 3, Berlin: Gustaf Schlawitz, 1866]). This dogmatics first appeared in 1657, twenty years after Gerhard died in 1637, and was edited by his son. All references are from the fourth volume of the Preuss edition of his *Loci*.

5. Gerhard provided citations from the Reformed fathers to show that they were agreed that sacraments as signs did not confer grace. Zwingli held, "I believe—in fact, I know for certain—that all the sacraments are so far removed from conferring grace that they not even offer or dispense." For Calvin, "a sacrament is nothing else but an external testimony of divine kindness toward us, a testimony which represents spiritual graces with a visible sign." Beza answers his own question: "From where does that efficacy of the Sacraments come? In sum, from the operation of the Holy Spirit, not from signs except insofar as our inner senses are moved by those external objects" (ibid., 146 [18.23]).

6. See Oberman, *Luther*, 230. For Luther, infant Baptism revealed the true nature of Baptism, since in this sacrament the child received an alien righteousness. As Oberman observes of Luther's position, "A good Christian is always an infant in his dependence on God and in the way he is bound up with Christ and His Church" (ibid., 230).

7. Calvin saw a value in the sacraments as signs which Zwingli did not.

8. Roman Confutation: "The ninth article, concerning Baptism, ... is approved and accepted, [the Lutheran princes] are right in condemning the Baptists ..." (quoted from Tappert, 178; *BKS*, 246).

tradition on their side, an argument they did not fail to use. The Anabaptist denial of infant Baptism was rooted in the question of the certainty of salvation, which for them depended on the believer's conscious awareness, an awareness which they understood as the essence of saving faith. For Lutherans, the certainty of salvation was found in Baptism. Its saving efficacy did not depend on the faith of the one administering it or the one receiving it. "Therefore only presumptuous and stupid persons draw the conclusion that where there is no true faith, there also can be no true Baptism" (LC IV.58).[9]

For the Anabaptists, Baptism served as confirmation of what God had already accomplished in the believer through a direct working of the Holy Spirit, a position which remains in force with Baptists today.[10] While today's Baptists are not theologically descended from the sixteenth-century Anabaptists and should not be confused with them, especially in the call for societal change through revolution, they hold to the same fundamental views in denying baptismal regeneration and infant Baptism. On that account what the Confessions say about those who deny infant Baptism has not outlived its usefulness.

In the theology of Calvin, Baptism served to signify not only what God had done and was doing, but, in the case of infants, what He was going to do (though this point is not entirely resolved in his theology, as the various editions and revisions of his *Institutes* illustrate). In the first edition of *Institutes* (1536), he seemed to follow Luther in ascribing faith to infants in Baptism, but whether he meant the same thing is another question.[11] Since God's important and necessary work of creating faith in the heart was accomplished by the Holy Spirit without any mediating activity, Baptism for Calvin was simply a sign of what God had already done in the believer.[12]

---

9. Tappert, 444; *BKS*, 703.

10. Stanley J. Grenz, *Theology for the Community of God* (Nashville: Broadman and Holman, 1994), 659–80. "Through [Baptism], we both announce the importance of Jesus' story for all believers and of our own initial public confession of faith in Christ" (ibid., 659). See also Augustus Hopkins Strong: "Christian Baptism is the immersion of a believer in water, in token of his previous entrance into the communion of Christ's death and resurrection, or, in other words, in token of his regeneration through union with Christ" (*Systematic Theology* [1907; reprint, Boston: Griffth & Rowland Press, 1912], 931).

11. "Therefore, the opinion stands firm, that no men are saved except by faith, whether they be children or adults. For this reason, baptism also rightly applies to infants who possess faith in common with adults" (trans. Ford Lewis Battles [Grand Rapids, MI: William B. Eerdmans, 1975], 101). In the 1539 edition of *Institutes* Calvin speaks of children having the seed of faith and being baptized in regard to their future faith, a position which is not Luther's. This point is discussed in the chapter on infant faith.

12. This persists as the Reformed position on Baptism. See for example Peter Toon: "Paul assumes that the internal work of the Spirit accompanies the external act of baptism . . . as believers are washed by the water, they receive the gift of the indwelling of the Spirit" (*Born Again* [Grand Rapids, MI: Baker Book House, 1987], 45). Toon is an Anglican clergyman.

Anabaptists went further and encouraged those who had been baptized as infants to obtain what they considered the authentic Baptism of the New Testament. In this way Baptism became an act of the believer who by this rite gave a pledge of good faith, obedience to a command of God and subservience to His will. With this understanding, the rite with water was viewed as part of the believer's sanctification, since by submitting himself to this churchly rite he was showing submission to God in order to please Him.[13]

For the Reformed and the Anabaptists Baptism was necessary as a good work flowing out of a willing heart. Calvin asserted that the Holy Spirit's work paralleled the sacraments and thus signaled what God was doing. He also incorporated the Anabaptist idea that Baptism indicated the believer's good intentions toward God. A sacrament "is a testimony of God's favor toward us, confirmed by an outward sign, with a mutual testifying of our godliness toward him."[14] For the Reformed in general, Baptism was not necessary as the channel or means through which God approaches the believer with salvation.

Here the distance between the Lutherans and the Reformed is profound. While one must in fairness distinguish the differences between the Reformation Anabaptists, the Baptists, who came later, and the Reformed, who insisted on Baptism even for children, they share a common ground in their understanding that Baptism is not, strictly speaking, a way in which God confers grace upon the recipient. They are unanimous in their condemnation of the Lutheran position, which they often identify or deliberately confuse with that of Roman Catholicism.

The differences over Baptism in the early Reformation period served to show the basic theological breach dividing Lutherans from Zwingli and the Anabaptists. Disagreements over Baptism were the first to divide those who opposed Rome.[15] Even before disagreements on the Lord's Supper led to a permanent split between Zwingli and Luther in 1529 at Marburg, equally critical differences on Baptism had led Thomas Müntzer and Andreas Carlstadt to separate themselves from Luther. Several years earlier Zwingli had overcome whatever doubts he had about administering Baptism to infants. The refusal of the Anabaptists to baptize infants and their insistence on "rebaptizing" (the word "Anabaptist" means to rebaptize) those who had been baptized as infants went squarely in the face of the then-still-accepted ancient church custom. The Reformed denial of Baptism as a means of grace was not

---
13. Calvin, *Institutes* IV.XV.15. Baptism is called "a surer exercise of faith." Calvin also asserts here, in commenting on Ananias's words to Paul to wash away his sins in Baptism (Acts 22:11), that Baptism does not in itself forgive sins, but confirms for Paul God's promise of forgiveness, to which promise his faith is directed.
14. Quoted in Felix B. Gear, *Our Presbyterian Belief* (Atlanta: John Knox, 1980), 63.
15. See Oberman, *Luther*, 228–29.

obvious, since they insisted on infant Baptism, though for reasons that were hardly acceptable to Lutherans, as will be shown. They have always been at a loss to justify the practice. Ultimately, differences regarding infant Baptism are not seen as divisive of church fellowship among the various Reformed denominations today.[16] It is not unusual for ministers and members to switch allegiance between churches which differ on this question.

Not only did the Anabaptist practices ecclesiastically and culturally disrupt any possible unity during the Reformation among the opponents of the Roman papacy, but they had grave political consequences in determining the constituency of the Holy Roman Empire of the German Nation and hence for all of western Europe. Baptism provided not only membership in the church but citizenship in the empire, a situation which remained in place until Napoleon's secularization of the state in the early nineteenth century. During the period of the Reformation and for several centuries thereafter, Baptism provided a legal basis for society. Up until recent times this situation has remained in place in the Scandinavian countries. In certain cases a special arrangement was made for Jews, but otherwise, Jews and Muslims who remained unbaptized were denied full legal rights. After conquest by Christian nations, subjugated populations routinely submitted to Baptism to avoid exile and to obtain citizenship. Such was the case when Ferdinand and Isabella subdued the remaining Muslims in Spain in 1492, and the practice was carried over in the conquest of the Americas. Baptized Native Americans also became subjects of the Spanish crown. Yet the medieval alliance between church and state was not a motivating force in the confessional Lutheran discussion of Baptism and of its suitability for infants. Lutherans never favored enforcing infant Baptism on the people to maintain civil and cultural unity. Even as recently as the mid-twentieth century, the role that infant Baptism plays in the relationship of church and state has been discussed by theologians.[17]

At the heart of the Reformation differences on Baptism was whether Baptism was commanded by God as a way to accomplish His gracious activity among us (Lutheran) or as a way in which we express our fidelity to Him (Anabaptist or Reformed). Zwingli and Calvin insisted on infant Baptism. Still, in spite of their insistence on infant Baptism, their fundamental theology seems to have had more in common with the

---

16. See for example Wayne Grudem, *Systematic Theology* (Grand Rapids, MI: Zondervan Publishing House, 1997), 982–83. Sacraments for the Reformed are adiaphora, and questions of their administration cannot separate Christians from one another. Thus, denominational membership and confessional subscription are not obstacles in receiving Holy Communion.

17. E.g., Karl Barth, *Church Dogmatics*, 5 vols., trans. G. W. Bromiley (Edinburgh: T. & T. Clark, 1969), 4/4:169–70.

Anabaptists than with the Lutherans whom they resembled in actual practice.[18] Lutherans and Reformed were doing the same thing but for different reasons. Similar practices covered up basic theological differences. The Reformed saw infant Baptism as necessary because it is the church's response to the command of God, and not as a necessary means of God's gracious dealing with sinners. Whether or not infants are included in Baptism is a secondary question for the Reformed, because they can be saved without Baptism, which is not, strictly speaking, a means of grace. Calvin did not allow for emergency Baptism! Here it again becomes evident that, in the Reformed system of theology, sacraments are adiaphora.

At issue between Lutherans and the Reformed was whether Baptism should be understood as Law or Gospel, even though this question was not addressed precisely in these terms. Is Baptism an act that we perform to satisfy a divine requirement like the Ten Commandments (Anabaptist) or is it a gracious activity of God toward us (Lutheran)? Luther is clear in seeing it as a form of the Gospel and never tires of saying that Baptism is God's work (LC IV.4, IV.8, IV.31). "Baptism is not our work, but God's" (LC IV.35).[19] Luther does use language which may at first glance suggest that he sees Baptism as "Law," but all he intends to say is that it has God's authority behind it. Luther designates Baptism as God's ordinance (*Gottes Ordnung*) and His command (*Gebot*). For the Reformed, "ordinance" stands for the Law, but for Luther, both terms are synonymous with "Word," which he actually defines as Gospel (LC IV.60).

In Lutheran theology, ordinance does not mean a moral requirement which Christians must fulfill to please God. Where this confusion of meanings does take place, the Gospel (Baptism) becomes Law. *This is not the Lutheran understanding.* Simply because Baptism has its foundation in Christ's death and resurrection, it must be Gospel. Where this

---

18. Article 27 of the Thirty-nine Articles of the Church of England, with which the Episcopal Church is in full communion, may allow for baptismal regeneration. Baptism is called "a sign of Regeneration or New-Birth, whereby, as by an instrument, they that receive Baptism rightly are grafted into the Church" (John H. Leith, ed., *Creeds of the Churches: A Reader in Christian Doctrine from the Bible to the Present*, 3d ed. [Atlanta: John Knox Press, 1982], 275–76). If "church" here means the *una sancta*, then Baptism is clearly a means of grace. But "church" can also be read in a Reformed sense, as the outward or external fellowship. While Article 27 may lack full clarity, the rite of Baptism in the *Book of Common Prayer* itself teaches baptismal regeneration and infant faith, and, like the Lutheran rites, the questions are addressed directly to the child (New York: Thomas Nelson & Sons, 1944). This illustrates that classical Anglicanism, due to its unique historical development, is not simply Calvinist or even Reformed in general in its confession, but persists in combining elements of Calvinist, Lutheran, and even Roman Catholic theologies. Hence the umbrella term Reformed does not include Anglicanism, even though the Church of England does indeed include in its confessions many Reformed elements.

19. Tappert, 441; *BKS*, 698.

Christology does not fully inform the content, benefits, and significance of Baptism, it will be interpreted as an obligation to fulfill the Law and thus the fundamental nature of the sacrament is removed. When Lutherans insist on this interpretation, they are most likely to be called sacramentalists or Romanists by the Reformed. But Lutherans insist on this meaning not for the sake of a rite, but for the sake of Christ. For Luther, "ordinance" and "command" used in connection with Baptism refer to the Gospel and its authority which have been established by God to bring salvation to men. It is not a synonym for the Law as it is used in the Law-Gospel dialectic so essential for Lutheran theology.

To put it quite simply, Baptism is not Law; thus, it is not a work we do to fulfill God's requirements. Baptism pleases God, not in a moral sense, but because through it Christ establishes His church and brings His kingdom. Despising Baptism is far worse than disregarding God's moral requirements, because Baptism brings all of God's grace, including God Himself, to the believer. It is one thing not to do what God requires and quite another thing to despise His gracious activity in Jesus Christ. The latter carries the greater consequences.

Scriptures can speak of commands, precepts, and even law to refer to God's entire revelation (Ps 1:1). Baptism certainly belongs to what Christ has commanded, but it is like the command to believe. The imperative is an invitation without threat of punishment. Where the threat of punishment lurks, the Gospel has given way to the Law. There are other instances where commandment language can refer to pure Gospel. The law of Christ is, after all, the Gospel (Rom 8:2, 10:4; Gal 6:2). When law, command, and precept are used in this context, they refer to God as their author and the permanency of these rites for the church. Confusion here can lead to false teachings. Marcion took advantage of this double use of the word "law" to deny the Old Testament's authority in the second-century church. Medieval Christianity took a reverse position and designated the Law as Gospel, with the result that the people were left without the promises of God. Baptism belongs to the Gospel, and the divine imperative attached to it is one of solicitous request. As the vehicle of salvation, Baptism simply cannot be understood as an arbitrary decision on the part of God to place another obstacle in the way to salvation, nor can it be removed. Luther has no difficulty in saying that "Baptism is forever" (LC IV.77).[20] He compares the command to baptize with the Fourth Commandment requiring that honor be given to parents, and concludes that the command by itself would require Baptism. Both Law and the Gospel have God as their author. Even in the case of the Law, God reveals that ordinary flesh and blood are mother and father (LC IV.38–40). Baptism, like the command

---

20. Tappert, 446; BKS, 706.

to honor parents, has God's authority behind it, but it possesses a promise which heaven and earth cannot comprehend. It "gives forgiveness of sins, God's grace, the entire Christ and the Holy Spirit with His gifts" (LC IV.41).[21] On this point also Lutheran theology is clearly distinguishable from the Reformed.

For Calvin, children were sanctified because of their birth from believing parents and were entitled to Baptism. Baptism does not serve as a medium of regeneration, but only confirms their status within a family and an accompanying divine activity in their lives.[22] Thus for the Reformed the lack of Baptism, whether in infants or adults, did not present the problem of salvation as it did for Lutherans and Roman Catholics. Since for the Reformed Baptism administered by the laity, especially women, had to be repeated by the regular minister, its rite and its proper execution constituted its essence. There was nothing in the water itself. Lutherans understood Baptism in sacramental terms, that is, the act of Baptism actually *did* something. By its place in Article II of the Augsburg Confession, Baptism was given a prominent position. Without Baptism original sin damns those *qui non renascuntur per baptismum et spiritum sanctum*. The implication is clear that without Baptism salvation is not bestowed. A remedy was found in Baptism which was necessary for salvation: [*Baptismum*] *sit necessarius ad salutem* (AC IX).

The first reference to the practice of Baptism in the Augsburg Confession is not deduced from a specific command of God, but is derived from its being the only escape from God's universal condemnation of all sinners, including children. Its necessity comes from God's offering it as His solution for sin. Exceptions and prerogatives to salvation apart from Baptism belong to God and not to us. Original sin is so devastating that without divine intervention in and through Baptism, all persons on earth, including children, are damned to eternal death. The Lutheran argument for Baptism's necessity from universal depravity is itself not intended to make other reasons for its practice inconsequential. Rather the doctrine of universal depravity requires an equally pronounced doctrine of univeral grace which then is made available to all, including infants, in Baptism. The doctrine of total depravity in the Lutheran Confessions is the presupposition for their understanding of mankind, sin, Christology, justification, and theology in general. In fact, without the doctrine of original sin the foundational Christian doctrines cannot be understood fully. Denial of original sin leads to a weakening and eventual destruction of the entire system of Christian theology. Without original sin, man is seen in some sense as capable of self-re-

---

21. Tappert, 441–42; *BKS*, 699.
22. Calvin, *Institutes* IV.XV.15.

demption. Christ's work is seen no longer as substitutionary atonement but as an example of good works for the Christian, a position taken by Pelagius, Abelard, and the Enlightenment theologians.[23]

The necessity of Baptism does not flow from an isolated command or word of God detached from the incarnation but finds its meaning and origin in Christ's work of atonement, which embraces all people. While individuals are baptized confessing their own sin and faith, each comes because he has been included under God's *universal* condemnation of sin. Individual or separate sins are only particular forms of a prior condition of general human sinfulness. He is there *as sinner*, but importantly he is only a part of a sinful humanity: "All men are born with sin" (AC II.1).[24] The universality of human sin, which is limitless in its scope, anticipates the universality of divine grace which is realized for the individual in Baptism. Where the meaning and content of Baptism are seen apart from Christ's atonement, it can degenerate into being understood as no more than a church rite, as held by the eighteenth-century Enlightenment theologians. Even saying that it is commanded by Christ may not be enough in forming its definition, since such a command or ordinance can be understood as Law, as discussed above in regard to the Reformed position.

Essential to Baptism is its origin in Christ's death and resurrection, since His death was a death to sin and His resurrection was for His vindication (justification). So in Baptism the faithful die to sin in His death and are raised to justification in His resurrection: "[Baptism] is simply the slaying of the old Adam and the resurrection of the new man, both of which actions must continue in us our whole life long" (LC IV.65).[25] Christ is not only one component of Baptism, but is its *essence*. So Luther: "Whoever rejects Baptism rejects God's Word, faith, and Christ, who directs us and binds us to Baptism" (LC IV.31).[26] Christ's benefits are applied in Baptism, because in His death Christ had us in view. His death was in a very real sense our Baptism. Or, to reverse the sentence, we were baptized when He died. Lutherans understand the Word which sanctifies the water in Baptism not in a magical sense, but as the involvement of Christ in the water. It is, as Luther says, "Christ's Baptism" (LC IV.35).[27] He is *necessarily* there with His Father and Spirit so that it is carried out in the name of the Father and the Son and the Holy Spirit.

---

23. See Gustaf Aulen, *Christus Victor*, trans. A. G. Hebert (London: SPCK, 1953), 112–13; 149–52.
24. Tappert, 440; *BKS*, 697.
25. Tappert, 445; *BKS*, 704.
26. Tappert, 440; *BKS*, 697.
27. Tappert, 441; *BKS*, 698.

Baptism as the Remedy for Original Sin

Though Lutherans and Roman Catholics are agreed in seeing Baptism as a regeneration, they differ in what this regeneration involves. The Lutherans, in seeing Baptism as the remedy for original sin in children, distanced themselves from the Roman Catholic position which saw grace poured into the soul (*gratia infusa*) to give the recipient, most often a child, a new character (*habitus*). The *Catechism of the Catholic Church* still speaks in these terms: "Baptism imprints on the soul an indelible spiritual sign, the character, which consecrates the baptized person for Christian worship."[28] Baptism must go beyond an individualizing of salvation since it brings the baptized into the church where God is worshiped, but speaking of "an indelible spiritual sign" only corresponds to the Roman Catholic view that the grace of Baptism is a substance *materially* or *organically changing* the person. The view that regeneration effects a change in substance, that is, a renewal, was held by Osiander and condemned by the Formula of Concord (Ep. III.15 and SD III.47–49). Suggesting that Baptism involves a mystical or substantive change is a "sacramental" modification of Osiander's understanding. For the Lutherans, Baptism initiates not a *substantive* change, but a *new relationship* with God whereby the believer is brought into the realm of salvation (Ap. II.35–37). It does not remove original sin, so that man now has a clean slate; rather, it is the continued and permanent promise of God to the believer.[29] "Therefore Baptism remains forever" (LC IV.77).[30]

Furthermore, the Lutheran doctrine of original depravity is much more severe than in Roman Catholic theology, which today grants that even those without faith in Christ might merit salvation. In other words, the Roman Catholic concludes that man is bad, but not so bad that he cannot please God. This is not simply a question of whether God can allow mercy to non-Christians, but whether man has moral capabilities recommending him to God, a position Lutherans of the Reformation firmly denied.[31] Baptism was confessed as an absolute requirement: "Moreover, it is solemnly and strictly commanded that we must be baptized or we shall not be saved" (LC IV.6).[32] While the Roman Catholics in the Confutation accepted the Augsburg Confession on Baptism, they did not accept it on original sin. A more detailed presentation of how the Lutherans understood Baptism came not in the article in the Apology devoted to that subject (IX), but in their defense of

---

28. Para. 1280.
29. Leif Grane, *The Augsburg Confession*, trans. John H. Rasmussen (Minneapolis: Augsburg Publishing House, 1987), 46–47.
30. Tappert, 446; BKS, 706.
31. For a discussion of this see John R. Stephenson, *Eschatology*, Confessional Lutheran Dogmatics, vol. 13 (Fort Wayne, IN: The Luther Academy, 1993), 109–10, n. 25.
32. Tappert, 437; BKS, 692.

original sin (Ap. II.35–37). Baptism does not eradicate sin or concupiscence, but removes its guilt. It embraces all of life, and not only original sin and those actual sins committed before Baptism. Lutherans saw more in Baptism than did the Roman Catholics, who attributed some of its effects to Penance and Confirmation, and in a certain sense to purgatory. Roman Catholics rightly saw Baptism as a solution for original sin, but not as that sacrament which embraced the totality of Christian life.[33]

Lutheran theology juxtaposes sin and justification (redemption). In both cases all of humanity stands before God in judgment. Accountability to and before God, *iustificari coram Deo*, lies at the heart of the Lutheran understanding of sin (AC II) and salvation (AC IV). This individual accountability as sinner and redeemed before God occurs in Baptism. God's universal judgment of the world for sin and his corresponding universal verdict of justification are individualized for the believer in Baptism, in which rite he recognizes himself first as a sinner and then as among redeemed. He is buried and raised with Christ, and so he is both condemned and released. Baptism occurs once, but it provides the foundation for all of the Christian life and is coterminous with it. The baptized in the act of Baptism confesses himself as sinner, and in turn God acknowledges him as saint, *simul iustus et peccator*. When one removes original and universal sin from the equation, as do the Reformed and especially the Baptists, one's view of the sacrament of Baptism is fundamentally altered. Roman Catholics with their doctrines on Penance and Confirmation allow the focus to be taken away from Baptism itself. Baptism for Lutherans is more than the sacrament of entrance into the Christian community, but is what being Christian is all about. It continually calls the baptized to respond in faith, and so it belongs to the present and the future as it does to the past.[34]

Baptism was not a controverted article in those intra-Lutheran debates leading to the writing of the Formula of Concord, but the first article of this confessional symbol carefully detailed the doctrine of to-

---

33. Luther wrote of the Roman Catholic doctrine of Penance that it "deprives Baptism of its value, making it of no further use" (LC IV.82; Tappert, 446; *BKS*, 707). Rome still holds the same position today. See *Catechism of the Catholic Church*, para. 1446: "Christ instituted the sacrament of Penance for all sinful members of his Church: above all for those who, since Baptism, have fallen into grave sin, and have thus lost their baptismal grace and wounded ecclesial communion. It is to them that the sacrament of Penance offers a new possibility to convert and to recover the grace of justification. The Fathers of the Church present this sacrament as 'the second plank [of salvation] after the shipwreck which is the loss of grace.'" Luther condemned this doctrine in Jerome. The *Catechism of the Catholic Church* finds it in Tertullian. In any event, Luther's critique is still valid.

34. For a discussion of Luther's position on Baptism as the all-embracing sacrament see Trigg, *Baptism*, 197.

tal human depravity. Historically, where the article on original sin is compromised, Baptism loses its value and soon falls into disuse, as happened in Enlightenment Europe. Where the doctrine of original sin and universal depravity is discredited, other reasons for infant Baptism have been adduced to support its continued practice; however, the fundamental definition of Baptism as a forsaking of sin and entering God's kingdom is lost. On the other hand, a complete understanding of human depravity does not guarantee a proper understanding of Baptism. Calvin's solution to depravity was the divine election which could be known only through the Spirit's inner testimony; hence there was no necessity in his theology to have a sacramental understanding of Baptism. Universal sin is the presupposition for Baptism, but does not detail its content.

Christianity is understood by Lutherans as a religion of the Gospel in the sense that God directs *all* of His efforts to the redemption of fallen mankind. Man's depravity can perhaps be discerned through observation, though its universal and total pervasiveness is not apparent to all. Philosophers have had a variety of opinions about just how evil or good the world is. Twentieth-century existentialists have often gone to the edge of despair. On the other side, the humanist tradition of the Renaissance came to full flower in the optimism of the eighteenth-century Enlightenment with its glorification of reason. Article II of the Augsburg Confession finds the origins of universal sin in the fall of Adam, and condemns as Pelagian attributing any positive saving virtues to mankind.[35] Primary for the Augsburg Confession was whether man could please God in matters of salvation. Secondary to its doctrine of universal depravity and in a sense separate from it was the issue of the ability of man to function rationally and morally in the world, which was affirmed (AC XVI). Thus, while the Augsburg Confession commends and even requires participation in the civil sphere, its real interest lies in how man relates to God. At issue is not how good man can be in society but how evil he really is within himself. The Confessions do not intend to develop a philosophy of total human depravity as an independent locus in theology so that mankind is left in despair, but only as the necessary background for the demonstration of God's grace in Christ.

In Lutheran theology divine wrath is never left unaddressed, as if it were a permanent or intrinsic attribute of God, but is presented in an-

---

35. "Pelagian" is a term used to describe the heretical teachings of Pelagius, a fifth-century British monk, who taught that man was morally neutral and could just as easily choose the good as the evil. Past actions did not affect future ones. Pelagianism is used to describe any theology which sees man as contributing something to his salvation, even though as an historical designation this may be less than accurate. Lutherans freely used this term to condemn the use of the free will as a factor in salvation (FC SD II.2–5; Tappert, 536; BKS, 870–73).

ticipation of His love and grace.³⁶ Since divine wrath finds its conclusion in divine love, the idea of a limited atonement has no place in Lutheran theology. Divine wrath is essential for understanding the atonement, in which it is completely absorbed, but its proclamation does not reveal God's fundamental attitude toward mankind. It is a work foreign to God's nature, *opus alienum*, necessary to prepare for the revelation of grace in the Gospel to which Baptism belongs. In other words, God wants to do something good in the Law, even though the hearer could never know that unless he hears the Gospel! The article on original sin holds the promise of salvation through Baptism and the merits of Christ in the background (AC II). In Lutheran theology, the universal and complete moral depravity of mankind requires God's intervention into the human dilemma, which takes place for the individual in Baptism. The argument here is not so much logically or theologically abstract, but concrete, or in a sense existential. Baptism's necessity builds upon the awareness of the helplessness of the human condition and is recognized as God's solution to this dilemma. From the side of humanity, Baptism is recognized as necessary: "We must be baptized or we shall not be saved" (LC IV.6).³⁷

Lutherans are not alone in seeing that Baptism is necessary, but this necessity is viewed differently by others. For Roman Catholicism, Baptism functions in eradicating the past, but must be supplemented for future sins. Calvin sees Baptism as confirming God's prior activity, while the Anabaptists (as well as today's Baptists) see it as a pledge which God requires of us in a show of good faith. This was only a variation of Zwingli's position, which committed baptized children to a Christian lifestyle and their parents to giving these children a Christian education. Lutheran theology holds that in Baptism God's universal judgment over each person's sin is overcome by God's redemption in Christ.

---

36. Classical Reformed theology stills holds that Christ's atonement is not as extensive as God's wrath, even though more recent exponents of the theory of Calvin's limited atonement theory have attempted to soften this position. See for example Grudem: "Did Christ pay for the sins of all unbelievers who will be eternally condemned, and did he pay for their sins completely on the cross? It seems that we have to answer no to that question" (*Systematic Theology*, 601). Limited atonement has many ramifications, the first of which is a faulty view of God which understands Him more in terms of wrath than love. Secondly, it reflects the Reformed failure to recognize that Christ's human nature is entirely permeated with the divine nature (*genus maiestaticum*). Christ's atonement by definition must be as extensive as God is. The Reformed view of a limited atonement does not allow this. Thirdly, it understands the atonement not in terms of a trinitarian act which necessarily involves all of what and who God is, but a barter in which the Father accepts the Son's atonement (payment) only for some sins, but not all. Lutheran theology sees God's love in Christ extending far beyond and covering divine wrath. Baptism focuses this love into the lives of sinners. In these terms Lutherans speak of Baptism's necessity.

37. Tappert, 437; *BKS*, 692.

Burial and resurrection with Christ is more than analogical; it is real and actual. The sentence of death over sin is carried out in Baptism, and the gift of the resurrection is given. This is not symbolic but real. The Augsburg Confession's brief article on original sin is in itself a complete theology in miniature. It begins with Adam's fall, mankind's continuing in sin, the eternal damnation as the consequence of this sin, the remedy provided by the Holy Spirit in Baptism, Christ's merits, and condemnation of man's attempt at self-justification through his own works (AC II).

> Our churches also teach that since the fall of Adam all men who are propagated according to nature are born in sin. That is to say, they are without fear of God, are without trust in God, and are concupiscent. And this disease or vice of origin is truly sin, which even now damns and brings eternal death on those who are not born again through Baptism and the Holy Spirit.
>
> Our churches condemn the Pelagians and others who deny that the vice of origin is sin and who obscure the glory of Christ's merit and benefits by contending that man can be justified before God by his own strength and reason.[38]

For the Augsburg Confession, Baptism belongs to a larger sequence of God's plan for the world, and cannot be understood merely in a personalistic sense of providing comfort, though of course it does precisely this. Even for Calvin, Baptism provided assurance for the believer, though more in the sense of a symbolic gesture. In Lutheran theology, Baptism focuses the universal sin of Adam into the life of the baptized as his own sin, and then presents the historic moment of the cross of Christ for the redemption and justification of the baptized. Before recognizing Baptism as a "Christ event" for the baptized, it is first of all an "Adam event," in which the baptized identifies with the first parent and acknowledges his sin as his own. Through Baptism, Adam's sinful children become God's justified children through Christ. Baptism is truly a rebirth (*renascuntur per baptismum*). Salvation, which is essential to understanding Baptism, is more than a verbal promise or assurance of a future forgiveness; it is a present reality, because Christ Himself is present in the water of Baptism. This christological reality is the essence of Baptism; it gives shape to the rite, and in this way Baptism incorporates the baptized into Christ.

The doctrines of universal depravity and of the necessity of divine grace provide an adequate basis for the Lutheran doctrine of Baptism, especially in requiring its application to infants. This hardly means that Lutherans later did not develop the doctrine of Baptism from the biblical texts themselves. In their defense of infant Baptism the Lutheran Confessions do not make use of the pericopes about children in the

---

38. Tappert, 29; *BKS*, 53.

synoptic gospels, which later became and have remained crucial for the Lutheran position. Luther did incorporate Mark's pericope in his baptismal rite. The arguments of the Anabaptists and later the Baptists required that Lutheran theology expand into exegetical discussions. Their faulty interpretations had to be met squarely for the sake of the people, since distortions of the Bible are often used to dissuade Lutherans and others from having their children baptized. Pericopes about the blessing of the children are discussed elsewhere.

Infant Baptism is a practical matter, since its practice depends largely on the parents and other responsible adults to bring their children or those of others to Baptism. Pastors can preach about Baptism, but others present themselves or bring others to Baptism. In the articles on original sin (AC II) and Baptism (AC IX), the Reformers were not dealing with abstract theological issues but with the practical matter of large segments of the population coming under Anabaptist influence and thus not having their children baptized. What was at stake for the Reformers was the salvation of these children, a question vitally important at a time when more children died in infancy than reached maturity. The chance that unbaptized children might live into adolescence was not great. Depriving children of Baptism was, for the Lutheran Reformers, nothing less than consigning them to damnation. Refusing Baptism to children was a practical matter with critical consequences. This practice might be compared to one in the modern secular world in which children are deprived of life through abortion. Whatever problems Luther had with Rome, its churches at least baptized infants, and in doing so they were recognized as church.[39] In denying Baptism to infants, the Anabaptists could not with the same certainty be recognized as church. The Lutherans did not back away on this issue and in 1577 in the Formula of Concord (SD XII.11) they made their condemnation of the Anabaptists more explicit. Condemned is the error of the Anabaptists "that unbaptized children are not sinners before God but righteous and innocent, and hence in their innocence they will be saved without Baptism, which they do not need. Thus, they deny and reject the entire teaching of original sin and all that pertains thereto."[40]

Practical as this issue was, beneath the surface lay two opposing perspectives on Christianity, each with different views on sin, anthropology, and salvation itself. These differences surfaced in their views on the sacraments, thus reflecting these fundamental theological differ-

---

39. During the sixteenth century, church and state were joined in the union of the *Corpus Christianum*, and the beliefs of the ruling authorities were factors in determining the practice of religion. Children born within towns and lands controlled by Lutherans or Roman Catholics could be assured of Baptism. Where the Anabaptists took control, infant Baptism was forbidden.

40. FC SD XII.11; Tappert, 634; *BKS*, 1094.

ences. Since by Luther's death in 1546 Calvin was not yet a major figure in theology, his baptismal theology and his reasons for infant Baptism are not examined in the Confessions written by Luther or Melanchthon. Since neither Zwingli nor Calvin saw Baptism as a remedy for original sin, they could not attach to it the necessity that the Lutherans did. Their reasons for its practice seem contrived. To support infant Baptism, both Zwingli and Calvin made use of their interpretation of the Old Testament practice of circumcision as providing entrance into the external community of Israel, though each differed from the other in how Baptism was understood. Calvin did see Baptism as a divine pledge, which was not Zwingli's position. Luther also used circumcision in his discussion on Baptism, but for him it was more than entrance into a religious community. Like Baptism, circumcision "was also a sacrament, that is, a sign of eternal salvation for those who believed."[41] For Luther Baptism was a continuation of God's sacramental activities in the Old Testament. The pillar of fire, the cloud, and the mercy seat were no less means of grace than Baptism.[42] Calvin on the other hand saw Old Testament promises chiefly in terms of physical, temporal rewards for those who obeyed the Law. God's spiritual purposes of the Old Testament were restricted to messianic predictions and types.[43] In the New Testament God rewarded His people spiritually.

For the Calvinists, theological reasons for practicing infant Baptist in the sixteenth century were less important than making sure the practice continued in the face of the objections of Anabaptists, whose populistic appeal was effective in stirring up rebellion among the landless peasants. Maintaining a society controlled by ecclesiastical principles, including the practice of infant Baptism, was part of the Calvinist system of maintaining an ecclesiastically ordered society. They agreed with the Anabaptists in denying any regenerative power to the act of Baptism itself, but they could hardly argue for its practice on the grounds of its necessity for salvation. Thus they had to find other arguments to support its continued use.

It should be noted that the Formula of Concord (SD XII.4) includes among the condemned errors of the Anabaptists one which might in a more limited way be applied to the positions of Zwingli, Calvin, and the Reformed in general:

> That the children of Christians, because they are born of Christian and believing parents, are holy and children of God even without and prior to

---

41. *AE* 3:110.
42. *AE* 1:309.
43. Trigg, *Baptism*, 54–55. Also J. Samuel Preus, *From Shadow to Promise: Old Testament Interpretation from Augustine to Luther* (Cambridge, MA: Harvard University Press, 1969), 155–56.

baptism. They do not esteem infant Baptism very highly and do not advocate it, contrary to the express words of the promise which extends only to those who keep the covenant and do not despise it (Gen. 17:4–8, 19–21).[44]

Here the Formula is addressing the Anabaptists, but Zwingli and Calvin shared their view that because of their Christian parents, children were holy before and apart from Baptism. On that account they did not advocate an emergency Baptism for a child in danger of imminent death. Every Lutheran pastor knows that, also among Lutherans, many bring their children to be baptized for reasons which strongly resemble those used traditionally by the Reformed. For some it is a matter of family tradition. This situation can be corrected only by careful pastoral instruction, and in some cases not at all. Inconsistencies between practice and doctrine are as old as Paul's epistles, and not even Luther could overcome them. Baptism cannot be denied or delayed simply because those desiring it for their children are inadequately or even mistakenly informed. Lutherans have contented themselves that the Reformed have Baptism, even if the latter cannot support their theological reasons for it. Our liturgy is quite clear in providing original sin as the basis for Baptism: "We learn from the Word of God that we all are conceived and born sinful and so are in need of forgiveness. We would be lost forever unless delivered from sin, death, and everlasting condemnation."[45] Thus, the argument that original sin provides a basis for Baptism is part of the church's common liturgical life.

Apart from the pressing questions of infant Baptism as an issue dividing Lutherans and Anabaptists, differences in practice pointed to a fundamentally different understanding of Christianity. It would be difficult to find agreement in any one article of faith. Certainly the Lutheran Confessions never express any agreement, nor do they desire to do so. Where agreement on the universality of sin and its condemnation cannot be reached, then all the other articles of the faith are open to different interpretations or even denial. Even the assertion that children of Christian parents are saved without faith or only in anticipation of future faith (an argument essential to the Reformed) compromises justification by faith alone, the article by which the church stands or falls. This assertion also ridicules the doctrine of original sin in making exceptions, a kind of spiritual nepotism. Certainly the idea that God loves people because of family connections has no biblical support. In fact, Baptism inaugurates a new family relationship.

Modern Baptists present a more pressing problem. In refusing Baptism to infants they deny the universality of sin and its consequences,

---

44. Tappert, 634; *BKS*, 1094.
45. *Lutheran Worship* (St. Louis: Concordia Publishing House, 1982), 199.

as well as denying that children can have faith. So they deprive them of Christ's benefits which can be given only to faith. Such a denial of Baptism places us no longer at the periphery but at the center of the Christian faith. Differing practices surrounding infant Baptism continue to bring fundamental differences to the surface. The theological descendents of Zwingli and Calvin in the Reformed churches of today agree in practice with Lutherans in administering infant Baptism, but ideologically they are closer to the Baptists. A theology which does not see Baptism as a remedy for original sin is inimical to the Lutheran Confessions.

Though today's Baptists are justified in claiming they are neither the Reformation period Anabaptists nor their descendants, they do agree with them on the reason for not baptizing children. Those who practice only adult Baptism today, perhaps teaching the total depravity of humanity but making an exception for children, find themselves in a contradiction. They interpret depravity or sin as only a conscious decision of the will, which of course is not what the words "total depravity" mean. Consistently, faith is also defined as a conscious decision of the will. Such so-called decision theology cannot long coexist with a theology which requires infant Baptism. Those Baptists who oppose abortion but deny faith to infants are inconsistent.

The Lutherans did indeed take a critical position against the Roman Catholic understanding of the depth of universal depravity and its definition of grace as an infused substance (*gratia infusa*), especially as it was operative in Baptism, but both parties required Baptism.[46] Post–Vatican II Roman Catholicism gives reason a higher role in conversion, and views as possible salvation apart from faith in Christ. This is clearly Pelagianism, and at least a modified form of universalism. Such exceptions of salvation outside the church have had no effect on Roman Catholic practice, however. Their children are still baptized. In question among Roman Catholics today is their traditional belief that unbaptized infants are consigned to *limbus infantium*, a place between heaven and hell. Without the sacramental grace of Baptism, so it was argued, they were unacceptable in heaven, but they were not sufficiently depraved to deserve hell.[47] More recently the *Catechism of the Catholic Church* (1994) takes a modified stance and claims that we can "hope that there is a way of salvation for children who have died without Baptism."[48]

---

46. Leif Grane holds that in regard to Baptism, "the Council of Trent clearly keeps itself free of Pelagianism" (*Augsburg Confession*, 48–49). The problem arose over justification and the different understandings of grace.

47. This was accepted by some as Roman Catholic dogma as late as 1976. See e.g. Robert C. Broderick, *The Catholic Encyclopedia* (Nashville: Thomas Nelson Publishers, 1976), 349–50.

48. Para. 1261.

The Anabaptist refusal to baptize infants because they are not morally accountable and the traditional Roman Catholic doctrine of the *limbus infantium* reflect a common understanding that infants or children stand in a different moral relationship to God than does the rest of the human race. It is still a matter of how one understands original sin. The Lutheran understanding of Law and Gospel, especially as the Gospel was expressed in Baptism, never allowed for the luxury of the *limbus infantium* or of excusing infants from being morally accountable to God (*coram Deo*), but required that Baptism be seen as necessary, making the difference between eternal life and death. The Apology (IX.2) holds that the promise of salvation to children "does not apply to those who are outside of Christ's church, where there is neither Word nor sacrament, because Christ regenerates through Word and sacrament."[49] Here the key term is "church" and not "Christian family." Since the Christian can never escape the fact and reality of original sin as long as he lives, Baptism has continued meaning for him.

---

49. Tappert, 178; *BKS*, 247.

2

BAPTISM AS DIVINE COMMAND

Lutheran theology sees universal depravity as the problem which God intends Baptism to answer, but it derives the necessity of its practice from the dominical command of Mt 28:19 to baptize all nations (Ap. II.2; SC IV; LC IV.3–9). Luther's confessional writings, rather than Melanchthon's, take up the issue of the Matthew 28 passage. The Small Catechism states briefly that Baptism is not only water connected with God's Word but a water that is enveloped, taken into, surrounded by a command of God. Because a number of things that were self-evident for Luther in his confessional writings have in later times become contested, they should be addressed in contemporary theology.

Though eighteenth-century Rationalists had no difficulty seeing Baptism as a command of Jesus, they saw it as binding only on the apostles.[1] A more difficult problem arose with the quest for the historical Jesus, especially in the quest's understanding of His resurrection as an event in history. The command to baptize is attributed to the resurrected Lord, and so those without firm convictions about the resurrection were forced to find another origin for these words. Even those for whom the resurrection of Jesus was incontestable faced the same question in considering whether these were the authentic words of the resurrected Lord or whether they were perhaps attributed to Him by the later church, one or two generations after the resurrection.[2]

Still another fundamental question is how the evangelist Matthew sees Baptism within the program of his entire gospel. Do we have here an isolated passage used as a proof text to demonstrate a dogmatical truth developed later and taught by the church, or can the passage be seen as an integral part of Matthew's gospel and hence the preaching of Jesus?

---

1. For example, Julius August Ludwig Wegscheider, *Institutiones Theologiae Christianae Dogmaticae*, 3d rev. ed. (Halle: Gebauer et Filii, 1817), 364–65.

2. Doubts about the historical authenticity of the trinitarian baptismal formula are raised by Edmund Schlink, *The Doctrine of Baptism*, trans. Herbert J. A. Bouman (St. Louis: Concordia Publishing House, 1972), 26–30. Heiko Oberman claims that the Anabaptist criticism of the necessity of Baptism is supported by modern research which "has recognized that Luther's central biblical passage, the baptismal commandment, was added to the gospels of St. Matthew and St. Mark only later. The baptismal commandment is a teaching of the early Christian community" (*Luther*, 231).

MATTHEW 28:19 AS COMMAND TO THE CHURCH
FOR LUTHER

Luther's use of Mt 28:19 in the Large Catechism as an objective working of God's grace, not dependent on man (not even his faith), is a result of his confrontation with the Anabaptists, who insisted on seeing Baptism as man's good work or as his obligation in the sense of it being an obedient response to God. Luther places Baptism on the same level of necessity as the Ten Commandments and the Lord's Prayer. It "is of divine origin, not something devised or invented by men," and, like the first three parts of the Catechism (the Ten Commandments, the Creed, and the Lord's Prayer), it is "not spun out of any man's imagination but revealed and given by God himself" (LC IV.6).[3] (Notice that Luther views the Creed, that is, the Apostles' Creed, as given by Christ!) For Luther, Christ is God and whatever God says must be obeyed. The divine Word puts a value on the most inconsequential things. If God attached His Word to a piece of straw, that Word would have to be obeyed and that straw honored.

Christ not only commands Baptism, He also does the baptizing. Luther's intention in asserting the objectivity of the working of divine grace in Baptism is not to regard faith as unnecessary for salvation, but rather to *connect* the faith necessary for salvation *with* the water of Baptism. Faith believes in the Word of salvation, which is Christ Himself and His Gospel in the water. In Lutheran sacramental theology, Christ is present in such a way that from *within* the sacrament He is both the dispenser of grace and the *object* of faith. The Lutheran position contrasts sharply with that of the Reformed, for whom the sacramental action is performed on earth while Christ is worshiped in heaven.[4] The connection between Christ, the command to baptize, and the Baptism itself is so firm that, according to Luther, "whoever rejects Baptism rejects God's Word, faith, and Christ, who directs us and binds us to Baptism" (LC IV.31).[5] Baptism is in its entirety a christological event, since Christ is the one who commands it, is present in it as the one who performs it, and is the one who is believed.

Luther himself never suggested that Baptism be administered to unbelievers, and he never suggests that infants in their Baptism are unbelievers. "Without faith Baptism is of no use, although in itself it is

---

3. Tappert, 437; *BKS*, 691.
4. Calvin holds that while the benefits of salvation are obtained through Christ's death and resurrection, they are bestowed neither by Christ nor by Baptism, but by the Holy Spirit. The Father is called the cause of salvation, the Son the matter, and Spirit "the effect of our purification and regeneration" (*Institutes* IV.XV.6).
5. Tappert, 440; *BKS*, 697.

an infinite, divine treasure" (LC IV.34).[6] He nevertheless asserts that just as unbelief does not invalidate the Sacrament of the Altar, so it does not invalidate Baptism. Luther's assertion that the Baptism of infants would be valid even if they did not believe, and that it would not have to be repeated later in life when conscious faith was present (as the Anabaptists insisted), is offered by him only as a hypothetical example to affirm the objectivity of this sacrament (LC IV.55). For Luther it was not simply a matter of asserting the objectivity of the sacrament, but rather the certainty about Christ whose person and acts have an existence apart from faith or unbelief. Nevertheless, Christ in the sacrament or in any other form becomes efficacious for salvation only through faith. The Lutheran Confessions do not distinguish between the Baptisms of adults and infants regarding what they are, do, or require, as if one Baptism required faith and the other not. There is only one Baptism commanded by Christ, which is necessary for salvation and requires both remorse over sins and faith. In the Lutheran Confessions the doctrine of Baptism is chiefly that of infant Baptism. There were two reasons for this. Sociologically, only in rare cases in the Middle Ages were adults baptized.[7] Theologically, the Baptism of infants has become the norm for the Baptism of all others, as they are most fit for the kingdom of God, a point that will be elaborated below.

BAPTISM AS LAW OR GOSPEL OR BOTH?

The question arises whether Baptism is Law or Gospel, because the Lutheran Confessions understand Baptism as a command of God (German, *Befehl*; Latin, *praeceptum*). Sometimes the sacraments are called God's ordinances, a term properly used to refer to rites accomplished in the church for her benefit, but improperly used to refer to ways in which we please God by fulfilling His law. The matter is not resolved simply by asserting that the sacrament is necessary for salvation, since without explanation both the fulfilling of the Law and the believing of the Gospel can be said to be necessary for salvation, though obviously in different senses. The Law offers salvation to those who fulfill it, though no one of us is able. The Gospel gives salvation without our works. In understanding Baptism, a distinction must be made between what is necessary for salvation under the Law and what is necessary for salvation under the Gospel. Without this distinction, the baptized person may in his confusion believe that by undergoing the liturgical rite, he is doing God a favor.

---

6. Ibid.
7. Toon, *Born Again*, 85.

Luther understood Mt 28:19 in its entirety as a command spoken to the apostles and still binding on the church. From this command he finds the foundation for the confessional understanding of Baptism. His seeing Mt 28:19 as the basis for a baptismal theology is supported by the internal evidence of the gospel itself. The command to the apostles to make disciples out of the nations or Gentiles through Baptism is derived from the imperative "make disciples." The words "teaching them to observe [keep] all things whatsoever I commanded you" are applied by the evangelist to the entire corpus of Jesus' teachings that He has delivered to them for His church. Luther's understanding of Baptism as a command for Christ's church is the proper reflection of the simple grammatical understanding of this pericope that Christ was in fact giving a command to His disciples. Luther uses this understanding of Mt 28:19 as a binding command on the church to condemn the Anabaptists, who by exempting themselves from this command in refusing to baptize children and by stating that it was unnecessary demonstrated that they were not following Christ's command. Since this passage was the foundation for the establishment of the church, those who disobeyed it were in danger of being judged disobedient to God and in fact may have been surrendering their claim to be Christians, that is, believers in Christ who show their faith in Him by believing His Word.

Does Luther's act of placing Mt 28:19, 20 in such a crucial position, both for building his theology of Baptism and for judging the position of others, bring this passage into the realm of the Law rather than the Gospel? Identifying the command as an "evangelical imperative" does little to clear up the problem and may confuse the issue even more. As mentioned, the concept of divine command is found twice in this pericope. The imperative to make disciples out of the nations is fulfilled first when the Eleven baptize the nations and then when they teach the new disciples all that Jesus has commanded. The statement or charter with which Christ establishes His church and lays down the working procedures for it must clearly belong to the Gospel and not the Law. The imperative to make disciples out of all nations by Baptism is simply the charter statement on and by which Jesus establishes His church: it describes how the promise made to Peter (Mt 16:18) that Christ will build His church is carried out. Ignoring or disobeying the command to make disciples by baptizing is tantamount to a rejection of the Christian message. Such refusal is not simply a sin on the same level as breaking the moral law as set forth in the Ten Commandments. Failure to follow the command to baptize is more dangerous, since attacking or failing to carry out Mt 28:19, 20 is an assault on the very foundation of the church. Luther was well aware of the vital nature of this passage, as indicated by his violent attack on the

Anabaptists, whom he found to be in direct contradiction with it. For contravening the Law, there is salvation in the Gospel, but for the despising of the Gospel (that which is God's own solution to the Law), there is no solution.

The concept of obedience or the life of sanctification accompanying Baptism has been deduced from "teaching them to *obey* everything I have commanded you" (Mt 28:20 NIV; emphasis added). The intent of these words, however, is not to speak about the Christian life, but about the nature or quality of Jesus' teaching as divine Word of God.[8] The ordinary New Testament word for "law" as a requirement for salvation is *nomos* (νόμος), which may also mean the written revelation of God in reference either to the Books of Moses (*torah*, תּוֹרָה) or what we call today the Old Testament. The word used here by Jesus is related to the *entole*, which refers to words spoken as coming from God Himself, regardless of the specific content of that word or message. The use of this word in its verbal form identifies the entire gospel of Matthew as the Word of God that must become the content of the apostolic proclamation to the nations and which the nations, now baptized, must believe.

BAPTISM NOT AN ISOLATED SACRAMENT

The Lutheran Confessions do not regard Baptism as an isolated sacramental act. At the time of the Reformation, the generally agreed-upon position of the Roman Catholic Church was that Baptism forgave original sin and actual sins, those committed before receiving this sacrament, but that it had no effect on those committed later. Penance restores those who have lost their baptismal grace and "offers a new possibility to convert and recover the grace of justification."[9] Purgatory provided a final purification.[10] The Roman Catholic Church "also commends almsgiving, indulgences, and works of penance undertaken in behalf of the dead."[11]

For the Lutheran Confessions, Baptism was a sacrament that actually gave the forgiveness of sins. Here there was agreement with the Roman Catholics. However, unlike their Roman Catholic adversaries,

---

8. See Eugene C. Chase, Jr., "The Translation of the Greek Words Τηρέω and Φυλάσσω in the New International Version, and Its Implications for Theology Today," *Lutheran Theological Review* 6 (Spring/Summer 1994): 21–36. In commenting on this translation's rendering of Mt 28:20, Chase remarks that the use of the word "obey" instead of "keep" may suggest "the outward obedience itself is seen to be the most important aspect of what Jesus is saying." An inward keeping means cherishing (ibid., 35). The Great Commission, which includes Baptism, is often set forth before the people as Law, the very thing against which Chase warns.
9. *Catechism of the Catholic Church*, para. 1446.
10. Ibid., para. 1030–32.
11. Ibid., para. 1032.

the Lutherans believed that Baptism projected this forgiveness into the Christian's entire life. Thus, in the Small Catechism Luther can speak of Baptism having the daily effect of drowning the evil nature remaining in the baptized and allowing a new man, the Christian, to come forth to a life of good works, pleasing to God. In the Large Catechism (IV.71) he can speak of "the old man [who] daily decreases until he is finally destroyed."[12] Leif Grane explains the teaching of the Augsburg Confession in this way: "The significance of Baptism is dying to sin and the resurrection of the new person in the grace of God. This does not happen completely until bodily death occurs; thus all of life is a spiritual Baptism without ceasing until death."[13]

It would hardly be accurate to say that Luther or the Confessions eliminated the third sacrament, Penance. In the Large Catechism, Luther, rather than disposing of Penance, incorporates it into Baptism, so that Baptism is not only an isolated sacramental act initiating the Christian into the fellowship of the church, but a sacrament to which the Christian can daily return. The distance between the time of the Baptism and the time when the sin is committed does not diminish Baptism's efficacy in offering forgiveness. Luther could confidently say, "Therefore Baptism remains forever" (LC IV.77).[14]

Whether Penance is embraced by Baptism (as for Luther in the Large Catechism) or whether as the continued life of repentance it remains a separate sacramental action, as with Melanchthon in the Apology (XIII.4), is immaterial for the faith life of the church. Even though Luther saw Penance as part of Baptism and not a separate act, it was Luther and not Melanchthon who provided as part of the Small Catechism (V) a section on how the people are to confess their sins and receive absolution. This absolution was to be followed by "amendment of life and forsaking of sin" (AC XII.6).[15] Luther placed his section on confession and absolution after his section on Baptism to show that they were a continuation of Baptism, and before the section on the Lord's Supper to show that repentance was prerequisite for receiving Christ's body and blood. Since Luther made confession a separate section in the Small Catechism, he may have given the impression that he viewed it as a separate sacramental act. Regardless, he viewed confession and absolution as sacramental, since he saw in them the extension of Baptism into the life of the church.

---

12. Tappert, 445; *BKS*, 705.
13. *Augsburg Confession*, 105.
14. Tappert, 446; *BKS*, 706.
15. Tappert, 35; *BKS*, 67.

3

THE BIBLICAL ORIGINS OF BAPTISM

The Confessions do not attempt to provide an exhaustive interpretation of significant Bible passages for Baptism, preferring to argue from the basis of the universality of sin and grace. Such exegetical studies are part of the confessional heritage, however, as the confessors and especially Luther offer this wider support in their writings. A more elaborate discussion of the biblical evidence becomes more important in a religious environment in which the Baptists are effective in convincing others that this evidence supports their position that Baptism is not a sacrament. For the institution and benefits of Baptism, Luther in his catechisms uses Mt 28:19 and the longer and contested ending of Mark (16:16): "He who believes and is baptized shall be saved."[1] For the benefits of Baptism, Luther uses Ti 3:5, and for a description of its working in the life of the Christian, he cites Rom 6:4. These passages have a focus similar to the now-contested Mk 16:16, so a confessional truth is not suspended without adequate biblical foundation.

---

1. Most ancient texts do not contain the section, so the matter is not absolutely settled. One exception to the prevailing opinion that Mk 16:9–20 is not from the pen of the evangelist is voiced by William R. Farmer in *The Last Twelve Verses of Mark* (London and New York: Cambridge University Press, 1974). Using critical techniques, Farmer holds that Mark appended these verses after the main body of the gospel had been completed. Mark, aware that his conclusion (16:8) was unsatisfactory, especially in comparison with Matthew 28, added verses 9 through 16. Farmer arrives at his conclusion by comparing the controverted section with the rest of the gospel, and finds nothing stylistically unique here. Thus the evangelist Mark might well be the author of the controverted appendix.

This section also does not contain anything which is theologically unique. Its content has parallels in both Mark and the rest of the New Testament. Apart from arguments for and against this section's authenticity, it is not unlikely that the words "he who believes and is baptized" (Mk 16:16) were actually spoken by Jesus and were first part of the oral tradition. Their importance was recognized, and they were then appended to the gospel. John 20:30 and 21:25 claim that most of the words of Jesus did not find their way into the written gospels. The verses of Mk 16:9–20 made their way into this gospel after the major section reached its present form. Hence Mk 16:16, as it is cited in Luther's Small Catechism, can be used without adjustment or comment.

Werner Elert, who with Paul Althaus, Jr., and Hermann Sasse is recognized as one of the three great twentieth-century German confessional scholars, offers another approach. He opines that an early church scribe noted the absence of Baptism in this gospel's conclusion and attempted to correct it by adding the now controverted section. He also notes that Mark, by describing Jesus as the one who baptizes with the Holy Spirit (1:8), is aware of Christian Baptism. He provides similar arguments for John and Luke and for Paul's epistles, where explicit commands to baptize are also lacking (*Der Christliche Glaube*, 5th ed., enlarged and with a foreword by Ernst Kinder [Hamburg: Furche-Verlag, 1960], 442–43).

The Biblical Origins of Baptism

Since for the Lutheran Confessions Mt 28:19 is the fundamental focus, the question that must be raised is whether the command to baptize is a sacramental innovation in the New Testament without precedent in the Old. In other words, is the command to baptize an isolated sacramental imperative attached at the end of Matthew, or does Baptism bring together into itself previous "sacramental" activities of God?

Both Lutheran and Reformed theologies find a basis in the events and rites in the Old Testament for New Testament Baptism. Where Lutheran theology sees the rites of both testaments as means of grace, Reformed theology does not. Both positions consistently apply their principles, which of course are diametrically opposed to each other. Providing an agreed-upon definition of "sacrament" and then projecting it back into the Old Testament is problematic. While we are convinced that Baptism and the Lord's Supper are *the* sacraments of the church, our concept of sacraments cannot be so narrowly defined as to prevent us from seeing that God has always worked sacramentally with His people. Sacraments are not really New Testament innovations, and yet the Old Testament rites do not share in the incarnation and atonement in the way that Baptism and the Lord's Supper do. Rather, the Old Testament rites and even certain historical events anticipate New Testament sacraments. As Luther notes, the Flood and the Exodus prefigure Baptism.[2] While such Old Testament liturgical rites and historical occurrences cannot exhaust the meaning of Baptism, they can inform it.

Paul's reference to Baptism as "the circumcision made without hands" and "the circumcision of Christ" (Col 2:11–12) is quite important. Comparing Baptism with circumcision is complicated, however, by the Reformed view which connects circumcision to their concept of covenant, which assures salvation to the children of believers. Covenant as a mode for understanding Baptism was basic to Zwingli. He explicitly denied that Baptism actually conferred anything, but held that it was only a sign of faith and conversion.[3] His ideas were those of the Anabaptists, for whom he is the spiritual father. Karl Barth claims Zwingli for his own also. At first Zwingli was inclined to give up infant Baptism, but found a reason for continuing the practice in the Old Testament rite of circumcision, which knitted Israel together as a nation. This argument assumed that the old covenant was of equal value and authority with the new.[4] Calvin also moves from the Old Testament circumcision to his understanding of Baptism,[5] but, unlike Zwingli,

---

2. *AE* 53:97.

3. From *Huldrych Zwinglie sämtliche Werke*, quoted in Ulrich Gäbler, *Huldrych Zwingli: His Life and Work*, trans. Ruth C. L. Gritsch (Philadelphia: Fortress Press), 128.

4. Ibid., 125–31.

5. "Certainly, if circumcision was a literal sign, the same view must be taken of baptism, since, in the second chapter to the Colossians, the apostle makes the one to be

Calvin goes further in seeing both as divinely given external pledges or badges; however, neither rite bestows grace.[6] Both Zwingli and Calvin saw one covenant embraced by the external signs of circumcision and Baptism, and failed to see either rite as a means of grace.[7] This misinterpretation of circumcision, and with it Baptism, is based on a particular view of covenant which requires human participation, as if God and man were partners in a contract or an agreement. On this point Barth admitted an affinity with the Reformed theologians which he did not find with Luther. Since the Reformed rely so heavily on the Old Testament circumcision in their defense of infant Baptism, it would be tempting for Lutherans to abandon its use in developing a biblical theology of Baptism. Many Lutherans have done this with the covenant, and dismissed it as a valid category in understanding Christ's death and His Supper. They assume that the Reformed view of covenant as a pact or treaty requiring human participation is that of the Old Testament, and hence find the term theologically inappropriate. This Lutheran capitulation to the Reformed view of covenant concedes that their definitions are right, and the Lutherans thereby forfeit valid biblical data and deny their own heritage derived not only from Luther but also from Johann Gerhard.[8]

Paul's comparison of Baptism to circumcision centers on rejection of sin and inclusion in Christ (Col 2:11–12). Baptism removes sin, as circumcision removes the flesh of the body, and incorporates the baptized into Christ's death and resurrection as circumcision incorporated its recipients into the saving community of Israel. Old associations are put away and a new life is inaugurated. This passage is the only place in the New Testament where circumcision is used as a model of Baptism. The connection between Galatians and Colossians is uncertain, but it may be that, in the face of Judaizers within the church, Paul argued that Baptism had finally taken the place of circumcision. Our Confessions make use of this passage, but not for Baptism.[9] Luther in his *Lectures on Genesis* used circumcision to advance his understanding of Baptism, especially of infants and their faith (see chapter 10).[10] Both

---

not a whit more spiritual than the other.... For [Paul's] object is to show that baptism is the same thing to Christians that circumcision formerly was to the Jews" (*Institutes* IV.XVI.11).

6. Ibid., IV.XVI.4.

7. Trigg, *Baptism*, 217.

8. Gerhard's discussion on the sacraments in his *Loci Theologici* was assigned to locus 18, circumcision and Passover to 19, and Baptism to 20.

9. Ap. XII.46; Tappert, 188; *BKS*, 260. The passage is used to show that true repentance consists of contrition and faith.

10. Gerhard had Luther's *Lectures on Genesis* at his disposal in developing his own ideas on Old Testament sacraments (*Loci Theologici* 4:184 [locus 18, para. 46]; 4:177 [locus 18, para. 64]), and it is not surprising that their views are similar. For example, Baptism

circumcision and Baptism are marked by external weakness and are masks under which God works. It is not that Luther does not see any value in the external sign. The sign points to the reality within it. Gerhard followed Luther in affirming that circumcision no less than Baptism was a means of salvation,[11] with both requiring faith.[12] Both circumcision and Baptism involve suffering[13] and are not only rites of initiation into the covenant but *are the covenant itself*. Lutheran theology uniquely sees Baptism as coterminous with the Christian life, and Luther used circumcision to illustrate this.[14] The destructive and saving effects of water in the Old Testament provided a point of departure for both Peter and Paul in their presentations of Baptism. This view seems naturally connected to Baptism, since the Greek word *baptizo* (βαπτίζω) means to apply water.

First Peter 3:18–22 brings together three items: a primitive form of the Apostles' Creed, the waters of the Noahic flood, and Baptism. After speaking of Christ's sacrifice as a death for sins accomplished by the just for the unjust to bring us to God, Peter continues with Christ's descent to the prison to preach, to those who had not listened to Noah's proclamation of the Gospel many years before, His resurrection, ascension, and session at God's right hand. In his reference to Noah, Peter refers to the water of the Flood not primarily as a destructive force (the expected meaning), but as the saving agent that lifted the ark up and

---

and circumcision cannot be equated, but both exhibit Christ's presence (4:141 [locus 18, para. 10]) and are sacraments of initiation (4:160–61 [locus 18, para. 44]). Gerhard shows his dependence on Luther in seeing such things as the Old Testament sacrifices and the rainbow as sacraments. Unlike New Testament sacraments, the Old Testament ones are limited in respect to time, but they are still sacraments in which Christ is present. Roman Catholic and Reformed positions on the sacraments were usually at odds, but they were agreed that grace was not given in the Old Testament rites. This position had been set forth by the Council of Florence in 1439 and affirmed by the Council of Trent, 1545–60, and defended by the Roman Catholic theologian Robert Bellarmine. Gerhard's insistence that Old Testament sacraments were effective means of grace set him apart not only from the Reformed, but also from the Roman Catholics (4:174 [locus 18, para. 60]). A fuller discussion on the Old Testament rites and events as sacraments, including their relation to creation, is anticipated in a separate volume on the sacraments in the Confessional Lutheran Dogmatics series. See also David P. Scaer, "Sacraments as an Affirmation of Creation," *Concordia Theological Quarterly* 54 (October 1993): 241–64.

11. *Ergo circumcisio fuit salutare medium, per quod non solum praeputium carnis, sed etiam cordis in infantibus fuit oblatum* (*Loci Theologici* 4:178 [locus 18, para. 64]).

12. *Ergo sacramenta V.T. itidem fuerunt efficacia media spiritualium beneficiorum credentibus collatorum* (ibid., 182 [para. 69]).

13. *AE* 3:143, 136, 170–71, 102, 135.

14. Trigg says of Luther's position, "Baptism then not only is the sacrament of initiation to the covenant. Like circumcision, it *is* the covenant. After wandering away, the wanderers return to baptism or circumcision; there is no idea that as signs of initiation they can have no further use. In another way both signs determine the nature of life under their covenant as death and resurrection. . . . Through the sign of baptism as through circumcision, the Church is born. As the sign of initiation, baptism must play its part in defining the limits of the Church" (*Baptism*, 45).

saved it from destruction. The otherwise destructive waters of the Flood are compared to Baptism that now saves Christians, that is, the church: "Baptism . . . now saves you" (1 Pt 3:21). The Flood is the divine judgment against unbelief, and becomes the *means* for saving eight souls, that is, Noah and his family, from whom as the last remnant on earth God will construct a new humanity. Luther draws the conclusion that the ark was the church which is lifted up by the waters of Baptism. Like Paul's use of circumcision, the attention is on an inauguration, a new beginning, an initiation. In 1 Peter salvation is caused specifically by water (διεσώθησαν δι' ὕδατος). By further retrospection, the waters of creation on which the world was built (2 Pt 3:5) may provide the foundation for the waters of Baptism in which God brings forth a new creation. This understanding may be suggested in Ti 3:5, where the phrase "washing of regeneration" brings to mind the Genesis account of creation with the word *palingenesia* (παλιγγενεσία). Quite literally, the Christian is created again by Baptism.[15]

Paul's statement in 1 Cor 10:1, in describing Israel's birth as a nation through the Baptism of the sea and the cloud, resembles 1 Pt 3:20, 21 in seeing water as God's agent. Israel's founding fathers are "baptized into Moses in the cloud and the sea." The language here is clearly baptismal, and resembles the typical New Testament language of Christians being baptized into Christ. Though the word "water" is not used, its presence is obvious from the words "sea" and "cloud." They are water. The Israelites left the old life of Egypt behind them, and by passing through the sea entered into a new life. What God had begun by their passing through the sea was continued by the cloud that surrounded and enveloped them. Baptism inaugurates and remains. The baptism into Moses was more than an initiation; it established Israel as God's people and nation.

Passover, the commemoration of the coming through the sea, was assumed into Easter (1 Cor 5:6–8). On that feast celebrating Christ's resurrection, the church baptized the catechumens and admitted them to the Holy Communion. Paul's resurrection discourse (1 Corinthians 15), which may have been intended to inform their celebration of Easter, is connected with Baptism, though the Corinthian practice is aberrant (v. 29). Moses is introduced as a Christ figure who stands in the place of Christ. Here he is not the stern law-giver, but the person through whom God gives salvation to His people and into whom the people must be incorporated if they are to share in the blessings which God

---

15. Abraham Calov, in commenting on the FC SD III.18–19, uses language reminiscent of the Genesis creation account: *Illa vero in novum hominem mutamur, et ad imaginem Dei in justitia et sanctitate sitam renovamur. Regeneratio praecedit, renovatio sequitur, quia per fidem justificati renovamur et sanctificamur*, etc. (quoted in Philippi, *Kirchliche Glaubenslehre*, vol. 5, no. 2 [Stuttgart: Samuel Gottlieb Liesching, 1864], 213).

bestows through him for their benefit. "All passed" through the sea (1 Cor 10:1–2) suggests that children can be baptized, a point which is not lost upon the Baptists![16] Significantly, Luther uses both the Flood and the passing through the sea in the "Flood Prayer" of his baptismal liturgies:

> Almighty eternal God, who according to thy righteous judgment didst condemn the unbelieving world through the flood and in thy great mercy didst preserve believing Noah and his family, and who didst drown hardhearted Pharaoh with all his host in the Red Sea and didst lead thy people Israel through the same on dry ground, thereby prefiguring this bath of thy Baptism . . .[17]

A completed doctrine of Baptism cannot be drawn from Old Testament references, but here too God was acting graciously through means, namely, circumcision and water, to make Israel His own. Circumcision, the flood waters lifting up the ark, and the passing through the sea were initiation acts through which God was saving His people. The New Testament writers saw that in Baptism God was *not* doing something entirely new, but was only perfecting and completing what He had already done. The question is not whether Baptism was found in the Old Testament. Quite evidently it was not. But God was acting *sacramentally* with His people to inaugurate them into a new life. The New Testament writers were aware of this, and incorporated Old Testament understandings into their presentation of Baptism. God was forgiving the sins of His people through these acts. This is what God's grace means![18] Though the understanding of God's acting graciously toward His people in Baptism originates with Jesus, the prophets provided the New Testament writers with the foundation for their teaching on Baptism.

THE BAPTISM OF JOHN

The person of John the Baptist serves as the link between God's sacramental dealings with the first Israel and His unique dealing with the church, His new Israel, through Baptism. John's baptism stands at the dawn of the new era in which Israel is reborn as God's new people. Discussion of God's sacramental dealings with Israel and the baptism of John may be of no immediate practical value, since these activities have long since ceased. They are of immense dogmatic and homiletical

---

16. G. R. Beasley-Murray, *Baptism in the New Testament* (Grand Rapids, MI: William B. Eerdmans, 1962), 181–85.
17. *AE* 53:97, 107.
18. Concerning circumcision, Adolf Hoenecke says, "Sie hat geistliche Wirkung, vermittelt Gnade" (*Ev.-Luth. Dogmatik*, 5 vols. [Milwaukee: Northwestern Publishing House, 1909–17], 4:69).

The Biblical Origins of Baptism

value, however, not only in understanding the nature of Christian Baptism, but in maintaining that God's sacramental dealing with His people did not begin with the New Testament era. Christian preaching on Baptism can be shaped by the Old Testament. Pieper and Hoenecke link the baptism of John and later Christian Baptism because both are instituted by God and bestow the forgiveness of sins.[19] All four gospels give a prominent place to John's baptism as a prelude to the post-resurrection Baptism of Jesus. At the time of the writing of Matthew (3:1, 11:11–12) and Luke (7:20, 33), John is called the "Baptist," (Ἰωάννης ὁ βαπτιστὴς), a title indicating not only that baptizing or using water was the most identifiable characteristic of his ministry, but that he was "the baptizer" through whom God gave this sacrament to the church and the world. By being baptized by John, Jesus changed the dimensions of that ritual in two ways: He gave definition to the baptism of John first by being baptized and then by His death and resurrection, and so elevated the baptism of John into Christian Baptism. What happened in John's baptism of Jesus recurs in Christian Baptism. Luther thinks along these lines:

> In the same manner, and even much more, you should honor and exalt Baptism on account of the Word, since God himself has honored it by words and deeds and has confirmed it by wonders from heaven. Do you think it was a jest that the heavens opened when Christ allowed himself to be baptized, that the Holy Spirit descended visibly, and that the divine glory and majesty were manifested everywhere?[20]

An examination of this passage from Luther shows that he understands the efficacy of Baptism in terms of what happened at the baptism of Jesus.[21] Here Luther anticipates current exegetical approaches in letting the Baptism of Matthew 28 be informed by that of John in chapter 3. In the baptism of John the water was joined to the Word, and the Trinity in whose name Christian Baptism is offered appears.[22] Luther includes this thought in the "Flood Prayer" of his baptismal liturgy:

> ... who through the baptism of thy dear Child, our Lord Jesus Christ, hast consecrated and set apart the Jordan and all water as a salutary flood and a rich and full washing away of sins . . .[23]

Matthew places the pre-Easter baptizing of John and Jesus on the same level. The Fourth Evangelist places the baptisms of John and Jesus

---

19. Pieper, *Christian Dogmatics*, trans. and ed. Theodore Engelder, John Theodore Mueller, and Walter Albrecht, 3 vols. (St. Louis: Concordia Publishing House, 1950–53), 3:288–89; Hoenecke, *Ev.-Luth. Dogmatik* 4:83.
20. LC IV.21; Tappert, 439; *BKS*, 695.
21. As is acknowledged also by the Baptist Frederick Dale Brunner, *The Christ Book* (Waco, TX: Word Publishing, 1987), 87–88.
22. *AE* 8:145.
23. *AE* 53:97.

side by side as parallel and not competing activities (Jn 4:1–3). The ministry of each is described as a preaching of repentance, since the kingdom of the heavens is near (Mt 3:2, 4:17). Jesus, and perhaps Peter, Andrew, and Nathaniel as disciples of John, had been baptized by him (Jn 1:35–51). For John and for Jesus, before His crucifixion, this preaching of faith and salvation was accompanied by baptizing, that is, the use of water, through which activity these believers in the Coming One were incorporated into God's saving activity. There is nothing to suggest that John preached chiefly a message of Law and damnation, and Jesus a message of the Gospel and love. Both preached about what God *was about to do* in Jesus. In one sense John stands with the Old Testament prophets in speaking of what God will do, and in another sense he stands with Jesus as he actually introduces the characteristic form of Christian Baptism that includes the preaching of the Gospel, the confession of sins, and the application of water by divine authority (Mt 21:25). Both Jesus and John are authorized by God. The components of John's baptism are not only external signs, but ones that affect the core of human existence. Mark says specifically of John's baptism that it worked the forgiveness of sins (Mk 1:4), a phrase attached by Matthew to Christ's blood in the Supper (Mt 26:28).

If the meaning and working of Christian Baptism were totally exhausted by the conferring of the forgiveness of sins, then it would be easy to draw an equation between John's baptism and Christian Baptism, but this simply is not so. Christian Baptism incorporates and then expands on John's baptism. Matthew 28:19 presupposes Jesus' death and resurrection, which provide the foundation for Baptism. By this rite the believer is incorporated into these saving events. This Baptism requires faith not in the Coming One, but in the One who by His cross has already come, and comes still by the water and His blood (1 Jn 5:6). Paul presents Baptism in the context of Jesus' death and resurrection, to which Peter adds His ascension and session at God's right hand. The baptisms which were administered by John, Jesus, and their disciples before the resurrection could only anticipate Jesus' death and resurrection for the recipients of these baptisms; thus such preparatory baptisms did not in fact incorporate them into that death and resurrection.

The problem of the effectiveness of John's baptism in the post-resurrection community surfaces in Acts 19:1–7, where Paul finds in Ephesus Christians, identified as disciples, who have received John's baptism but are ignorant of the Holy Spirit. They are called disciples because they believed in John's message that Jesus was the Coming One. Thus they are not classified as unbelievers, but as disciples who believe the Gospel. Though they have believed in Jesus and were baptized in John's baptism, they are now baptized in the name of the Lord Jesus, that is, the Father-Son-Spirit, and speak in languages foreign to them. Even a superficial reading does not permit a one-for-one identification between the pre- and post-Easter baptisms. These disciples in Ephesus are given *another* Baptism.

Another question can be asked, whether *all* who were baptized before the resurrection, including the wide circle of Jesus' followers in Palestine, for example the five hundred brethren (1 Cor 15:6), were given another Baptism. There is no record or even suggestion of another Baptism for the pre-resurrection followers of Jesus in Acts 1 or 2, where the apostles preach and baptize but are not baptized again. To what extent was the pre-Easter baptism valid or effective? Perhaps the solution is that those who knew the earthly Jesus and had been witnesses to His resurrection were accounted and regarded as participants in His resurrection and did not have to be baptized in the name of the Lord Jesus. At Pentecost, by the outpouring of the Spirit, the baptism given by John became the Baptism of Jesus. The baptism of John was, as his preaching was, anticipatory and thus incomplete. Both his preaching and his baptizing looked forward to what God was soon going to do in Jesus' death and resurrection. His was not a Baptism in the name of Jesus, and so a full revelation of God as Father-Son-Spirit was not given. This could be given only after and then through the crucifixion in which the Father offered up Jesus who gave His Spirit to the church in Baptism. The ignorance of the Ephesus disciples about the Holy Spirit could hardly have been an intellectual ignorance, that is, that they never had heard the words "Holy Spirit," since John describes Jesus as baptizing with the Holy Spirit. Rather, they were unaware of the post-Easter situation in which the Spirit testified to the death and resurrection of Jesus as completed acts of salvation. The miraculous speaking in foreign languages of God's work is a repetition of the Pentecost miracle, to demonstrate that they have been received completely into the apostolic fellowship of the church. Though a one-for-one identification between John's baptism and Christian Baptism cannot be made, the former gives form, and in a certain sense substance, to the latter. John A. T. Robinson correctly says of Jesus' Baptism that "it is John's baptism raised to a higher power—water and spirit, as he foretold."[24] The outward liturgical shapes of both baptisms are the same; that is, water is applied to believers upon a confession of their sin and belief. The Coming One is "fleshed out" by the crucifixion and resurrection, which now forms the substance of Christian Baptism. Christians are not merely baptized into

---

24. *The Priority of John*, ed. J. F. Coackley (Oak Park, IL: Meyer-Stone Books, 1987), 185. Robinson draws his argument from Armitage Robinson's comments on Jn 3:3–5: "When Nicodemus was told, 'Except a man be born of water and spirit he cannot enter the kingdom of God,' he would necessarily be reminded of the Baptist's works and words: the whole of John's mission lies behind the saying" (*The Historical Character of John's Gospel* [London and New York: Longman's Green, 1929], 24–25).

Christ, but into His death and resurrection, and to them God is revealed as Father-Son-Spirit.

THE BAPTISM OF JESUS BY JOHN

The baptism of Jesus by John is a factor in Luther's definition of Baptism. Its inclusion in all four gospels indicates its importance. With this event the salvation accomplished by Jesus begins. This point is reinforced in the first three gospels with the opening of the heavens and the voice from heaven identifying Jesus as God's Son. The Fourth Evangelist says that John saw the Spirit coming down on Jesus as a dove (Jn 1:32). In Matthew, John's refusal to baptize Jesus is countered by Jesus' insistence that only in this way will God's saving righteousness be completed (Mt 3:15). It simply will not do to regard John's baptism as a mere outward liturgical formality, a ritual without internal substance, since by this act Jesus becomes *sacramentally* involved with sinners. His baptism by John becomes for Jesus the *sacramental* participation in His own death, so that now He can call His death His baptism: "I have a baptism with which to be baptized and I am under great distress until it is completed" (βάπτισμα δὲ ἔχω βαπτισθῆναι, καὶ πῶς συνέχομαι ἕως ὅτου τελεσθῇ; Lk 12:50; my translation). The deaths of the disciples will also become their baptisms. As listeners of John (and also the later church) went into their respective baptisms confessing their sins, so Jesus in His baptism confesses His identity with sinners so that He becomes sin for us (Paul) or the chief sinner Himself (Luther).[25] This sin spells for Jesus not only an ordinary death but a death in the place of and for sinners. His baptism is a vicarious death for sinners. Just as Christian Baptism has its roots in God's saving acts in the Old Testament, so also the command of Mt 28:19 is not simply divine, isolated sacramental imperative, but a necessary reality built upon John's baptizing Jesus into His death. This death in turn is a baptism for Jesus and the foundation of Christian Baptism. All those who are baptized in the name of the Lord Jesus participate with Him in this one death. The Nicene Creed's "one baptism for the remission of sins" also presup-

---

25. "Jesus submitted to the baptism of John and thereby announced his solidarity with the generation which repented prior to the appearance of the messianic era. His submission to the baptism was therefore an early expression of his consciousness of being the humiliated Son of Man. Thus, there is a factual connection between his submission to the baptism of John and the *logion* in Mk 10:38, where Jesus likens his own death to a baptism. This solidarity with the guilty race, to which Jesus gave expression by submitting to the baptism of sinners unto repentance, implies the necessity of his rejection and death. The baptism of repentance is in itself a death which must precede the actual new life in the kingdom of God" (Regin Prenter, *Creation and Redemption*, trans. Theodor I. Jensen [Philadelphia: Fortress Press, 1967], 464).

poses that Christ's death is the one death for all. The Word gives the water its sacramental force to forgive sins; but this Word is not a message sent from a distant heaven, but the *actual* presence of the God-Man, Jesus Christ, standing in His baptism with and in the place of sinners and who Himself becomes "the baptizer" and invites them to share in His death. Consider Luther: "[God] appears to you in Baptism. He baptizes you himself and addresses [absolves] you himself."[26] Not only is there continuity between the baptism of John and Christian Baptism; together with the death and resurrection of Jesus they constitute one reality.

Mark is the only gospel that includes the question to James and John, "Are you able . . . to be baptized with the baptism with which I am baptized?" (Mk 10:38–39).[27] The use of "baptize" and "baptism" six times in the short discourse suggests that the evangelist has a sacramental interpretation in mind and is not simply overusing a figure of speech.[28] Death is for Christ the ultimate baptism, since in His death and resurrection He undergoes a transformation, surrendering His life for others and regaining it for the justification of sinners.[29] Baptism in the name of the Lord Jesus thus comes to its fullest expression in the death of the baptized and his resurrection with Christ.

---

26. *Ipse Deus revera adest, baptisat et absolvit* (*AE* 5:21). One can only hazard a guess why the translators of *AE* rendered *absolvit* as "address" and not "absolve."

27. Mark 10:38–39 blends Mt 20:22–23 and Lk 12:50: "But Jesus said to them, 'You do not know what you are asking. Are you able to drink the cup that I drink, or to be baptized with the baptism with which I am baptized?' And they said to him, 'We are able.' And Jesus said to them, 'The cup that I drink you will drink; and with the baptism with which I am baptized, you will be baptized' " (ὁ δὲ Ἰησοῦς εἶπεν αὐτοῖς οὐκ οἴδατε τί αἰτεῖσθε. δύνασθε πιεῖν τὸ ποτήριον ὃ ἐγὼ πίνω ἢ τὸ βάπτισμα ὃ ἐγὼ βαπτίζομαι βαπτισθῆναι; οἱ δὲ εἶπαν αὐτῷ δυνάμεθα. ὁ δὲ Ἰησοῦς εἶπεν αὐτοῖς τὸ ποτήριον ὃ ἐγὼ πίνω πίεσθε καὶ τὸ βάπτισμα ὃ ἐγὼ βαπτίζομαι βαπτισθήσεσθε). Luke 12:50 connects suffering with Baptism and Mt 20:22–23 connects suffering with the cup, possibly a reference to the Lord's Supper. Mark 10:38–39 sees suffering in terms of both the cup and Baptism. It is quite arguable that Mark kept Matthew's order by putting the cup first and then inserting the Baptism reference from Luke. Of course this cannot be proven, but what does seem evident is that suffering was described in sacramental terms.

28. The Baptist exegetical scholar Beasley-Murray is, not surprisingly, uncomfortable with a sacramental interpretation of these verses, but he is aware of the possibility (*Baptism*, 72–77).

29. Concerning the use of Baptism in this passage, C. S. Mann notes that "in ordinary Greek [water] was the common expression to denote being flooded or overwhelmed," and cites Lk 12:50 as an example (*Mark*, The Anchor Bible, vol. 27 [Garden City, NY: Doubleday, 1986], 412). "The Mk 10:38 passage corresponds to a testimony of Papias that James and John were martyred by the Jews, but this tradition is highly suspect. James's martyrdom had already taken place by the time Mark was writtten. James and John, like Peter and the other disciples, are not only aware of the violent death which awaits Jesus, but express their willingness to share in it" (ibid.).

4

THE EFFICACY OF BAPTISM

FOR THE FORGIVENESS OF SINS: THE CONFESSIONAL POSITION

The Small Catechism lists the benefits of Baptism as effecting the forgiveness of sins, delivering from death and the devil, and granting eternal salvation (SC IV.2). In the Large Catechism Luther further elaborates: "In Baptism, therefore, every Christian has enough to study and to practice all his life. He always has enough to do to believe firmly what Baptism promises and brings—victory over death and the devil, forgiveness of sin, God's grace, the entire Christ, and the Holy Spirit with his gifts" (LC IV.41).[1] Basic to the Lutheran understanding of Baptism's effects is its bestowal of the forgiveness of sins, which assumes the presence of all of God's other benefits.

Luther was only developing a theme found in the New Testament, that Baptism gives the forgiveness of sins: "Repent, and be baptized . . . for the forgiveness of your sins" (Acts 2:38). Indeed, wherever the phrase "forgiveness of sins" is used in the apostles' preaching in the New Testament, the reference with few exceptions is to that forgiveness given in Baptism. The benefits of Christ's death are available in Baptism, and thus no attempt should be made to play the cross of Jesus and this sacrament against one another. The Gospel is preached so that people can believe and be baptized for forgiveness. That people should hear preaching and remain unbaptized is foreign to the New Testament. This necessary relationship between Baptism and forgiveness, which is derived from the New Testament and is essential to Luther's theology, especially in the Large Catechism, is problematic in neo-Evangelical and Reformed Protestantism in general, where faith as a conscious and deliberate decision of the will is held as the prerequisite for being "saved."[2] This understanding of faith as a conscious decision results in a low regard for Baptism, especially as it applies to infants and young children. Those baptized as infants are taught that it is inadequate and must be completed through a conscious decision, as

---

1. Tappert, 441–42; BKS, 699.
2. ". . . For water baptism does not effect identification, but presupposes and symbolizes it" (Henry C. Thiessen, *Lectures in Systematic Theology*, revised by Vernon D. Doerksen [Grand Rapids, MI: William B. Eerdmans, 1979], 320).

might happen in the rite of confirmation,[3] a "decision for Christ," or, in the case of charismatic groups, a "Baptism in the Holy Spirit." This popular view of Baptism as essentially unnecessary has many prominent theological proponents. In our time Karl Barth distinguished between a Baptism of the Holy Spirit and a Baptism by water, and thus provided fuel for those with a low estimation of this sacrament.[4]

For Luther, Baptism is commanded by God, but such divine command does not exhaust the foundation and the basis of this sacrament. Concerning Mt 28:19 and Mk 16:16, he writes: "Observe, first, that these words contain God's commandment and ordinance. You should not doubt, then, that Baptism is of divine origin, not something devised or invented by men."[5] Since Baptism is given by the command of the risen Lord, it is necessary for the church (if it is indeed to be the church) and is always a complete act in itself, regardless of who the administrants and recipients may be. In Roman Catholicism, Baptism grants forgiveness only for past sins; for later sins it needs to be supplemented by the Sacrament of Penance. This view of Baptism provides the basis for the Roman Catholic system of sacraments in which later sacraments supplement the earlier ones. Confirmation, Penance, and Extreme Unction each give a grace which Baptism does not. Thus, in Roman Catholicism Baptism provides entrance into the church but does not remain as the Christian's foundation for the certainty of salvation. Similarly, while positions vary among the Reformed, they are agreed in concluding that Baptism does not effect salvation—that the baptized must look beyond his Baptism for the reality both of the Spirit in his life and for the certainty of his salvation. Thus, in regard to salvation, both for Roman Catholicism and for Reformed Protestantism Baptism is never an act which is complete in itself. Though the former holds that something happens in Baptism and the latter views it only in symbolic terms, in both systems the baptized must look beyond his Baptism to another reality for the certainty of salvation.

In contrast, Lutheran theology views Baptism as complete in itself, as containing the totality of the Christian life. Both the daily repentance of the Christian and his receiving of forgiveness through such means of grace as preaching, private confession and absolution, and the Sacrament of the Altar are grounded in the objective reality of Baptism which remains throughout the life of a Christian. As Luther writes in the Large Catechism,

---

3. For a critique on confirmation as a separate rite, see Robert W. Jenson, "Part Two: The Two Sacraments," in *Christian Dogmatics*, ed. Carl E. Braaten and Robert W. Jenson, 2 vols. (Philadelphia: Fortress Press, 1984), 2:328–29.

4. *Church Dogmatics* 4/4. He divides his volume on Baptism into two chapters, "Baptism with the Holy Spirit" (3–40) and "Baptism with Water" (41–213).

5. LC IV.6; Tappert, 437; *BKS*, 691–92.

> Repentance, therefore, is nothing else than a return and approach to Baptism, in order to resume and practice what had earlier been begun but abandoned.
> I say this to correct the opinion, which has long prevailed among us, that our Baptism is something past which we can no longer use after falling again into sin. We have such a notion because we regard Baptism only in the light of a work performed once for all. Indeed, St. Jerome is responsible for this view, for he wrote, "Repentance is the second plank on which we must swim ashore after the ship founders" in which we embarked when we entered the Christian church. This interpretation deprives Baptism of its value, making it of no further use to us. Therefore the statement is incorrect. The ship does not founder since, as we said, it is God's ordinance and not a work of ours. But it does happen that we slip and fall out of the ship. If anybody does fall out, he should immediately head for the ship and cling to it until he can climb aboard again and sail on in it as he had done before.[6]

Thus Jonathan Trigg correctly characterizes Luther's view when he states that "to marginalize baptism by confining it to the past is to destroy the Gospel, because the Gospel of forgiveness through faith in Christ and the covenant of baptism are one and the same."[7]

For Luther, faith receives the benefits of Baptism but does not belong to its essence.[8] For Roman Catholicism, Baptism is operative without faith (*fides*, meaning assent).[9] In Reformed Protestantism faith belongs to the definition of Baptism; it is something which the believer does. Calvin, who seems to come close to Luther in seeing a lifelong significance in Baptism as a sign, ultimately sees Baptism as a human response.[10] Lutheran theology requires faith for Baptism to be effective, but it does not belong to the definition of what this sacrament is. The forgiveness of sins is present in Baptism as an accomplished and completed reality demanding and creating faith.[11] But, though it does not constitute what Baptism is, faith must be present to receive Baptism: "Without faith Baptism is of no use, although in itself it is an infinite, divine treasure."[12]

FOR THE FORGIVENESS OF SINS: THE NEW TESTAMENT POSITION

This connection necessarily entailed in a confessional Lutheran understanding of the relationship between Baptism and forgiveness has its

---

6. LC IV.79–82; Tappert, 446; *BKS*, 706.
7. Trigg, *Baptism*, 149.
8. LC IV.35; Tappert, 441; *BKS*, 698.
9. See Trigg, *Baptism*, 208–9.
10. See ibid., 214–19.
11. LC IV.35; Tappert, 441; *BKS*, 698.
12. LC IV.34; Tappert, 440; *BKS*, 697.

The Efficacy of Baptism

origins in the New Testament. John, as described by Mark, "appeared in the wilderness, preaching a baptism of repentance [contrition and faith] for [the purpose of receiving] the forgiveness of sins" (κηρύσσων βάπτισμα μετανοίας εἰς ἄφεσιν ἁμαρτιῶν; Mk 1:4). Baptism was for John, as it was for Jesus in His pre-Easter ministry, not an empty symbolic liturgical rite, but the divine presence in the water actually offering the forgiveness of sins. A variety of opinions has been offered on the nature and efficacy of John's baptism, and complete agreement even among Lutheran theologians may not be possible, but our position cannot be that it was only a symbolic act, the view which characterizes the Reformed view of the sacraments in general. John's baptism of Jesus cannot be thought of merely as symbolic, for Jesus submitted Himself to it and by it assumed the burden of the whole world (Jn 1:32–36). In this baptism Jesus appeared as a sinner among real sinners and pointed to His death as the one baptism in which all sins were absorbed (Mk 10:39; Lk 12:50). Jesus' submission to John's baptism informed and gave shape to this ritual, and then by His death and His resurrection transformed it.

If the sacraments are defined simply as a proclamation of the forgiveness of sins (a definition with which the Reformed would be comfortable), then it might be possible to equate the pre- and the post-resurrection baptisms. But such an equation does not take into account the death and resurrection of Jesus as factors in the formation and definition of Christian Baptism. John's baptism directed the baptized ahead to what God was going to do, and so it fit the idea of an Old Testament ritual in providing an outline of what God was going to do and not what He had already done in the death and resurrection of Jesus. Still fundamental to both baptisms is the idea of forgiveness and a new relationship with God for the baptized, ideas which were carried over from John's baptism into Christian Baptism. Thus, John's baptism brought the Old Testament to a conclusion, and like the rites of the Old Testament it required a preaching of the Law and proclaimed the forgiveness of sins as the Gospel. It anticipated Christian Baptism and was assumed into it.

While noting the differences in these baptisms, the similarity of the formulas in both baptisms cannot be overlooked. Peter's baptismal invitation, "Repent, and be baptized every one of you in the name of Jesus Christ for the forgiveness of your sins" (Acts 2:38), resembles John's in all three synoptic gospels, with little variation. For example, as recorded both in Lk 2:3 and in Mk 1:4, John preached "a baptism of repentance for the forgiveness of sins." The clear meaning is that John preached that sins were forgiven in his baptism. We make the point about John's baptism offering the forgiveness of sins simply to show that the Lutheran position is firmly grounded in New Testament evidence.[13]

The phrase "for the forgiveness of sins" throughout the apostolic missionary sermons in Acts refers to what Baptism gives for those entering the Christian community. Before the high priest, Peter preaches that Jesus died and rose "for the forgiveness of sins" (Acts 5:31). Peter preaches the same message to the household of Cornelius and they are baptized (Acts 10:43–48). This New Testament understanding that Baptism forgives sin is carried into the Apostles' and Nicene creeds. When the Apostles' Creed says, "I believe in the Holy Ghost, . . . the forgiveness of sins," it is referring to the working of the forgiveness of sins in Baptism. The Nicene Creed is more explicit: "I acknowledge one Baptism for the remission of sins." This phrase, "Baptism for the remission of sins," is virtually identical to Mk 1:4. From the ancient creeds, the idea of forgiveness in and through Baptism is taken into the Lutheran Confessions, for which the Apostles' and Nicene creeds remain foundational.

This necessary correlation between Baptism and the creed is reinforced by the use of the creed in preparing candidates for Baptism in

---

13. Note must be made of *The Living Bible,* which by means of false translation robs Baptism of its sacramental meaning. Bordering on acceptability is its translation of Acts 2:38, "Each one of you must turn from sin, return to God, and be baptized in the name of Jesus Christ for forgiveness of sins," providing that turning from sin is contrition and returning to God is belief. Its translation of Mk 1:4, "[John the Baptist] taught all should be baptized as a public announcement of their decision to turn their backs on sin, so God could forgive them," is completely unacceptable. By manipulating the translation *The Living Bible* gives the impression that each of these baptisms was completely different. John's baptism, according to *The Living Bible,* is something *we* do! If such a translation is allowed to stand, then John's baptism, as a declaration of the forgiveness of sins, can in no way be allowed to inform Christian Baptism, which is not a human action but a divine work. The other and intended option for the translators of *The Living Bible* is that Christian Baptism should be interpreted in the light of John's, namely, as no more than an individual's announcement of moral resolution to live a better life. Its translation of 1 Pt 3:21 is a clear example of the moralistic understanding of Baptism, in which the accent is on what we do for God rather than what He does for us.

Suggesting that John's baptism dealt with a decision not to sin and that Christian Baptism has to do with forgiveness is nothing else than a form of dispensationalism, the belief that God has different plans of salvation for different periods of time. People were saved by moral rectitude in the period before Christ came (Law) and by grace after His coming (Gospel). Not only does this deny that salvation is by grace through faith, but it allows for another way of salvation besides Jesus Christ. *The Living Bible* offers a somewhat less offensive translation of the Acts passage, as noted above. In spite of the improvement, however, this translation allows for the Baptist notion that Baptism is a final and necessary step by which the Christian pleases God. Cf. Stanley J. Grenz: "Baptism, however, is more than a mere demonstration of our obedience, it is a meaningful oath of fidelity" (*Community of God,* 685). Both passages, the one referring to John's baptism and the one referring to Christian Baptism, use the same vocabulary to refer to the forgiveness of sins in connection with this sacrament.

the post-apostolic church. Faith is required for Baptism, and this faith is confessed before Baptism in the form of the creed, though its length has varied since then from place to place. Luther's form of the creed in his baptismal liturgy is much shorter than ours, but the outline is the same. Clearly our practice of using the creed in the form of questions and answers before the administration of Baptism has New Testament origins and is more than a ritual inherited from the ancient church, though it is surely this. In this way Baptism establishes the historical continuity, that is, the *catholicity*, of the church.[14] Those who received pre-resurrection baptism heard John preach about the Coming One, confessed their sins, and received this baptism for the forgiveness of sins. In the post-Easter church, those who were baptized also came confessing their sins, a practice taken over from John's baptism that remains in place in our own baptismal liturgies. Instead of confessing their faith in the Coming One, as those who were baptized by John did, believers in the post-resurrection church now acknowledged that "He who was to come" had indeed come in Jesus. Any accommodations with modern Jews over the question of whether the Messiah (Christ) has or will come contradicts the very foundation of Christian Baptism, which allows for no other identification for the Messiah than that He has come in the person of Jesus. By the resurrection "God has made [Jesus] both Lord and Christ" (Acts 2:36). In His death and resurrection God's kingdom had been realized, and by Baptism the candidate or the catechumen acknowledges this and is incorporated into it.

At first the Christian faith was expressed simply by confessing that Jesus was the Christ, the One in whom God's promises had been actualized. Hence the Book of Acts speaks of being baptized "in the name of Jesus." In such a formula was implicit the understanding that Jesus was God's Son, through whom forgiveness and the Holy Spirit were given (Acts 5:38-39). There is good reason to believe, as discussed in chapter 5, that the Father-Son-Holy Spirit formula was used from the very beginning as the one liturgical formula. This conclusion is further supported by the formula's inclusion in the Didache (VII.1), a document which some scholars date as contemporary with our New Testament.[15] Baptism in the name of Jesus was understood within the trinitarian reality. He was God's Son who in His baptism had been endowed with the Spirit (Mt 3:16-17), and who now in Baptism makes believers the children of His Father. He who was equipped with the Spirit to fight

---

14. Trigg makes this observation in regard to Luther: "First, [Baptism] defines the entire community of the baptized as those to whom the word of promise of forgiveness of sins is addressed.... Secondly, baptism divides men and women by the response they make to that word and call" (*Baptism*, 199).

15. In *The Apostolic Fathers*, trans. Kirsopp Lake, Loeb Classical Library, 2 vols. (Cambridge, MA: Harvard University Press, 1985), 1:319-21.

Satan (Mt 4:1) now gives them His Spirit (Mt 28:20). With the death and resurrection of Jesus, God's kingdom no longer lay in the future, as it did in John's baptism, but became accomplished reality, now given in Christian Baptism. Though the shadow and outline of what God was going to do in Jesus was present in John's baptism, it left its recipients looking for something more. What was implicit there became explicit in the Baptism which Jesus gave to His church through the apostles.

FOR THE FORGIVENESS OF SINS: THE CREEDS AND THE LITURGY

Though the present form of our Apostles' Creed is dated several centuries after the Nicene Creed was formed at Constantinople in 381, an earlier form containing the phrase "the forgiveness of sins" was in place in Rome already in the middle of the second century.[16] Certain New Testament references (e.g., 1 Pt 3:18–22 and Rom 6:4) suggest that precursors of this creed were firmly in place as part of the baptismal ritual in the earliest apostolic churches.[17] Around the rituals of Baptism and the Eucharist our New Testament writings came into existence; thus, these sacraments provided the historical context for these documents. These earliest liturgies were themselves of apostolic origin, derived from the preaching of Jesus, and echoed the apostles' own preaching. Thus, the content of Baptism was not really new for the baptized, but rather brought him into the reality of the message which was preached to him. The God who had offered His Son and endowed Him with the Spirit brought the believer into the trinitarian reality by means of a Baptism in the name of the Father and of the Son and of the Holy Spirit. Not only did God authorize Baptism, but through it acted upon the believer. From the earliest apostolic period, Baptism, confession of sins and faith, and the forgiveness of sins formed an indissoluble unity. Our Nicene Creed had its origins as a baptismal creed, which had found a place in the Eucharist in the East already by 318.[18] In the West, Charlemagne introduced the creed into the Eucharist by the ninth century. What was origi-

---

16. J. N. D. Kelly, *Early Christian Creeds*, 2d ed. (New York: David McKay, 1960), 156.
17. Ibid., 13–29.
18. Now discredited is the theory of F. J. A. Hort and Adolph von Harnack that Eusebius was responsible for the Nicene Creed. This assumption depended on the misreading of one of his letters describing the Council of Nicea. J. N. D. Kelly provides the evidence that the Nicene Creed had its origins in a local baptismal creed of Syro-Palestinian provenance (ibid., 227). Its use was regularized in the East by Justin II in 568 and in Spain in 589 by Reccared, king of the Visigoths. Influenced by the Spanish liturgy, Irish monks brought it into Charlemagne's courts before 800. Only after Henry II was crowned emperor in Rome was the Nicene Creed used regularly in the eucharistic liturgy there. What was originally a baptismal creed developed into an anti-Arian sign of orthodoxy (ibid., 348–57).

nally a baptismal and then a eucharistic creed is included with our Lutheran Confessions. So, in a real sense the confessional life of the Lutheran church has its source in Baptism. Its recitation as part of the regular Sunday service of Holy Communion serves as a statement of what Christians confessed at their Baptisms.[19]

Confessing the creed was a statement that Baptism still determined the parameters, foundation, and content of the believer's life. Behind such public confessions of faith which remain in the traditional liturgy is the idea that the believer accepts as true what God reveals, but with it the more fundamental idea that he *remains in his Baptism*. The believer does not leave his Baptism behind as he anticipates the sacrament of Christ's body and blood. Rather, Baptism is the necessary presupposition and prerequisite for the Holy Communion. Because he is baptized, the Christian is able to accept Christ's invitation to share in the sacrament of His body and blood.

This principle has led some Lutherans to reconsider the ancient church custom of communing infants, which is still in vogue in the Eastern Orthodox church.[20] One sacrament does not replace another, but each prepares, presupposes, and incorporates others. Participation in the Holy Communion is also a confession that those who receive it are baptized. The sacramental dimensions of the liturgy surround the believer with Christ. The idea that Confirmation or Penance is necessary or gives another kind of grace destroys the sacramental union be-

---

19. While the Apostles' Creed is considered the baptismal creed and the Nicene Creed the eucharistic creed, the latter has its origins in the former. This is a liturgical and not strictly a theological distinction, and either one may be used for the Eucharist. Nothing more is required for Baptism than what is required for the Lord's Supper. For a fuller discussion of this historical development see ibid., 344–57.

20. Both the Roman and Eastern Orthodox churches see Baptism, Confirmation (chrismation), and the Eucharist as the initiatory sacraments. Customarily Rome reserves the latter two for a more mature childhood and adolescence. The Eastern Orthodox administer all three at infancy. The issue of whether Communion should be administered to baptized infants is now being raised among Lutherans. Fundamental to their argument is that in the New Testament and ancient church, these sacraments belong together. See for example three articles in *Lutheran Quarterly* 10 (Autumn 1996): Craig R. Koester, "Infant Communion in the Light of the New Testament" (233–39); Todd W. Nichol, "Infant Communion in the Light of the Lutheran Confessions" (241–47); and Marc Kolden, "Infant Communion in the Light of Theological and Pastoral Perspectives" (249–57). Also see "Should Babies Be Communed?" edited by Ronald B. Bagnall, in *Lutheran Forum* 30 (Winter 1996): 16–35. For an article opposing the practice, see Edward Kettner, "The Practice of Infant Communion," *Lutheran Theological Review* 1 (Fall/Winter 1988–89): 5–17. Among the arguments used against infant communion are infants' lack of conscious faith and inability for self-examination. Similar arguments are used by Baptists to deny them Baptism. The argument that the benefits of the Lord's Supper are available in Baptism fails to note the unique character of each sacrament, and, if pressed too far, this argument might be used by adults to avoid receiving Communion. It seems unlikely that the practice will be inaugurated among Lutherans, though the age of the first Communion has been lowered in some churches.

tween Baptism and the Lord's Supper which supports and defines the church. Where sins are confessed before the Holy Communion, this is done not as an isolated act but in the context of Baptism. Confession and absolution, which belongs to Lutheran piety and liturgical practice, has meaning in that it brings the essence and power of Baptism to the surface. Baptism is more than an historic moment in the believer's life: it is the reality in which he lives. The baptismal assurance that sins are forgiven is not the memory of a past act, but a description of the believer's current situation.

As Luther writes, "To appreciate and use Baptism aright, we must draw strength and comfort from it where our sins or conscience oppress us and must retort, 'But I am baptized! And if I am baptized, I have the promise that I shall be saved and have eternal life, both in soul and body.'"[21] This faith or confession which is the prelude to Baptism comes to clear and regular expression in the recitation of the creeds, especially during the liturgy of the Holy Communion. Removal of the creeds from the regular liturgy not only suggests that the doctrine preserved in these creeds is not fully appreciated, it also shows that the present significance of Baptism in the believer's life is lost. Along with the creed, all trinitarian references within the liturgy reflect the faith of the church as the community of the baptized. Such references to Baptism can be found throughout the New Testament, and their inclusion in our liturgy indicates the continuity between apostolic times and ours. Clearly the trinitarian invocation, "in the name of the Father and of the Son and of the Spirit," has its origin in the command to baptize. Still other trinitarian references point to the baptismal reality in which the church lives and worships. "The grace of the Lord Jesus Christ, the love of God, and the communion of the Holy Spirit" could hardly have any reference other than a baptismal one.

BAPTISM AS THE ENCOMPASSING REALITY

Baptism is the reality in which early Christians knew God and His forgiveness; it both described and set the parameters for their entire existence. Luther deserves the credit for putting Baptism in its proper place: "In Baptism, therefore, every Christian has enough to study and to practice all his life."[22] Luther's intent is not that the Christian would meditate on an isolated ritual, but that he would reflect on the *content* of

---

21. LC IV.44; Tappert, 442; *BKS*, 700. Consider also Trigg on this point: "For Luther, as we have seen, there can be no resting secure on past faith, past holiness, or past spiritual achievement. Justification requires faith, baptism requires a response—now" (*Baptism*, 172).

22. LC IV.41; Tappert, 441–42; *BKS*, 699–700.

The Efficacy of Baptism

Baptism: "[The Christian] always has enough to do to believe firmly what Baptism promises and brings—victory over death and the devil, forgiveness of sin, God's grace, the entire Christ, and the Holy Spirit and his gifts."[23] Luther places the entirety of the Christian life within Baptism.

Christians study and *practice* what Baptism presents. In his Small Catechism, Luther included the practice of the Christian faith when he said that Baptism signifies that the sinful self should each day die and a new creature be resurrected (IV.12). Baptism is not something which merely happened once; it is something which is *always happening*. Such thinking is unique to the Lutheran understanding of Baptism. It is without parallel in Roman Catholic thought, where the grace of Baptism must be reinforced, and in Reformed thought, where grace is never inherent in the act itself and thus the baptized must look within himself for signs of the Spirit's working. Eastern Orthodoxy speaks of Baptism restoring the original and natural form of freedom, and so this sacrament implies a call to freedom which for infants is only potential.[24] While Baptism remains effective in calling the baptized to freedom, Penance restores the fallen into the church. In Lutheran theology, the penitents in being restored to the church are returning to their Baptism. For Luther, Word, Christ, the Spirit, and water belong together, and so Baptism is complete in itself.[25]

If Luther says we cannot exhaust the meaning of Baptism, perhaps it is not too much to say that we will never exhaust what Luther says about Baptism. Of course, Luther is only plumbing what the New Testament says, and only those coming after him could realize the depths of his teaching on Baptism. Here in Baptism we receive the forgiveness of sins, not only as a divine reprieve from past crimes and misdemeanors, but as the victory over Satan which is ours due to our participation in the life of the Triune God. Consider these words of Luther again: Baptism gives "victory over death and the devil, forgiveness of sins, God's [the Father's] grace, the entire Christ [the incarnate Son], and the Holy Spirit and his gifts."[26] While with Luther we do not want to consider one means of grace superior to another, especially in relation to the forgiveness of sins, he does see Baptism as embracing everything which belongs to Christianity.[27]

---

23. Ibid.
24. See Meyendorff, *Byzantine Theology*, 194–97.
25. For an extensive Calvinist critique of the Lutheran doctrine, see Charles Hodge, *Systematic Theology*, 3 vols. (London: Thomas Nelson, 1873), 3:482–85, 599–609.
26. LC IV.41; Tappert, 441–42; BKS, 699–700.
27. Trigg confirms that Luther had a higher regard for the sacraments than did Calvin. Luther places "the preached word *alongside* the other external signs . . . and

Essential to confessional thought is that the Lutherans, especially Luther himself, do not construct a theology of the sacraments which predetermines how the Word or the sacraments will be defined. In the Augsburg Confession and the Apology Melanchthon places the article on the use of the sacraments (XIII) after the articles on Baptism (IX), the Lord's Supper (X), and Confession (XI). Reformed theology begins with a theology of the sacraments which predetermines and limits what can be expected of Baptism and the Lord's Supper.[28] What Luther thinks about the sacraments must be derived from what he says about Baptism, confession and absolution (which he sees as the practice of Baptism), and the Lord's Supper. The Reformed set up parameters according to which these sacraments are then defined. In other words, one might say that the Reformed have a theology of the sacraments, but their theology is not sacramental. For Lutherans the reverse is true. Lutheran theology is sacramental, but it does not insist on any one particular expression or form of sacramental theology. Only because of the necessity of taking a defensive posture over against Roman Catholicism and especially the Reformed positions on the sacraments has a characteristic Lutheran sacramental theology developed.

Luther's theology of the sacraments had to take into account his doctrine of justification by faith, which for him was at the center as the article which held together all the others. Justification never stood alone, but correlated all doctrines around Christology. Consistently, Luther understood Baptism in christological dimensions. Christ instituted this sacrament and constituted its content. If Christ's institution of the sacrament is not accompanied by the understanding of Him as its sole content, then Baptism could be understood as Law. Luther's expansive claims for Baptism are understandable in the light of his christological definition of it. Choosing between Baptism and Christ is a false alternative; Baptism is more than an instrument which leads to Christ, but it is the sacrament in which Christ is permanently present to the believer. According to Trigg, when Luther was confronted by the false antithesis of defining the church either by faith or by sacraments, he leaned in the

---

refuses to rank the means of grace" (*Baptism*, 217–18). Trigg points out that Calvin, in a probable reference to Luther, speaks of good men who claimed too much for the sacraments. Luther sees the blood of Christ at work in Baptism. Calvin keeps Christ's blood distinct from Baptism, so that the power of Christ's blood cannot be predicated of Baptism. "For Calvin the washing of the water and the cleansing in the blood of Christ are utterly distinct, and the power of one must not be predicated of the other" (ibid.). The Geneva reformer held Christ's divine and human natures operated together (*communicato operatum*), but not through each other (*genus apotelesmaticum*), as Lutherans held. Calvin's Christology found a parallel in his doctrine of Baptism, in which the Spirit worked along with but distinct from the application of water.

28. So Hodge, *Systematic Theology* 3:490–525.

The Efficacy of Baptism

direction of the sacraments: "[Luther's] theology of Baptism is not least among those factors that pull in the opposite direction, towards a sacramentally defined church of the baptized."[29] Luther does not allow Baptism to be effective without faith, but his views on this sacrament reflected the objectivity and certainty of the Gospel, which could never be posited of faith. What Luther said about the sacraments, he was really saying about Christ. One does not rely on one's faith in the way that one relies on Baptism.[30] This sacrament defined the church for Luther. Not only is it not an extraneous ritual, it is conterminous with the faith and life of all Christians, and in this way defines, determines, and identifies the church itself.[31] Confessing the church—"I believe in one holy catholic and apostolic church"—is only recognizing what Baptism has accomplished: "I believe in one Baptism for the remission of sins." Baptism determines the life of the Christian and of the church. Luther when oppressed by sin could cry out *"Ego tamen baptizatus sum"*—"But I am baptized! And if I am baptized, I have the promise that I shall be saved and have eternal life . . . "[32]

GOING BEYOND FORGIVENESS

The phrase "the forgiveness of sins" does not, however, exhaust the New Testament's salvific understanding of Baptism. First Peter 3:21, used in Lutheran baptismal liturgies, bluntly states that "Baptism now saves"—words that stand in the middle of an early creedal formula which states that Christ has died for sins, is risen, ascended, and is now at God's right hand (vv. 18–22). So, noted here again is the essential unity between Baptism, faith, and the creeds. Luther in the Small Catechism makes use of Ti 3:5 in seeing Baptism as a washing of regeneration and a renewal of the Holy Spirit. Thus, in their definition of Baptism the Lutheran Confessions are not limited to those New Testament passages in which the Greek word βαπτίζω and its cognates are used.[33]

---

29. Trigg, *Baptism*, 6–7.
30. "Our know-it-alls, the new spirits, assert that faith alone saves and that works and external things contribute nothing to this end. We answer: It is true, nothing that is in us does it but faith, as we shall hear later on. But these leaders of the blind are unwilling to see that faith must have something to believe—something to which it may cling and upon which it may stand. Thus faith clings to the water and believes it to be Baptism in which there is sheer salvation and life, not through the water, as we have sufficiently stated, but through its incorporation with God's Word and ordinance and the joining of his name to it" (LC IV.28–29; Tappert, 440; BKS, 696).
31. See Trigg, *Baptism*, 50–58.
32. LC IV.44; Tappert, 442; BKS, 700.
33. Use of the word "washing" to refer to Baptism alerts us to two significant issues relating to this subject. First, opponents of a sacramental view often use the absence of the specific words "Baptism" and "baptize" to argue that there is no reference to this

The idea of Baptism as washing is also used by Paul in 1 Cor 6:3. In 1 Cor 6:1–11 Paul makes reference to Baptism not only as the rite necessary for entrance into the Christian community, but as that rite which gives this community its unique characteristic of both extending mutual forgiveness and denouncing immoral acts. The Corinthians could not bring lawsuits against other members of the community or live openly immoral lives, since such people do not inherit God's kingdom (1 Cor 6:10), a phrase which is used in the baptismal preaching of John and Jesus. Such behavior has become impossible for the Corinthians because of their Baptism; they "have been washed [baptized], sanctified [brought to faith] and justified in the name of the Lord Jesus and in the Spirit of our God" (1 Cor 6:11; my translation). Baptism remains the rite of initiation, but in such a way that it continues to determine the believers' life in the community.[34] Paul's order here, washing (Baptism), sanctification, and justification, reflects his understanding of the working of Baptism. Within Baptism—what he calls "washing"—comes the Spirit's complete activity of sanctifying, making holy, and claiming the baptized as His own. Where this has happened, the one baptized understands himself as being justified, accepted by God in Christ. Thus, Baptism is not only the sure foundation for faith, but is an act of the Holy Spirit shaping the believer's entire life. He is now the temple of the Holy Spirit and resolves to flee immorality (1 Cor 6:12–20).

---

sacrament in these texts, and thereby begin to attain their predetermined objective that the New Testament says little about Baptism. It must be noted sadly that many Lutheran theologians adopt the same posture and use the same arguments in regard to other texts. This challenge must be faced head-on. Secondly, acknowledging this use of the term "washing" permits the possibility of recognizing more references to Baptism in the New Testament. By taking a minimalistic attitude to locating biblical references to Baptism, we give the impression that our theology of the sacraments is hanging on by a few threads here and there. The Lutheran doctrine of Baptism is developed also from those pericopes where that specific word is not used. Consider John 3, where the word "Baptism" is not used. Calvin and Barth argue that "water" in Jn 3:5 is simply a reference to the Spirit and not Baptism! (Barth, *Church Dogmatics* 4/4:120–21). Barth cites Calvin's *Commentary on John*. Lutherans should follow the example of the Reformer and be willing to acknowledge the abundance of baptismal references. A hesitancy to do this may reflect an inherent and perhaps unrecognized Reformed influence.

34. For Luther, Baptism is present tense: "Do not hold such a a view, but understand that this is the significance of baptism, that through it you die and live again. Therefore, whether by penance or by any other way, you can only return to the power of your baptism, and do again that which you were baptized to do and which your baptism signified. Baptism never becomes useless, unless you despair and refuse to return to your salvation. . . . We are therefore never without the sign of baptism nor without the thing it signifies. Indeed, we need continually to be baptized more and more, until we fulfil the sign perfectly on the last day" (from *The Babylonian Captivity of the Church*; AE 36:69). For a full discussion of this see Trigg, *Baptism*, 201–2.

"BAPTIZED ON BEHALF OF THE DEAD": A FAULTY PRACTICE WITH SACRAMENTAL SIGNIFICANCE

A word must be said about the dogmatic significance of the problematical 1 Cor 15:29: "What do people mean by being baptized on behalf of the dead? If the dead are not raised at all, why are people baptized on their behalf?" Though no assured agreement seems possible for a passage which is properly called a *crux interpretum*, a plausible solution is that a highly sacramental view of Baptism was the reason for this unusual practice. The Mormon practice is of absolutely no dogmatic significance, since their religion is only a slightly veiled form of polytheism. Also not at issue here in the Baptism of the dead is baptizing comatose people, those on the verge of dying, or those who may have died already. From time to time there are reports that pastors have baptized the stillborn. We oppose Baptism before birth for the same reason we oppose it after death: rebirth suggests that the baptized has been born and is alive.

At issue is what kind of baptism was practiced in Corinth. Paul had already presented the outlines of a theology of Baptism. A baptism in the sea and cloud made Israel God's people (1 Cor 10:1–2). A more fully developed theology is given in 1 Cor 6:11–20, where Baptism is given in the name of the Triune God and effects justification and Christian living. Baptism "on behalf of the dead" is an essential part of Paul's defense of the resurrection: "If the dead are not raised at all, why are people baptized on their behalf?" (εἰ ὅλως νεκροὶ οὐκ ἐγείρονται, τί καὶ βαπτίζονται ὑπὲρ αὐτῶν; 1 Cor 15:29b). Thus, this practice hardly can be regarded as having no significance.

Johann Gerhard proposed that the Corinthians were baptizing not on behalf of but *over* the dead, that is, over their graves, which suggests that the church had already retreated to the catacombs or at least to conducting their services in graveyards.[35] Such clandestine services would have been necessitated by persecution, but there is no reference indicating that the Corinthians were experiencing this. Their use of the law courts suggests that they were citizens in good legal standing (1 Cor 6:1–6). Their celebrations of the Lord's Supper which had become so bacchanal hardly could have been held in subterranean tunnels; they were held in houses (11:20–22). Since outsiders were regularly attending their services (14:16), they were obviously worshiping openly without fear of arrest and imprisonment. They continued with pagan fune-

---

35. Johann Gerhard, *A Comprehensive Explanation of Holy Baptism and the Lord's Supper* (1610), trans. Elmer Hohle (Decatur, IL: The Johann Gerhard Institute, 1996), 135–37. Gerhard lists six other possible meanings besides this one, including the washing of dead bodies and the killing of the old Adam.

real rites (8:1–9) and perhaps even participated in the usual synagogue worship (12:3). Paul found some of their liturgical practices unacceptable, but nothing in this epistle suggests they were facing persecution and were escaping to the catacombs to worship over the bodies of deceased believers. Such a young congregation may have known of only a few deaths among its members, and so there were no cemeteries exclusively for Christians. Grammatically, "on behalf of the dead" is a more natural reading than "over the dead." So, Christ's body is given "on behalf of you" (τὸ σῶμα τὸ ὑπὲρ ὑμῶν) and not "over you" (1 Cor 11:24).

Deciphering "on behalf of the dead" also necessitates agreement on what is meant by "the dead." Were people being baptized in view of their fallen natures or their impending deaths? In other words, did these Corinthians look on Baptism as a deliverance from the state of being dead in sin, or were they perhaps acknowledging the power of Baptism ultimately to raise them from the grave? Baptism pointed to the future and final resurrection. This is Paul's understanding of Baptism, but this could not have been the understanding of those in the congregation who explicitly denied the resurrection.

Karl Barth suggests that Baptism on behalf of the dead is "a definitive assignment of Christians to the service of their fellowmen who do not yet have this hope and who are to this extent dead."[36] The context, however, is devoid of reference to works of sanctification. In combining several assumptions, his interpretation is rather complex and unnatural. Barth holds that these Christians were baptized so that people who were still dead in sin could be saved by their witness. First Corinthians 15 has in view the resurrection of people who are now actually dead in the sense that Christ also was dead. Since Christ was raised, so the dead in Christ will also be raised. Why should "dead" suddenly mean "fallen nature" or "unbeliever"? Consistency would require the absurd and unsupported interpretation that Christ was raised from His fallen nature. Barth sees Baptism not as a sacrament but as a human act, and his idea of commitment to others fits this view. For Barth, Baptism is a kind of ordination for all Christians to do church work.[37] The erroneous suggestion that Baptism gives the baptized a "ministry" is a view currently popular even among some Lutherans, though probably not through the influence of Barth.

The simplest way to understand this passage is that the Corinthians were in fact practicing Baptism by proxy on behalf of family members who had died before they heard the preaching of the Gospel. There is no reason to doubt Beasley-Murray's assessment that Baptism for the

---

36. *Church Dogmatics* 4/4:201.
37. Ibid.

The Efficacy of Baptism

dead matched no pagan belief, but that the Greeks simply had great respect for their dead.[38] In their vicarious Baptisms for the dead they were combining their newly acquired beliefs with their older views concerning the dead. Another plausible hypothesis is that they were being baptized vicariously for those catechumens who died before finishing the catechesis, the course of instruction given in preparation for Baptism. It was natural that they would be concerned about the salvation of those who died before completing the catechesis, and thus were baptized on their behalf.[39]

Donald A. Carson takes up the problem of interpreting 1 Cor 15:29 in regard to the Mormon practice of getting "baptized for the dead."[40] Though he finds no other reference to the practice in the New Testament or the earliest apostolic fathers, he suggests that a few may have had themselves baptized on behalf of a relative who "died after trusting the gospel before being baptized."[41] It was clearly an unusual practice. Carson holds to the Reformed position that "Christian baptism is part of that personal response, even as it is a covenantal pledge."[42] His view that these dead had already come to faith but had not been baptized is similar but not identical to the view that they were catechumens who died before completing the catechesis. Carson sees Paul's question about why the Corinthians are being baptized on behalf of the dead as rhetorical, akin to a Protestant asking, Why pray for the dead, if the dead are not raised? Or, it could be added, if their souls no longer exist.

Bernard Marie Foschini has surveyed forty interpretations of this controverted pericope, and favors the vicarious interpretation that the

---

38. Beasley-Murray, *Baptism*, 192.
39. I am indebted to C. S. Mann for the suggestion that vicarious Baptisms were provided for catechumens who died before they could receive their own Baptism. Without precise knowledge, this hypothesis seems as plausible as providing vicarious Baptisms for unbelieving dead relatives. The church has wrestled with the problem of believers dying without Baptism and posited "a baptism of desire" and "a baptism of blood," that is, a martyr's death. At the root of baptizing the dead or resorting to speaking of baptisms without water is an anxiety about the fate of others. Elsewhere we discuss the absence of Baptism, and the issue should not detain us here. Vicarious Baptisms were later condemned and persisted only among heretical groups. Unusual practices have grown up around the sacraments, and thus we should not be amazed by the aberrant practice of Baptism for the dead. Well known are the practices of baptizing entire tribes without ascertaining whether they believed, as well as baptizing the stillborn, unconscious unbelievers, and inanimate objects like church bells. The custom of placing the sacrament of Christ's body directly in the mouth became necessary when those who received it in the hand took it home as a kind of charm. Faulty practices are derived from what are in nearly all cases improper views about the essence of the sacrament. In several aberrations little attention is paid to whether faith is present in the recipient.
40. "Did Paul Baptize for the Dead?" *Christianity Today* 42 (August 10, 1998): 63.
41. Ibid.
42. Ibid.

Corinthians had developed a Baptism-like rite to commemorate the dead.[43] Equally compelling to this writer is the interpretation that the dead were never Christians, but relatives who died before Paul came. Whatever the answer to this question is, we take Carson's caution: "We really do not know." It is much more certain, however, that this really was a vicarious Baptism, whatever the reasons for its practice.

Putting aside the question of whether or not Paul condoned the practice, his argument shows that the Corinthians were caught in a practice which contradicted their explicit denial of the resurrection. These early Christians denied the resurrection, but believed that Baptism offered the forgiveness of sins and gave "life and salvation," to use Luther's phrase. They believed that Baptism actually *did* something. It effected salvation on the recipients, even if they were dead. If the Corinthians had examined their motives in this aberrant custom, as Paul required of them, they would have discovered that their baptismal practice was itself a profession in the general resurrection. In other words, their preaching which denied the resurrection stood at odds with their sacramental understanding of Baptism which affirmed it, even if it was being practiced erroneously for the dead. The Word informs and determines the shape of the sacrament. Here Paul points to the aberrant Corinthian practice of Baptism (sacrament) to correct their deviant proclamation that there was no resurrection (Word). Implicit in Paul's understanding of Baptism in 1 Corinthians 15 is that this sacrament places the baptized into the death and resurrection of Christ (especially v. 20).[44]

---

43. "Those Who Are Baptized for the Dead," *Catholic Biblical Quarterly* 12 (July 1950): 260–76 and (October 1950): 379–88; 13 (January 1951): 46–78, (April 1951): 172–98, and (July 1951): 276–83.

44. Beasley-Murray has an extensive treatment of this issue and agrees that these were Baptisms performed vicariously for the dead (*Baptism*, 185–92). He rightly shows that illustrations in the preaching of Jesus and the writings of Paul do not indicate approval. After all, God comes as a thief in the night. Troublesome for this Baptist scholar is that Baptism is here being handled sacramentally. He agrees with Bultmann that "baptism for the dead represents an unethical, sub-Christian sacramentalism" (ibid., 190). Beasley-Murray claims that this would be the only place where Paul sees Baptism as a sacrament, and that it would be better to assume that he is employing the "sacramentalism" of the Corinthians. Thus Beasley-Murray holds that Paul for the sake of the argument makes two concessions which he himself does not really believe. Paul approves neither of baptizing the dead nor of regarding Baptism as a sacrament. Beasley-Murray distances himself from Bultmann, who holds that Baptisms on behalf of the dead demonstrated the early church belief in the sacramental power of Baptism even for the dead. While there is no other place in the New Testament, let alone in the Pauline corpus, where there is the slightest indication that the dead should be baptized, there is a developed baptismal theology, regardless of how one defines this theology.

Another remote and barely defensible possibility overlooked by those denying a sacramental efficacy to Baptism is that "baptizing" refers not to a sacrament but to a required ritual Jewish washing for those who had touched dead persons. The controverted sentence would read like this: "If the dead are not raised, then what purpose does your ritual washing serve—this contact with the 'holy' is meaningless, unless that

A concluding note to this *crux interpretum*: Richard E. DeMaris has presented convincing and detailed archaeological and anthropological arguments supporting the view that the Corinthian Christians were combining their pagan beliefs with their newly acquired faith by being baptized vicariously for the dead.[45] A Graeco-Roman cult of the dead was firmly in place in Corinth. Sacrifices and feasts were held for dead relatives. Religious-type picnics were held at the graves, where food was left for the deceased, and sometimes drink libations were funneled by tubes into the graves. In this environment, the Corinthians who had become Christians naturally would still be preoccupied with the state of the dead. Church history is replete with Christian beliefs carried out together with older pagan practices. To attempt to carry out their obligations, especially to their deceased relatives, the Corinthians merged pagan "sacramental" rites with their newly acquired beliefs about Baptism. DeMaris suggests, with good reason, that Paul's experience with the Cornthinians being baptized on behalf of the dead may have played a role in his composition of Rom 6:1–11:

> If baptism for the dead necessarily raises the issue of the resurrection, as [1 Cor] 15:29 suggests, in Rom 6:11 we learn from Paul why it does: baptism joins the believer to the death and resurrection of Christ. Perhaps Paul's christological understanding of baptism was his way of hinting at a deficiency in the Corinthians' understanding of baptism for the dead, for the language of dying and rising with Christ represents a reversal of the journey from life to death. In a letter that went to Rome, we may catch Paul expressing his wish that the Corinthians would rethink their theology of vicarious baptism. Paul did not confront the Corinthians; he simply, deftly turned their theology on its head.[46]

Paul's baptismal theology reflected the world in which he lived, even as ours should. Historical evidence raised by scholars like DeMaris reconstructs the original situation in which Paul articulated his theology, and demonstrates the strong sacramental understanding of Baptism which was already in place in apostolic times. Even such opponents of the Lutheran position as the Baptist New Testament scholar Beasley-Murray recognize this. Rudolf Bultmann, perhaps the greatest

---

dead body is raised." Since Paul uses the "baptizing" vocabulary of the initiation rite of what we call Baptism, this option should not concern us. (I am indebted to discussions with the late C. S. Mann for much of this material, though I later found much of it in Johann Gerhard, as shown above.) Beasley-Murray and Bultmann rightfully see that here is a reference to sacramental efficacy, even though they believe that the Corinthians were wrong.

45. "Corinthian Religion and Baptism for the Dead (1 Corinthians 15:29): Insights from Archaeology and Anthropology," *Journal of Biblical Literature* 114 (Winter 1995): 661–82.

46. Ibid., 682.

opponent of retrieving the historical Jesus in our time, saw the strong sacramental implications in Paul's presentation of Baptism. These testimonies cannot be ignored in a religious situation in which Baptism is practiced as a ritual without saving significance.[47]

OTHER PAULINE REFERENCES

As the washing of Baptism is presented in 1 Cor 6:11 as a determinative factor for the life of the Christian congregation, in Eph 5:25–27 the washing in the Word is shown to make the church holy:

> Husbands, love your wives, as Christ loved the church and gave himself up for her, that he might sanctify her, having cleansed her by the washing of water with the word [τῷ λουτρῷ τοῦ ὕδατος ἐν ῥήματι], that he might present the church to himself in splendor, without spot or wrinkle or any such thing, that she might be holy and without blemish.

Baptism is not presented here as the rite of individual initiation, but as that act which makes the entire church acceptable to Christ. Since Baptism incorporates into Christ, the baptized take on the same characteristics as Christ. In this case, husbands baptized into Christ demonstrate the same love to their wives which Christ showed to His church, who is His bride.[48]

Along with the idea of washing, regeneration or new birth is a prominent New Testament dimension of Baptism. Article II of the Augsburg Confession speaks of the devastating effects of original sin: it "condemns to the eternal wrath of God all those who are not born again through Baptism and the Holy Spirit" (*qui non renascuntur per baptismum et spiritum sanctum*).[49] Luther carries over the word "regeneration" from the Vulgate of Ti 3:5 into his explanation of the effects of Baptism in the Small Catechism, a translation that has become customary in English renditions. The idea of regeneration in Article II of the Augsburg Confession makes Baptism the sacrament of initiation that stands as the necessary rite of passage from the old life into the new. Luther knows of the ending of the old life and the beginning of the new, as shown through his use of the imagery of killing the old man and the new man's resurrection in Christ (Rom 6:4). Conversion is understood in terms of death and resurrection, symbolized and realized in the act of Baptism itself.

---

47. Luther held that the Corinthians "had themselves baptized at the graves of the dead in token of their firm conviction that the dead who lay buried there and over whom they were being baptized would rise again" (*AE* 28:150).

48. Barth sees no reference to Baptism in this pericope. He holds that the true washing takes place at Golgotha and not in Baptism (*Church Dogmatics* 4/4:113–14).

49. Tappert, 29; *BKS*, 53.

This act or observance consists in being dipped into the water, which covers us completely, and being drawn out again. These two parts, being dipped under the water and emerging from it, indicate the power and effect of Baptism, which is simply the slaying of the old Adam and the resurrection of the new man, both of which actions must continue in us our whole life long.[50]

Regeneration refers quite specifically to the actual beginning of the Christian life in Baptism, and is interchangeable with rebirth or new birth, that is, the initiation into the church. Though Baptism inaugurates the Christian life once, its regenerating qualities remain in place for life. "Thus a Christian life is nothing else than a daily Baptism, once begun and ever continued."[51] This view contrasts with the Roman Catholic view, where Penance rather than Baptism serves as the refuge in which the Christian finds forgiveness.[52]

Titus 3:5 is used in both the Small and Large catechisms to support the idea of Baptism as "the washing of regeneration."[53] There is some question whether the regeneration in Titus has the same referent as that in the episode between Jesus and Nicodemus, ". . . unless a man is born of water and the Spirit . . ." (Jn 3:5). The Greek word translated in Ti 3:5 as "regeneration," *palingenesia* (παλιγγενεσία), may suggest a re-creation as much as it suggests a rebirth or regeneration. The sense would be that God in Baptism "begins again" in us with a new creation by reestablishing the Holy Spirit in our lives. The language here reflects the working of the Spirit in Gn 1:2, who now in Baptism is beginning a new creation. The thought of Ti 3:5 is not only that we are born again, but that God is creating us again and making us new in Baptism (λουτροῦ παλιγγενεσίας καὶ ἀνακαινώσεως πνεύματος ἁγίου). In a real sense, Baptism is the beginning of the new heavens and the new earth for the believer.[54] What God does in Baptism in bringing forth new creations is as impressive as the creation in Genesis. Understanding Baptism in Ti 3:5 as God's beginning a new creation in us through the Holy Spirit is not far removed from understanding a rebirth as in, for example, the Johannine writings.[55] Luther approaches the creation in Baptism not

---

50. LC IV.65; Tappert, 444–45; BKS, 704.
51. LC IV.65; Tappert, 445; BKS, 704.
52. "The forgiveness of sins committed after Baptism is conferred by a particular sacrament called the sacrament of conversion, confession, penance, or reconciliation" (*Catechism of the Catholic Church*, para. 1486).
53. LC IV.27; Tappert, 440; BKS, 696.
54. Compare the language of Rv 21:1, where the Greek word for new is used in connection with the renewed creation: Καὶ εἶδον οὐρανὸν καινὸν καὶ γῆν καινήν.
55. Rather than interpreting παλιγγενεσία as regeneration, Regin Prenter makes a forceful argument in understanding it as resurrection. He points out that in Matthew (19:28), Philo, and Josephus, it means resurrection: "This can mean only that baptismal regeneration and renewal are a foretaste, the beginning of the actual resurrection" (*Creation and Redemption*, 463).

The Efficacy of Baptism

through Ti 3:5, but in his imagery of drowning the old Adam so that a cleansed new man can come forth.[56]

JOHANNINE REFERENCES

The Johannine writings have the most fully developed presentation of Baptism as regeneration in the New Testament. Among American Protestants, regeneration or rebirth is commonly taken to mean a conscious decision for Christ, a moment that can be recalled in the memory without difficulty as the basis of Christian life. In classical Reformed theology, conversion is seen as God's work, but personal experience still plays a prominent role.[57] For Lutherans, Baptism itself regenerates and gives new life (creation). Baptism is not only the occasion for regeneration (a position which Calvin could accept), but also the cause.

Already in the prologue of John's gospel, God's children are spoken of as believers who have been born from God (ἀλλ' ἐκ θεοῦ ἐγεννήθησαν; Jn 1:13). A fuller elaboration of what is intended in this birth from God comes in the discussion between Jesus and Nicodemus about the necessity of a heavenly birth (Jn 3:1–12). Nicodemus is convinced by the miracles that Jesus is a teacher from God. Rather than commending him for his fragmentary knowledge, Jesus says that without rebirth or "a birth from on high," Nicodemus will not be able to recognize God's kingdom, that is, Jesus as the full embodiment of God. The evangelist seems to be making a deliberate play here on the Greek word *anothen* (ἄνωθεν), which can be translated as "again," or "from on high," as would be more customarily Johannine. For example, Jesus comes "from on high" (ἄνωθεν; Jn 3:31), not "again." The rebirth is in fact the birth that comes from on high, that is, heaven. To Nicodemus's query about the impossibility of old men being born again from their mothers, Jesus responds that the birth that permits men to see who Jesus really is

---

56. Karl Barth goes to great lengths to use the "new creation" translation against a sacramental view of Baptism. This view, according to Barth, was dependent on the understanding that it was identical to Jn 3:5. Since "re-creation" and not "regeneration" is the proper understanding—and we agree with Barth—he concludes that this is a reference to what happened in Jesus Christ and the outpouring of the Holy Spirit, and not to what he calls water Baptism (*Church Dogmatics* 4/4:114–16). Barth could have used the evidence to come to the exact opposite conclusion. As mysterious as rebirth is, a re-creation is greater. The great Baptist scholar Beasley-Murray, in many references to *loutron* (λούτρον) in his *Baptism in the New Testament,* takes it as a reference to Baptism and not to what God did in Jesus Christ; however, he does not tie down the regenerating activity to the water (e.g., 303). One suspects that Barth's exegetical conclusions are really no more than presupppositions basic to his theological system, namely, that God's act in Jesus Christ is the only revelatory one.

57. Grenz, *Community of God,* 536–41.

The Efficacy of Baptism

comes "of water and the Spirit" (Jn 3:5). This birth which is effected by the Spirit brings its recipients into the realm of God. Those who do not experience this birth belong to the flesh and are still not God's children.

A number of attempts have been made to deny the strong sacramental implications of this pericope, since it establishes Baptism as an essential part of a complete Christian life: "Unless one is born of water and the Spirit, he cannot enter the kingdom of God." Some who have followed Calvin's lead, including Barth, have taken the word "water" as simply another reference to the Holy Spirit.[58] Another attempt to skirt the sacramental meaning of the passage is to take the reference to water as a reference to natural, ordinary birth, as a woman's water breaks just before birth. What is required first is that a man be born from his mother and then later receive another birth from the Spirit, usually understood as a conscious experience in which the individual makes a decision for Christ. Such a rendering is strained, since the verb "to be born" appears only once, and only with difficulty could it refer to two birth experiences.[59]

Though the Greek words βαπτίζω and βάπτισμα, which are the roots for the English "I baptize" and "Baptism," are not used in this Nicodemus account, John's gospel prior to this point does use them. The person of John the Baptist is introduced as early as the prologue (Jn 1:6–8), and his ministry is described in Jn 1:19–34. Jesus' first disciples are those who followed John (Jn 1:35–42). Immediately following the Nicodemus account the evangelist relates how both Jesus and John were baptizing, the latter at Salim because of the abundance of water there (Jn 3:22–30). John, like other New Testament writers, is using the word "water" in reference to Baptism.[60] Where John writes "water and the Spirit" the Small Catechism has "water and word," and seems to be closer in expression, though not in idea, to Eph 5:26, "the washing of the water with the word."

The word "Baptism" is not strictly a native English word taken over from the Anglo-Saxon, but a word borrowed from Greek through Latin. We use the word "Baptism" as a *technicus terminus* for the first sacrament. Though Baptism was already in use in the apostolic church as a term for the first sacrament, it was not the only term used. While in English the sacrament with water is referred to exclusively as Baptism,

---

58. "By 'water and the Spirit,' therefore, I simply understand the Spirit, which is water" (*Institutes* IV.XVI.25). So also Barth, as mentioned above.

59. Beasley-Murray refutes a view commonly held among the Reformed, including the Baptists, that the Baptism by water refers to ordinary birth and not to regeneration. "From above" applies to "water and the Spirit" and not to the Spirit alone. He also mentions that Calvin's preference for understanding water as the Spirit came from his utter distaste for baptismal conversion (*Baptism*, 228, n. 2).

60. For a preliminary discussion of Baptism in Johannine literature see ibid., 216–42.

the New Testament uses "water," "washing," "new creation," and "born again," or, better, "born from on high" or "born from God." Thus, for example, in his first epistle John identifies those whose faith conquers the world as those who have born from God (1 Jn 4:5). They are the ones who have known Jesus in the water of Baptism (1 Jn 4:6). Wherever this usage appears in the New Testament, there is the assumption that the writer is referring to Baptism.

When Baptism is contrasted with the Lord's Supper, the benefits unique to it become clear. The Lutheran Confessions properly reflect the New Testament teaching that both sacraments work the forgiveness of sins, but to suggest that they are thereby interchangeable in how they work or for their use in the church would indicate a deficient understanding of each.[61]

In the Small Catechism Baptism is said to work the forgiveness of sins, while in the Lord's Supper the forgiveness of sins is given (SC IV.6 and V.8). Though for Luther Baptism permeates the entire Christian life and gives it its unique character, it is nevertheless the unique rite of initiation into the Christian community in a way that can never be replaced by the Lord's Supper, or for that matter faith. Baptism is the inaugural rite into the kingdom of God, a role which cannot be assigned to faith. Since the Christian is always sinner and saint, even in the middle and at the end of life he stands at the beginning.[62] The necessity of Baptism and its relationship to faith will be discussed below, but they are certainly not interchangeable or equal in any sense, as if one can perform the functions of the other. Through Baptism God creates and confirms faith, hence it is prior to faith. Baptism possesses an objectivity in which the Christian places his trust, and so provides faith with its certainty. In Reformed theology Baptism is an expression of faith: it is not only a covenant God makes with us, but a personal response of the faith of the one who is being baptized by which he makes a covenant with God. Hence in this view Baptism is a work of obedience, which faith does, and so in a real sense is a human work. In Lutheran theology Baptism is completely God's work. Unless this were so, the Christian could not look for salvation in Baptism. In spite of its continued validity in the life of the Christian and even for those who have fallen away from faith, Baptism remains a past event to which the Christian can and must return. Since Baptism is in every sense a birth, it is a non-repeatable, one-time act assuring us of our present condition as God's chil-

---

61. Karl Barth sees Jesus Christ as the only sacrament and effectually denies that anything else, including Baptism, is a sacrament. For Barth, since sacraments are only church rites without intrinsic value in bestowing grace, all such rites are of equal value (*Church Dogmatics* 4/4:201).

62. See Trigg, *Baptism*, 150–73.

dren and thus joint heirs with Christ, God's Son. It is not improbable that Paul's reference to Christians as God's adopted sons is a recollection of their achievement of this status through Baptism. At this time they entered God's family and were entitled to call upon Him as their Father: "God has sent the Spirit of his Son into our hearts, crying 'Abba! Father!'" (Gal 4:5). Baptism, not the Lord's Supper, places us within the family of God and gives us the privileges of Christ in addressing God as our Father. The Christian's right to call God his Father and to participate in the full liturgical rites of the church is not merely a dogmatical conclusion but is supported by the early church practice, which allowed for catechumens to know the words of the Lord's Prayer only after their Baptism. Then for the first time they were permitted to witness and participate in the church's greatest mystery, the Supper of the Lord. Luther is never at a loss for words in describing the abundant gifts of Baptism: "In short, the blessings of Baptism are so boundless that if timid nature considers them, it may well doubt whether they could all be true."[63] Rather than Baptism *obligating* the baptized to receive the Supper, he is now entitled by virtue of his Baptism to participate in it.

Eighteenth-century Rationalists preserved the Reformed view that Baptism was a reception into the outward, visible fellowship of the church rather than the actual bestowal of spiritual blessings.[64] On this basis they could find a justification for infant Baptism, since the children baptized within the church would benefit from their membership there and could come to faith later in adolescence.[65] Such a view in one form or another becomes necessary where a theology of Baptism has been weakened. A similar view was present already in the Middle Ages, during which Penance replaced Baptism in importance.[66] Enlightenment-era Rationalists in Protestant Europe were hardly sacramental in any real sense, but they required a rite of confirmation, if infant Baptism was to have any meaning. Though a sacramental medieval church

---

63. LC IV.42; Tappert, 442; *BKS*, 699. Adolf Philippi says that Baptism is the most effective form of the Word (*Kirchliche Glaubenslehre* vol. 5, no. 2, 220).

64. Calvin specifically denies any salvific significance to Baptism: "Nay, the only purification which baptism promises is by means of the sprinkling of the blood of Christ, who is figured by water from the resemblance to cleansing and washing" (*Institutes* IV.XV.2). In Lutheran theology Christ is found in the water of Baptism, and in Reformed theology our vision is shifted from the water of Baptism to Christ.

65. Such was the view of the influential nineteenth-century theologian Friedrich Daniel Ernst Schleiermacher: "Infant baptism is a complete baptism only when the profession of faith which comes after further instruction is regarded as the act which consummates it" (*The Christian Faith*, ed. H. R. Macintosh and J. S. Stewart, 2 vols. [New York: Harper & Row, 1963], 2:633). Julius August Ludwig Wegscheider, a Rationalist contemporary of Schleiermacher, understood Christianity in terms of cognitive knowledge and required that those baptized as infants determine for themselves if they wanted to join the Christian community. See Barth, *Church Dogmatics* 4/4:188.

66. Oberman, *Luther*, 231.

and post-Enlightenment Protestantism may be worlds apart in their respective understandings of the sacraments, they are agreed that Baptism by itself has an inherent insufficiency. Baptism does inaugurate the baptized into the fellowship of the church, but this is not the church understood merely as an association of persons whose membership can be measured by sociological criteria. Rather, Baptism ushers the believer into that church which has been redeemed by Christ (Eph 5:25) and in which all the benefits which God has bestowed on Christ become the possession of the baptized. Luther speaks of Baptism as the boundaries of the church, but those without faith belong to the false church. He mentions Ishmael, who could boast of circumcision but did not belong to the true church.[67]

Though it is customary in some circles to speak of levels of membership in the church (for example, baptized, communicant, and confirmed), the New Testament and Lutheran Confessions recognize only the baptized as members. The church which Christ has redeemed and washed with Baptism includes husbands and wives, children and parents, and slaves and masters (Eph 5:21–6:9), and there is no distinction in regard to benefits. This church manifests itself only where the Gospel of Christ is preached and Baptism and the Supper are celebrated.

Baptism and the Lord's Supper also differ from each other in how they attain the same goal of offering the forgiveness of sins to the church. Just as Baptism remains a past event in the life of the Christian, though its efficacy and benefits always remain present realities for the believer, it makes the baptized a participant in the *past, historical* events of salvation, the cross, resurrection, ascension, and session at the right hand of God. Christians are buried and raised with Christ as historical events in the past, and on this account Paul can say that they are dead to sin and alive to God in Christ (Rom 6:10–11). They receive the benefits of Christ's death and resurrection, since they are made participants in them through Baptism. The preaching of the Gospel has for its content the death and resurrection of Christ, but it is never said by Paul or any other New Testament writer to take the believer into the tomb by death and out of it through resurrection, as Paul says of Baptism. The new life bestowed on the baptized is in a very real sense the manifestation of Christ's death to sin and His resurrection to God, and the beginning of the final resurrection. Denial of the resurrection in Corinth may have come from confusing the resurrection in Baptism with that of the Last Day. These were not two *different* resurrections, but the resurrection in Baptism was part and parcel of Christ's resurrection, and the final one. The Lord's Supper also has its foundation in the cross, but it projects the death of Christ

---

67. Trigg, *Baptism*, 56–58.

and His atonement into the worshiping life of the congregation. The eating and the drinking are for Paul a proclamation of Christ's death (1 Cor 11:26). Baptism thrusts the believer into the past, and the Supper makes the atonement of Christ contemporary to him. Since Baptism involves the believer as part of Christ and His redeemed church, nothing should be contained in the baptismal liturgy of the church to suggest that the members of the congregation are the ones who are receiving the baptized into the membership of *their* church. The pastor who baptizes is not standing in the place of an association, congregation, or community, but in the place of Christ. Giving the impression that Baptism is an act of the congregation and not solely of Christ destroys the concept that the church is a heavenly reality and that Baptism bestows the heavenly blessings.[68]

Only when Baptism is viewed as an act of the church as an association of like-minded persons or as an act of the believer performed by his will does it become possible to speak of being baptized more than once. Mainline denominations, of course with the exception of some Baptists, are agreed that those baptized in other denominations should not be given another Baptism when they come from one denominational family to theirs, though the Roman Catholics have frequently made an exception for themselves in conferring *conditional* Baptism.[69] Baptism is conferred again only on those who have been baptized in churches where the trinitarian confession is not part of the church's publicly stated confession, though this is not actually a rebaptism. Churches which are not Christian in the New Testament sense cannot administer Baptism.

A problem arises in pastoral practice when the pastor cannot determine for certain that Baptism was actually administered. This kind of situation can arise from faulty memory or records. In such cases Baptism *without* any conditions should be administered. Luther's objections to rebaptism are directed specifically against the Anabaptists, who claimed that Baptism in infancy was of no use.[70] Baptism, unlike the proclamation of the Word and the Supper, provides the certainty that the baptized has been included in Christ's saving activities. In cases

---

68. One questions the conclusion to the order of Baptism in *Lutheran Worship*: "We welcome you into the Lord's family. We receive you as a fellow member(s) of the body of Christ, (a) child(ren) of the same heavenly Father, to work with us in his kingdom" (204). Is it really fellow Christians who welcome the baptized into the kingdom? The idea that we are baptized to work with fellow believers may give a distorted picture of what the church is.

69. "The [Roman Catholic] Church recognizes as valid baptisms performed by non-Catholic ministers. Baptism is conferred *conditionally* when there is doubt concerning a previous baptism or the disposition of the person to be baptized" (Robert C. Broderick, *Catholic Encyclopedia*, 65).

70. Trigg, *Baptism*, 85.

where there is a lack of verifiable certainty that Baptism was actually administered, the individual can hardly be assured of his inclusion in Christ.

This uncertainty regarding one's salvation is nothing less than could be expected in the Reformed view and that of Schleiermacher (who was as influential in the nineteenth and twentieth centuries as were Luther and Calvin in the sixteenth and seventeenth centuries), which see no intrinsic benefit in the act of Baptism itself. For Calvin, the Spirit works separately in an action parallel to Baptism but not in Baptism itself. Calvin uses the word "illumination" to describe the Spirit's activity. For Schleiermacher the saving activity is attached to the community.[71] In utter contrast, and to the relief of our souls, the Lutheran Confessions locate the benefits of salvation in Baptism.

---

71. "Baptism as an action of the Church signifies simply the act of will by which the Church receives the individual into its fellowship; but inasmuch as the effectual promise of Christ rests upon it, it is at the same time the channel of divine justifying activity, through which the individual is received into the living fellowship of Christ" (ibid., 619). For additional discussion on this question, see Pieper's section, "Baptism a True Means of Grace" (in *Christian Dogmatics* 3:263–75).

Excursus

MINISTRY: AN EFFECT OF BAPTISM?

From either a confessional or an historical perspective, ordinarily there would be no reason to discuss ministry and Baptism together, but the claim is now made more frequently that Baptism is foundational for the office of the ministry.[1] This claim has been used as the basis for ordination of women pastors. Arguments finding the ministry as a derivative of either Baptism or faith are basically the same. Ministry is seen as nothing else than the Spirit's work of sanctification through Baptism in the believer's life, to which all can lay claim or at least aspire.[2] Karl Barth goes so far as to say that Baptism is an ordination. Though many Protestants, including some Lutherans, do not see the office of the ministry as distinct from being a Christian, it would be difficult to find very many who would be so blunt as to equate Baptism with ordination.

---

1. David L. Bartlett, in *Ministry in the New Testament* (Minneapolis: Augsburg Publishing House, 1993), proceeds precisely along these lines in demonstrating that the church has no need for an ordained ministry. He gives a favorable assessment to some contemporary Roman Catholic thought that roots ordination in Baptism (ibid., 12–14). Chapter II ("The People of God") of "Lumen Gentium," adopted by the Second Vatican Council on November 21, 1964, holds that the people by virtue of their royal priesthood participate in the offering of the Eucharist. It further holds that, having been incorporated into the church by Baptism, "the faithful are appointed by their baptismal character to Christian religious worship" (*Vatican Council II: The Conciliar and Post-Conciliar Documents*, ed. Austin Flannery [Wilmington, DE: Scholarly Resources, 1975], 361). Vatican II also adopted the Decree on the Lay Apostolate, *Apostolicam Actuositatem*, on November 18, 1965, which lays down the rationale for the lay apostolate and sets forth its peculiar obligations as well as those shared with bishops and priests. The lay apostolate engages in missionary work and may in certain circumstances do the work of a priest in teaching Christian doctrine (ibid., 766–92). Foundational for the lay apostolate is the royal priesthood, which is demonstrated from such passages as 1 Pt 2:4–10 and Eph 4:16. Though these and other passages might suggest a correlation between Baptism and the lay apostolate, references to these passages in the Decree on the Lay Apostolate are lacking.

2. John N. Collins wrote a monumental work disputing that ministry is the common possession of all Christians (*Diakonia: Reinterpreting the Ancient Sources* [New York: Oxford University Press, 1990]). His work was abridged into *Are All Christians Ministers?* (Collegeville, MN: Liturgical Press, 1992). Here he claims, "The dominant line of interpretation emerging from the modern [English Bible] translations is that the saints do the work of ministry, and this is in close accord with the contemporary view which has occasioned this book, that all Christians are ministers because they have been baptized into the ministerial condition" (ibid., 22). This view is also fostered in many modern commentaries, including one by Karl Barth's son Markus Barth (*Ephesians*, The Anchor Bible, vol. 34, nos. 1–2 [Garden City, NY: Doubleday, 1974]). It is also characteristic of Baptistic theology.

Ministry: An Effect of Baptism?

Since for Barth only Jesus Christ qualifies as sacrament, the distinction between church rites, including Baptism and ordination, is insignificant.[3] Strange as it may seem, considering ministry as an effect or gift of Baptism not only indicates the presence of false views about the ministry and ordination, but worse, the great things which this sacrament really does accomplish, such as forgiveness of sins and burial with Christ, are no longer recognized as sufficient gifts for the believer and are relegated to a level of unimportance. As important as ordination and the ministry are, they cannot be considered on the same spiritual level as Baptism. Already in the Middle Ages, in regard to spiritual gifts ordination was seen as an advance beyond Baptism in what it could do. So modern attempts to link and see a progression from Baptism to ministry are not new. Luther says that the blessings of Baptism are boundless (LC IV.42), but it does *not* make its recipients ministers! The ministry is a blessing to others and not to the ministers: "In order that we may obtain this faith, the ministry of teaching the Gospel and administering the sacraments was instituted."[4]

Proponents for the ordination of women, however, have offered arguments in support of this practice which are strangely similar to Barth's. Simply put, Baptism provides the basis for the ministry and so allows for all baptized, both men and women, to serve as ministers. Ministry is now viewed as an exercise of Christian faith which finds its basis in Baptism. Our Confessions treat the doctrines of the ministry and Baptism separately and make no necessary connections between them, except of course the understanding that the ministry is responsible for administering the sacraments, including Baptism. Those who are baptized do not by that Baptism become ministers.

For Barth, however, Baptism serves as an ordination into the ministry, and so it makes all Christians ministers. This reasoning is particularly popular among some Lutherans, especially those who are searching for a theological basis for the ordination of women; this argument is not pursued with great dogmatical and exegetical vigor, however, and no mention is made of Barth, for whom the view was essential. David Bartlett, whose book was published by a Lutheran publisher, sees ordination as an extension of Baptism: "The minister's baptism provides

---

3. "But all those baptized as Christians are *eo ipso* consecrated, ordained and dedicated to the ministry of the church" (*Church Dogmatics* 4/4:201). A fuller discussion of Barth's views on Baptism is left to another chapter.

4. AC V.1; Tappert, 31; BKS, 58. In the *Catechism of the Catholic Church*, Confirmation is said specifically to complete Baptism, imprint an indelible mark, and perfect the bond of the Holy Spirit (para. 1304). Penance is for those who have "lost their baptismal grace and wounded ecclesial communion" (ibid., para. 1446). "By the sacrament of Confirmation [the baptized] are more perfectly bound to the Church and are endowed with the special strength of the Holy Spirit" ("Lumen Gentium," 361).

Excursus

the identity that ordination only elaborates."[5] This assertion raises the question of how ordination differs from confirmation, which builds on Baptism. Not only does this view, which is reminiscent of Barth's, allow any baptized person to become a minister, but real differences between the laity and the clergy are removed. Women receiving ordination are only exercising a privilege which is already theirs in Baptism. So in a real sense they have not gained anything from ordination which they did not already possess in their Baptism. Ordination is in effect understood as a confirmation of Baptism or an intensification of its gifts. It is not surprising that some women ministers have found the view inadequate and unattractive. In their battle to be ordained, they have gained hardly more than a public recognition of what was already theirs. If all Christians become ministers in their Baptism, ordination becomes redundant and a superfluous rite. Bartlett goes precisely in this direction.

Since women are serving as ordained ministers in nearly all major Protestant denominations, including such tradition-bound ones as the member churches of the Lutheran World Federation and the Anglican Communion, finding a basis for this custom is moot for them. Seminary enrollment figures indicate that women may in a generation or two constitute a majority of the clergy in some churches, including Lutheran ones, and the image of the pastor as a male figure may belong to the quaint historical past. With the increasing number of women pastors, demonstrating that the ministry is derived from Baptism may already be of diminished interest. Churches which do not now ordain women, however, can expect that the argument based on the correlation between Baptism and the ministry will be raised by those supporting the ordination of women.

It may be overlooked that women's ordination for Lutherans, as it is for Anglicans (Episcopalians), is only a recent innovation. There is no long, historic theological tradition to support the custom, either among those whose heritage is derived from Rome, like the Lutheran and Anglican churches, or from the Eastern Orthodox, who will not even allow its discussion. For nearly twenty centuries churches of the *catholic* tradition did not ordain women priests or pastors.

Though the Norwegian government was the first to provide official authorization to ordain women for a Lutheran church in 1938, the first such ordination in that country took place twenty-three years later, in 1961. Other Scandinavian and then German churches followed suit, and in 1970 the first woman was ordained in North America. Initial resistance to ordaining women has disappeared, and vigorous dissent is no longer tolerated within church bodies that have approved the practice. Pastors unwilling to ordain women are simply ineligible to become bishops or assume professorships or a post of any kind. In addressing the

---

5. Bartlett, *Ministry*, 187.

Ministry: An Effect of Baptism?

issue of the ordination of women, it must be remembered that this practice was first required by government decree, and that theological arguments, including that for Baptism as a basis for ministry, followed only later. In North America governmental interference was never an issue, but interpretations of some biblical citations were shaped to fit feministic philosophies. For the churches now constituting the Evangelical Lutheran Church in America, the decision to ordain women was made strictly on theological grounds in which arguments from the doctrine of Baptism played a role.[6] At that time a substantial minority in the American Lutheran Church was not convinced by these arguments, and the vote authorizing women's ordination was very close. Though the issue is no longer debatable in the member churches of the Lutheran World Federation, it remains a cause of dissension among some churches associated with The Lutheran Church—Missouri Synod in the International Lutheran Conference. In spite of official pronouncements, calls for the introduction of the ordination of women have not subsided. A similar situation exists in the Roman Catholic Church. In spite of John Paul II's encyclicals against the practice, a majority of American bishops, priests, and laity reportedly finds no difficulty in having women ordained as priests.

Arguments from Baptism for the ordination of women are at best exegetically contrived and are recognized by some proponents themselves as inconsistent,[7] but this has not prevented their appeal, especially to those who see the office of the ministry as derived in some sense from the universal priesthood of all believers. The idea of the universal priesthood does not provide a basis from which the ministry is derived, but this argument was prominent in the endeavor to gain support for ordaining women. Since the ministry is a derivative of the universal priesthood as it takes form in the baptized congregation, so the reasoning goes, there is no real reason to prevent otherwise qualified Christians, including women, from becoming pastors. This argument takes on additional force since references to the royal priesthood (1 Pt 2:9) are taken from an epistle which many scholars recognize as a baptismal homily.[8] Of course this argument assumes that the priesthood, which is bestowed in Baptism, is identical to the ministry. Such

---

6. For a description of the history and theological and exegetical arguments leading up to the ordination of women in the American Lutheran Church and Lutheran Church in America, now the Evangelical Lutheran Church in America, see David P. Scaer, "May Women Be Ordained as 'Pastors'?" *The Springfielder* 36 (September 1972): 89–109.

7. See Daphne Hampson, *Theology and Feminism* (Cambridge, MA: Basil Blackwell, 1990), 26–27. This articulate and firmly committed proponent of the ordination of women claims that the alleged equality of male and female found in Gal 3:27–28 is contradicted by St. Paul himself in 1 Corinthians, where he speaks of male headship and the silence of women.

8. For a discussion of 1 Peter as a baptismal homily see J. N. D. Kelly, *A Commentary on the Epistles of Peter and Jude* (New York and Evanston: Harper & Row, 1969), 16–20.

reasoning can hardly be supported from 1 Peter itself, where a distinction between church and clergy is made (5:1–3).[9] Peter is a fellow elder (ὁ συμπρεσβύτερος) with other elders (πρεσβύτεροι). In our terms, he is a minister with other ministers. An elder in the New Testament is what we call today a minister, a pastor. With other Christians, Peter is a co-heir of salvation, but the baptized are not in any sense co-ministers with him. In addition, there is hardly any suggestion here or any other place in the New Testament that early Christians regarded their Baptism as equivalent to an ordination ceremony into the ministry, even though Bartlett makes this outrageous claim without evidence or argument. He does not seem to have been familiar with Barth's discussion, which at least would have added the weight of prestige to his argument.

In the debate against the ordination of women, Lutherans traditionally have used arguments from the orders of creation, by which God in creation assigned different functions to men and women. These orders allow certain qualified men, but not women, to become ministers. The argument that views the ministry as a derivative of Baptism holds that with the coming of Christ the orders of creation were abrogated for the baptized, and so the obstacles of the orders of creation barring women from ordination are removed.[10] Such an argument resembles ancient Gnosticism, which viewed redemption as a solution to a defective creation. Baptized Christians are equal in every respect, including their eligibility to become ministers, as it was argued by those churches now constituting the Evangelical Lutheran Church in America. It is not clear whether this argument assumes that Baptism makes everyone a minister, as Barth held, or simply makes everyone eligible, but the outcome of the argument is the same: women can be ordained. Lack of a unanimous view of the ministry among Lutherans has added confusion to the discussion, which has benefited the proponents of women's ordination.[11] This position, where its proponents find a need to defend it, continues to rely heavily, if not convincingly, on Gal 3:27–28: "For as many of you as were baptized into Christ have put on Christ. There is neither Jew nor Greek, there is neither slave nor free, there is neither male nor

---

9. First Peter's discussion of apostleship and ministry is found in 5:1–5; Kelly, *Epistles of Peter and Jude*, 99–102, 195–99.

10. Hampson dismisses the idea that St. Paul had any idea of an equality which did away with the orders of creation. New Testament texts speaking of the subordination of women rely on the Genesis account, which for her are no longer valid in the post-Darwinian age (*Theology and Feminism,* 27).

11. See David P. Scaer, "Augustana V and the Doctrine of the Ministry," *Lutheran Quarterly* 6 (Winter 1992): 403–24. Those who look for support in the Confessions for the ordination of women do not rely on the sections on Baptism, but on Article V of the Augsburg Confession, from which they conclude that all Christians are ministers. This interpretation is correlated with their view of Gal 3:27–28, where Baptism is mentioned.

female; for you are all one in Christ Jesus."[12] Finding a basis for ministry (whether for men or women) in the Galatians text is contrived, as even some proponents of women's ordination recognize. [13] St. Paul is speaking here not about the ministry but about the justification of the sinner before God, which is the major theme of this epistle. An Australian Lutheran theologian views the situation accurately:

> The equality that Luther speaks about is the equality of the redeemed *coram Deo*, Gal. 3:27f. But this does not immediately imply equal, in the sense of identical functions in the church. Every member of the church has the right, not the duty, to participate in the calling of a servant of the Word which is proclaimed on Christ's behalf. But there can be no confusion of offices and functions. . . . While the old *Übertragungslehre* of the last century will hardly be repeated in the same terms, we can expect a repetition of the claim that the public office is merely a delegated authority. And as the pleas for the ordination of women intensify we can expect repeated reference to this idea.[14]

This prediction was probably written before women were ordained in North America, and published shortly after it came true. The fundamental fault in any argument that sees every Christian entitled to become a minister is the fusion of the doctrines of justification, sanctification, and ministry. Where ministry is seen only as an exercise of faith, any obstacle to ordaining women is removed. Without in any way diminishing the foundational importance of Baptism as "the first and most important sacrament, without which the others are all nothing,"[15] it does not take the place of any other sacrament or rite, including ordination. Arguments for the ordination of women pastors based on the universality of Baptism are at best contrived, a conclusion which some of them may have reached. At least fourteen women pastors do not find that the Evangelical Lutheran Church in America and its theologians have offered them "a scripturally sound, confessionally faithful, theological rationale in defense of the ordination of women."[16] It seems that arguments from Galatians making Baptism the basis for ministry are unconvincing. They themselves are at a loss to put any forward.

---

12. The official document presenting arguments for the ordination of women, including those from the Galatians passage, was written by Fred Meuser, *The Ordination of Women* (Minneapolis: Augsburg Publishing House, 1970). This argument is revived by Bartlett, who reminds us that the barriers have come down (*Ministry*, 197). His extremely brief reference to the Galatians passage may indicate the slight exegetical support he finds for this position.

13. Hampson, *Theology and Feminism*, 27.

14. Victor Pfitzner, "'General Priesthood' and Ministry," *Lutheran Journal of Theology* 5 (November 1971): 107–8.

15. *AE* 41:195.

16. Ruth H. Ballard, Pamela J. Carnes-Chapman, Carol E. A. Fryer, et al., "Open Letter: Turning Down 'Stirring Up,'" *Lutheran Forum* 24 (May 1990): 9.

5

THE BAPTISMAL FORMULA: BAPTISM IN THE NAME OF THE TRIUNE GOD

Baptism in the New Testament is an initiation rite into the church performed with water and administered, according to Mt 28:19, "in the name of the Father and of the Son and of the Holy Spirit." A problem arises concerning the necessity of the trinitarian formula in connection with Acts, with its references to Baptism in the name of Jesus Christ (2:38, 10:48) but no reference to the Father and the Spirit. Some scholars have concluded that "in the name of Jesus" formulas of Acts were part of the earliest baptismal rite, and that the tripartite formula of Matthew 28 was a later development of church theology and cannot be attributed to Jesus.[1] This argument is used both by those who affirm and those who deny the resurrection of Jesus, though obviously the latter could hardly attribute the words to Him.[2] Two questions are involved here. First, can it be demonstrated that the "Father–Son–Holy Spirit" formula of Matthew's baptismal command is so foreign to the preaching of Jesus that it cannot be attributed to Him or the evangelist?[3] Secondly, is it really true that the remainder of the New Testament is devoid of references to a trinitarian Baptism?

If it were possible to excise the trinitarian formula of Mt 28:19 from the rest of that gospel, such a wording would seem more at home in the gospel of John with its highly developed Christology. The Logos, who shares in the nature of God, is God's instrument for the world's creation and takes on flesh (Jn 1:1–3, 14). However, isolating the trinitarian pericope from the rest of Matthew overlooks the fact that, even without this verse, this gospel offers an explicit and high Christology and has all

---

1. Schlink, *The Doctrine of Baptism*, 26–31.
2. Jenson argues for the authenticity of the trinitarian formula: "Exegetes often regard these passages as retrojection of the church's self-consciousness, but if there were indeed appearances of the risen Lord, there is no reason the giving of this mandate cannot have been among their incidents" ("Part Two: The Two Sacraments," in Braaten and Jenson, *Christian Dogmatics* 2:315).
3. William D. Davies and Dale C. Allison defend the authenticity of the text, but are compelled to place the entire gospel at the end of the first century (*Matthew: International Critical Commentary*, 3 vols. [Edinburgh: T. & T. Clark, 1988–97], 1:132–33). In the third and final volume these scholars maintain this position, but see no connection between it and the promise of the Spirit in Mt 3:11, nor do they allow for any advanced trinitarianism in the first gospel. Its use in the Didache points to the early use of this trinitarian formula in the Syriac, but in their view other formulas predominated (ibid., 3:684–86).

the components of a trinitarian theology.⁴ In the annunciation to Joseph, the trinitarian form emerges. An angel of the Lord, that is, of the Father, appears, saying that Mary's child is conceived by the Holy Spirit, and the evangelist explains that the Child's name, Jesus, signifies that He is the God who saves His people from their sins. As the Immanuel child, He is God with them (Mt 1:20–25). In the return from Egypt, Jesus is for the first time explicitly identified as God's Son: "Out of Egypt have I called my son" (Mt 2:15). The One to whom Mary gives birth (Mt 1:15, 25) is called both God and God's Son. The "Holy Spirit" of the trinitarian formula is also introduced in the same narrative (Mt 1:18, 20), and the only conclusion is that the evangelist wants the reader to understand these two pericopes as part of a larger whole.⁵ The Spirit in whose name Baptism is given is responsible for the incarnation of the Son. Even more explicit is the baptismal narrative, where the Spirit of God descends in the form of a dove and the voice from heaven claims Jesus as "my beloved Son" (Mt 3:16).⁶ Luther understood Jesus' Baptism as a trinitarian revelation, and combined it with Mt 28:19:

> There stood the Son of God in love, His grace to us extending;
> The Holy Spirit like a dove Upon the scene descending;
> The triune God assuring us, With promises compelling,
> That in our baptism He will thus Among us find a dwelling
> To comfort and sustain us.⁷

In connection with His Baptism, Jesus commits Himself to carrying out God's plan of righteousness (Mt 3:15) and receives the Spirit to assist Him (Mt 3:16, 4:1). Other references serve to show the unique relationship that Jesus as the Son has with the Father. Similarly, Matthew speaks of the Holy Spirit, the Spirit of God, or the Spirit of your Father. Particularly important in establishing the authenticity of the trinitarian formula in Matthew is v. 11:27: "No one knows the Son except the Father, and no one knows the Father except the Son and any one to whom the Son chooses to reveal him." It is not uncommon for some scholars to put an Arian twist on these words to avoid a developed trinitarian theology attributed to Jesus or the evangelist.⁸ Still, the tripartite formula of "Father-Son–Holy Spirit" in Matthew 28 is hardly alien to this gos-

---
    4. See Jack Kingsbury, "The Composition and Christology of Matthew 28:16–20," *Journal of Biblical Literature* 93 (1974): 573–84, and David P. Scaer's "The Relation of Matthew 28:16–20 to the Rest of the Gospel," *Concordia Theological Quarterly* 55 (October 1991): 245–67.
    5. Contra Davies and Allison, *Matthew* 1:200.
    6. For a discussion of the relationship of the baptism of Jesus in Matthew 3 and the trinitarian formula of Baptism in Matthew 28 see Bo Reicke, *The Roots of the Synoptic Gospels* (Philadelphia: Fortress Press, 1986), 80.
    7. "To Jordan Came the Christ, Our Lord," *Lutheran Worship*, 223.
    8. So Davies and Allison, *Matthew* 1:280–82.

pel. Rather, it brings together a description of God already offered throughout the gospel. The argument that the trinitarian formula of Mt 28:19 must be a later addition of the church has no real support from the document itself. Related to the authenticity of Matthew's use of the tripartite formula is the Didache, which many scholars see as contemporary with or even earlier than the composition of Matthew. This document does not use "in the name of Jesus" as a baptismal formula.[9]

The second question is whether only Matthew among the New Testament writers knows of the tripartite formula used in Baptism. First Corinthians is arguably more liturgically oriented than any of the apostles' other epistles. It addresses such aberrant worship practices as women preaching in the church, lack of proper dress, gluttony and drunkenness at the Lord's Supper, communing at the Lord's Table and those of pagans, preaching sermons denying the resurrection, and vicarious Baptisms for the dead. These aberrations have theological consequences, but they are still practical matters and not merely matters of abstract theological debate. Paul is capable of the lofty theological discourse of Romans and Ephesians, but in the Corinthian correspondence he is working with the nitty-gritty of congregational life. Baptism plays a prominent role in Paul's first letter to the Corinthians. This sacrament was a cause of division (1 Cor 1:10–17), the basis of Israel becoming God's people (10:2), and was being conducted to benefit the dead (15:29). Though he does not want to define his ministry within the terms of Baptism, Paul does concede that he was a baptismal officiant. He actually baptized Stephen's household (1 Cor 1:16–17), which may suggest that he administered Baptism to a congregation which had this particular person as its pastor or elder. Paul is at first uncertain about whether he had baptized others who are now members of other churches. What is important is that he actually did some baptizing himself and was acquainted with the baptismal formula. That the phrase "in the name of" was part of the formula is explicit in Paul's rhetorical question: "Is Christ divided? Was Paul crucified for you? Or were you baptized *in the name of* Paul?" (1 Cor 1:13; emphasis added). Christ was crucified for the Corinthians, and in His name they were baptized. Paul's reference to Israel being "baptized into Moses" suggests that Christians were "baptized into Christ." But the question remains whether the Corinthian Baptism was administered in the name of the "Father–Son–Holy Spirit." What about Paul? Did he know the trinitarian formula and, more importantly, did he use it?

---

9. Scholars are not agreed on the exact relationship of the gospel of Matthew and the Didache or their dating, but their common use of the trinitarian formula for Baptism not only suggests they are related, but confirms that this formula was in common use in the church by the end of the first century. For a discussion of this issue see ibid., 130–33. The "in the name of Jesus" formula does not enjoy such attestation.

He speaks about their being "washed . . . sanctified . . . justified in the name of the Lord Jesus Christ and in the Spirit of our God" (1 Cor 6:11), a tripartite formula strikingly similar to Matthew's "Father–Son–Holy Spirit." "God" is Paul's normal reference to the Father, as for example in the well-known benediction "The grace of the Lord Jesus Christ and the love of God and the fellowship of the Holy Spirit be with you all" (2 Cor 13:14). "Wash" is another term for Baptism, as discussed above, though the Reformed hardly concede this.[10] What connects this washing to Baptism is that the phrase "in the name of the Lord Jesus Christ" is virtually identical to one used in Acts, "in the name of Jesus Christ" (Acts 2:38, 10:48). In the New Testament Jesus is commonly called the Lord, the Father is called God, and the Holy Spirit, simply Spirit.[11] It cannot be concluded definitely that the Corinthians used the trinitarian formula, which was preserved by Matthew and the Didache, but the words "God," "Jesus," and "Spirit" may suggest it was part of the ritual.[12]

---

10. One happy exception is Baptist theologian G. R. Beasley-Murray: "The coincidence of language between 'you had yourselves washed . . . in the name of the Lord Jesus' and that used by Ananias to Paul, 'Get baptized and wash away your sins, calling on his name' (Acts 22:16), is so close as to make it difficult to dissociate the 'washing' of 1 Cor. 6:11 from baptismal cleansing" (*Baptism*, 163). Note Beasley-Murray prefers the middle to the passive voice for "you had yourselves washed." If he were right, the sentence would have to read, "You had yourselves washed, you had yourselves sanctified, you had yourselves justified." Even he reads "you were justified" (ibid., 164). Read all verbs in the passive, especially "you were baptized." Consider Luther. God baptizes! The alternative is blatant synergism.

11. Ibid., 162–63.

12. The question arises whether in 1 Cor 6:11 Paul correlated the divine names Christ, Spirit, and God with the activities of washing, sanctifying, and justifying: Jesus baptizes, the Spirit sanctifies, and God justifies. Justifying is more often used in the passive than active voice, but where the latter is used it is God, the first person of the Trinity, who justifies, e.g. Rom 8:33. That God and not Father is used in these cases may indicate that only after the believer comes to faith and is baptized, after he is personally justified, is he entitled to address God as "Our Father" (Gal 4:16). Where the passive is used, the reference is also to God. God justifies on account of Jesus, but it is God who does the justifying. Such an understanding derives from the doctrine of the atonement, in which the Father sends the Son and receives His sacrifice. The word "sanctifying" and its cognates are not so clear-cut. In 1 Thes 5:23 God sanctifies Christians. In several places Paul attributes this work to the Holy Spirit (1 Thes 2:13; Rom 15:16; see also 1 Pt 1:2). Actual baptisms are carried out by the apostles; however, Luther's view that Christ actually baptizes (washes) every Christian is the correct New Testament understanding. Obviously Jesus did not personally baptize anyone in the apostolic churches, but this was also the case in His own ministry, in which the disciples carried out this task in His place (Jn 4:2). All four evangelists are definite in saying that, in contrast to John the Baptist, Jesus will baptize and that this will take place with the Holy Spirit (Mt 3:11; Mk 1:8; Lk 3:16; Jn 1:33; see also Jn 3:22, 4:1). Note Eph 5:26: ". . . [Christ] might sanctify [the church], having cleansed her by the washing of water with the word." Here both sanctification and washing (baptizing) are attributed to Christ, but in the same sequence as in 1 Cor 6:11. He accomplishes sanctification through the water of Baptism. A division of labor among the persons of the Trinity cannot be sharply drawn, *opera Trinitatis ad extra indivisa sunt*, but New Testament writers characteristically attribute certain works to certain persons.

The Baptismal Formula

What is undeniable is that their baptismal theology was clearly trinitarian.[13]

First Corinthians 6:11 sheds light on the Baptisms in Acts administered "in the name of the Lord Jesus Christ."[14] Throughout the New Testament, but especially in Acts, God claims Jesus as His Son in the resurrection. The Lord Jesus is God's Son. Romans 1:4 states: "[Jesus is] designated Son of God in power according to the Spirit of holiness by his resurrection from the dead." Prior to the Baptism of the three thousand, Peter says that Jesus "[was] exalted at the right hand of God . . . having received from the Father the promise of the Holy Spirit" (Acts 2:33). Baptism was offered "in the name of Jesus Christ . . . [to] receive the gift of the Holy Spirit" (Acts 2:38), and as such it, like the resurrection, was a trinitarian event: God raised Jesus and gave Him the Spirit who now through Baptism was being given to believers (Acts 10:38). In the early church, Baptism in the name of Jesus was always trinitarian. Jesus was understood not only as Lord and Christ, but God's Son, and He gave the Holy Spirit to the baptized, as the Father had given the Spirit to Him in His baptism. Regin Prenter notes that Baptism in the name of Jesus "means, then, that baptism is performed with the purpose of bringing the baptized one into a total living fellowship with Jesus Christ, that is, into a participation in His death and resurrection."[15] Baptism by the Spirit into the body, that is, the church, also suggests that the Spirit was mentioned in the baptismal formula.

Charles Gieschen has offered evidence that "the name of Jesus" is a reference to "the name" of God which Jesus as God's Son possesses.[16] In other words, Jesus is entrusted with manifesting God. As the possessor of this name, Jesus is both the Revealer of God and the content of His revelation. Jesus provides access to God as triune. This may account for the fact that the name of the Triune God is given in the baptismal formula only after Jesus has both died and risen from the dead. Application of Gieschen's view to Acts would mean that "in the name of Jesus" was not and was never intended to be a liturgical formula for administering Baptism. He demonstrates that the earliest Christians, who were Jewish, transferred their respect for יהוה, the divine name, to the trinitarian formula and used it circumspectly. This practice may be based on the

---

13. Beasley-Murray states matters soberly: "This is insufficient evidence of the existence in Paul's time of baptism in the name of the Father, Son and Holy Spirit, but it provides a hint of the way in which the trinitarian formula arose, namely, by the enumeration of respects in which baptism in the name of the Lord Jesus involved the operation of the Father and the Holy Spirit" (*Baptism*, 167). Quite to the contrary, it could very well be the other way around. The classical and also liturgical trinitarian formula provided the *homiletical* basis for Paul's discourse. The trinitarian name actually meant that God was doing something to the baptized.

14. This observation is made by Beasley-Murray (ibid., 163).

15. *Creation and Redemption*, 465.

16. *Angelomorphic Christology: Antecedents and Early Evidence* (Leiden: E. J. Brill, 1998).

understanding that "the name" in the trinitarian formula, which is shared by the three persons of the Trinity, is the divine name (יהוה).[17] Hesitancy to vocalize the divine name would account for its being introduced only at the end of Matthew and not at all in the other New Testament writings, though certain other references surely seem to be circumlocutions, as will be shown below.

Justin Martyr in *I Apology* 61 cautions that only the baptizer should speak the divine name at Baptism. Only then would the trinitarian formula be made known to the catechumen. Baptism was for him the moment of God's revealing Himself as Father–Son–Holy Spirit. Walter Eichrodt, an Old Testament scholar, points out that, to the Hebrews, the nature of a thing is found in its name. To have the name of something or someone is to have a direct knowledge of it. So the act of revealing the name of the Father and of the Son and of the Holy Spirit to the baptized makes this God his own. This line of reasoning depends on the Old Testament, where the name is the expression of the individual character of the person.[18] So in Ps 54:1, God brings help by His name. It is a divine hypostasis in several Old Testament texts; thus, it is nothing less than God Himself or the instrument through which He works in the world.[19]

In Jn 1:12 Jesus as the Father's representative possesses the divine name. Through Him the Father is at work in the world.[20] This reference precedes the strong baptismal overtones found in v. 13. God's children are those born from God (ἐκ θεοῦ ἐγεννήθησαν), and so know Him and possess Him. The Baptism of Mt 28:19 not only is carried out by the authorization of the Triune God, something with which the Reformed would agree, but in Baptism that same name of God is invoked and revealed. God Himself is thus present to perform the Baptism, a thought which squares with Luther's thinking.

Gieschen's theory about the name of God and the hesitancy to use it may also account for the absence of the trinitarian formula in other New Testament books. Paul's implicit trinitarian terminology in his teachings on Baptism, as discussed above, may be part of early church piety which gave the same respect to the tripartite formula which was previously given to the Old Testament יהוה.[21] Lutherans have tradition-

---

17. Ibid., 70–78.
18. Walter Eichrodt, *Theology of the Old Testament*, trans. J. Baker, 2 vols. (London: SCM Press, 1967), 2:40.
19. Gieschen, *Angelomorphic Christology*, 70–78.
20. See ibid., 270–86. Gieschen discusses this matter in these pages. The name at which every knee bows (Phil 2:9–10) would be "Father–Son–Holy Spirit." Here Jesus Christ is confessed as Lord to the glory of God the Father. Similarly, in Rv 3:12, "I will write on him the name of my God, and the name of the city of my God, the new Jerusalem which comes down from my God out of heaven, and my own new name."
21. As noted above, Beasley-Murray sees a primitive form in 1 Cor 6:11 out of which a full trinitarian formula evolved (*Baptism*, 167). Gieschen's theory suggests a development in the other direction. Paul not only knew the trinitarian formula, but

ally used the phrase Real Presence in connection with their doctrine of the Lord's Supper. It would be confusing to use this phrase in referring to the presence and activity of the Triune God in Baptism; however, Christ with the Father and Spirit is no less present in Baptism than He is in the Supper. All this is intended not only in the phrase "in the name of the Father and of the Son and of the Holy Spirit," but also in the phrase "in the name of Jesus."

THE APPARENT ABSENCE OF BAPTISMAL COMMANDS IN MARK AND LUKE

In previous sections we have discussed the authenticity of Mk 16:16, a passage used by Luther in the Small Catechism to teach the efficacy of Baptism. Apart from the debate over whether or not Mk 16:9–20 was part of the original gospel, the inclusion of this pericope shows how important it was for its author that the resurrected Jesus speak explicitly about the role of Baptism in salvation. At issue is the authenticity of Mk 16:9–20, and not whether this pericope is explicit about the necessity of Baptism. It is quite clear! "He who believes and is baptized will be saved" (Mk 16:16).

Since the conclusions to both Matthew and Mark contain explicit references to Baptism, the question arises whether there is a possible reference to Baptism in Luke's conclusion. Within the context of Luke's own characteristic vocabulary in his gospel and Acts, a baptismal allusion in trinitarian language in Lk 24:47–49 becomes evident. A baptismal command, remarkably similar to Matthew's, would have been recognized by Luke's hearers in these words: ". . . and that *repentance and forgiveness of sins* should be preached *in his name to all nations*, beginning from Jerusalem. You are witnesses of these things. And behold, *I send the promise of my Father* upon you" (καὶ κηρυχθῆναι ἐπὶ τῷ ὀνόματι αὐτοῦ μετάνοιαν εἰς ἄφεσιν ἁμαρτιῶν εἰς πάντα τὰ ἔθνη. ἀρξάμενοι ἀπὸ Ἰερουσαλὴμ ὑμεῖς μάρτυρες τούτων. καὶ [ἰδοὺ] ἐγὼ ἀποστέλλω τὴν ἐπαγγελίαν τοῦ πατρός μου ἐφ᾽ ὑμᾶς).

For us a closer examination may be necessary. There are surface similarities between Lk 24:47–49 and Mt 28:19–20. Both gospels include all nations (πάντα τὰ ἔθνη) in the apostolic task. Mark specifies "the whole creation" (16:15).[22] While the tripartite formula of "Father and Son and Holy Spirit" (τὸ ὄνομα τοῦ πατρὸς καὶ τοῦ υἱοῦ καὶ τοῦ ἁγίου πνεύματος) is missing in Luke's commission, it is nevertheless trinitarian,

---

used it only for baptizing. It also lends credence to the theory that the gospel of Matthew was a catechesis with liturgical rubrics on how certain rites, including Baptism, were to be administered.

22. Mark knows of the phrase πάντα τὰ ἔθνη (13:10), and it would seem strange, if he were the author of Mk 16:9–20, that he used "all creation" (πάσῃ τῇ κτίσει).

carried out in the name of Jesus, that is, the name of the Triune God which Jesus reveals. This meaning emerges in the promise of Jesus to send the Promise of the Father, that is, the Holy Spirit. In Acts 1:4 the Spirit is referred to as the Promise of the Father (τὴν ἐπαγγελίαν τοῦ πατρός), as He is in Acts 2:33 (τῇ δεξιᾷ οὖν τοῦ Θεοῦ ὑψωθείς, τήν τε ἐπαγγελίαν τοῦ πνεύματος τοῦ ἁγίου λαβὼν παρὰ τοῦ πατρός). Here each divine person performs His essential role, but the text indicates a deeper significance. The Son's sending of the Father's Spirit reflects the more profound inner trinitarian mystery in which the Son is begotten of the Father, while the Spirit proceeds from the Father and the Son (*filioque*). Jesus as the Father's Son is both the agent and the source of the Spirit. Luke's text is as important as Matthew's for understanding the role of the Trinity in Baptism. In Matthew we see the final and full revelation of the Trinity to the baptized. Luke shows how this revelation came.

Already with John the Baptist repentance is connected with a baptism for the forgiveness of sins (κηρύσσων βάπτισμα μετανοίας εἰς ἄφεσιν ἁμαρτιῶν; Lk 3:3; cf. Mt 3:2; Mk 1:4). Now Luke connects repentance to the Baptism of Jesus administered by the apostles. Both Matthew and Luke, as well as Mark, agree that the commission is given to the Eleven, that is, the original surviving disciples of Jesus, whose names are listed in each of these synoptic gospels (Mt 10:1–2; Mk 3:14–18; Lk 3:12–16). Luke mentions no number, but clearly intends the original disciples. It is striking that all three synoptic gospels make use of the "name" in their closing section. Where Matthew attaches the "name" to the Triune God, that is, the divine name, Luke speaks of repentance preached in the name of Jesus, while Mark mentions demons cast out by the same name (Mk 16:17). Most commentators agree that Mark's longer ending (16:9–20) is in some sense dependent on both Matthew and Luke. The reference in Mark's longer ending to Baptism as necessary for salvation, "He that believes and is baptized shall be saved" (Mk 16:16), which was so prominent in Luther's thought (SC IV), is just as dependent on Luke as on Matthew. Thus it reflects the unified testimony of the apostolic church in which all three synoptic gospels came into existence. The command to the apostles recorded in Matthew, to go and baptize the Gentiles, becomes in Luke a description of what the apostles will do: ". . . that repentance and forgiveness of sins should be preached in his name to all nations" (Lk 24:47). Mark's longer ending, "He that believes and is baptized shall be saved" (Mk 16:16), sets forth the dogmatic necessity of Baptism and concludes the synoptic testimony.

OTHER REFERENCES TO THE NAME

A reference to the community which possesses His name through Baptism may be found in the promise of Jesus to be present where two or three are gathered in His name (εἰς τὸ ἐμὸν ὄνομα; Mt 18:20). These are those to whom the divine name of the Triune God has been made known by Jesus, who is present among them in their identity as both a baptized and a eucharistic community (Mt 28:20).[23] An early testimony to the significance of the divine name in Baptism is found in Jas 2:7, in the context of the actual ritual: "Is it not they who blaspheme that honorable name which was invoked over you?" (τὸ καλὸν ὄνομα τὸ ἐπικληθὲν ἐφ᾿ ὑμᾶς).[24] With good reason, Massey H. Shepherd, Jr., claims that the name of the Lamb and the Father which is placed on the forehead in Rv 14:1 "is intended to remind the hearer of the divine name said over him at his baptism."[25] In Rv 3:5 Jesus confesses the Christian, as He does in Mt 10:32: "So every one who acknowledges [confesses] me before men, I also will acknowledge [confess] before my Father who is in heaven." In Revelation the Christian bears the name of Jesus, presumably in Baptism. Though in Matthew Jesus confesses the one who confesses Him, the similarity suggests that this also has a baptismal reference. The RSV, by translating ὁμολογήσω "I will acknowledge," loses the credal and confessional thrust intended in this word.

The apostolic and post-apostolic sources saw the name as God working through Christ in the world. Some Protestant denominations, especially the Baptists, find no difficulty in baptizing those who have already received Baptism, and in many cases require and encourage

---

23. The similarity between Mt 18:20 and 28:19–20 is striking. Both use the εἰς τὸ ὄνομα formula and promise the presence of Jesus. Davies and Allison suggest that Jesus is present as the glory of God (*Matthew* 3:790). Applying Gieschen's hypothesis, the Christian community gathers in the name of the Triune God, the name which Jesus has given to the community in Baptism.

24. Jean Danielou, *The Theology of Jewish Christianity*, trans. and ed. John A. Baker (London: Darton, Longman, & Todd, 1964), 150. See also David P. Scaer in *James, the Apostle of Faith*: "The name of the Triune God given in Baptism is the guarantee of God's presence in the church for the salvation of His people. Christians are absorbed into Christ's name by Baptism, and all churchly activity is carried out in His name" ([St. Louis: Concordia Publishing House, 1984], 77–78). Additional information on the significance of the divine name can be found in Richard N. Longenecker, *The Christology of Early Christianity* (Grand Rapids, MI: Baker Book House, 1970), 41–46.

25. *The Paschal Liturgy and the Apocalypse* (Richmond: John Knox Press, 1960), 90. Shepherd is cautious in recognizing other possible references to Baptism in Revelation. For example, "I know your works; you have *the name* of being alive, and you are dead" (Rv 3:1; emphasis added here and following). The giving of the name, the baptismal white garments, and the confessions are brought together in Rv 3:5: "He who conquers shall be clad thus in *white garments*, and I will not blot his *name* out of the book of life; I will *confess* his name before my Father and before his angels." (Similarity of language to Mt 10:32–33 may suggest that this also has a baptismal reference.) At last the baptized "shall see his face, and *his name* shall be on their foreheads" (Rv 22:4). An allusion to infant Baptism may be found in Rv 11:18, where the great and the small fear the name of God, that is, the divine name given in their Baptisms. A correlation between God's name on the foreheads and the names written in the Book of Life suggests that candidates were named in the same rite of Baptism in which they learned the divine name.

rebaptism, especially if it was first administered in infancy. They rightly understand that Baptism is commanded by God, but wrongly see it as a pledge of the believer's obedience to a divine law. For them multiple Baptisms demonstrate the believer's fidelity to divine law. Such rebaptism can only be considered blasphemy, because it shows contempt for the divine name of the three persons of the Trinity and their work in the world through Baptism.[26] As Luther says, "Whoever rejects Baptism rejects God's Word, faith, and Christ, who directs and binds us to Baptism."[27]

THE TRINITARIAN BAPTISMAL FORMULA AND ITS NECESSITY

There can be no dispute over whether water must be used, since the root words "baptizing" and "baptism" (βαπτίζω) mean "using water." The dispute exists over whether the tripartite formula of Matthew must be used in every case. Baptism is the possession of the trinitarian community, those who confess by the Spirit's working that Jesus Christ is Lord (1 Cor 12:3) to the glory of God the Father (Phil 2:11). Where a community does not identify itself by this confession, it cannot stand in succession with the original apostolic community, and hence it is not trinitarian in the New Testament sense. Thus, for example, such groups as Mormons, Unitarians, and Swedenborgians may use the tripartite baptismal formula with water for initiation into their communities, but their rites may not in any way be equated with the Baptism commanded by Christ and practiced by the original apostolic communities. Baptisms of Gnostic groups, who in many cases provided their own formulas, were not recognized by the early church. Both Pieper and Walther are quite definite on this view.[28] On the other hand, it may happen that

---

26. Administering Baptism to those have already received Baptism not only has theological implications for how one understands this doctrine, but has repercussions in an ecumenically sensitive environment. The church administering such a Baptism is in effect saying that another church is sub-Christian, that is, it does not have the fullness God intends. Confessional Lutherans certainly take this position over against the Reformed celebration of the Lord's Supper, but not regarding their administration of Baptism. Though Rome has formally recognized Baptisms by other churches, it was not uncommon that her priests administered Baptism to converts from other denominations. James Nuechterlein, in discussing the dimensions of catholicity, claims that while the Roman church does not re-administer Baptism and ordination to those who have received these rites in the Eastern Orthodox Church, the Eastern Orthodox do not reciprocate ("Catholics at Home," *First Things* 73 [May 1997]: 8). Lutherans have contested the multiple Baptisms of the Baptists. This concern may have to embrace some Roman Catholics and Eastern Orthodox, though an ecumenical climate has changed these negative attitudes.
27. LC IV.31; Tappert, 440; *BKS*, 697.
28. Pieper, *Christian Dogmatics* 3:262–63. Pieper quotes Walther's view, articulated

the precise "Father–Son–Holy Spirit" formula may not be used in a recognized trinitarian community simply because the words have inadvertently been dropped or misread. In such a case there would be no question that a true and right Baptism had taken place. Problematic are those groups with an undeveloped doctrine or where the original Christian confession has been denied openly and consistently. Examples of the former may be ad hoc congregations in which the focus is on emotional worship, with little attention to what is really believed. Under the Rationalistic influence of the Enlightenment, many eighteenth- and nineteenth-century European clergy openly denied the Trinity, but continued to use the traditional liturgy with the trinitarian formula for administering Baptism. Some congregations in New England have claimed affiliation at one time or another with the Congregationalists, Baptists, and Unitarians, frequently at the same time. Unless there is specific information, pastors receiving members from such historically confused confessions may have to assume that a genuine Baptism has not taken place.

The water which constitutes Baptism, "used according to God's command and connected with God's Word,"[29] involves the entire revelation of the crucified and resurrected Christ, who is the Father's Son and who works in the church through the Holy Spirit. Mere recitation of a formula under any circumstance cannot assure that a Baptism has taken place. On the other hand, misspeaking a formula does not detract from an otherwise valid administration of the sacrament. In the Middle Ages, priests who were not at home in Latin, so it was said, might have misspoken the baptismal formula out of ignorance. *In nomine Patris et Filii et Spiritus Sancti* might have become *In nomine Patriae et Filiae et spiritui Sancti*, quite literally, "In the name of the fatherland and the daughter and the Holy Spirit." Such priests read the Mass and other liturgical forms without knowing their precise meaning. They may have suffered from a moderate form of illiteracy, but they were not ignorant of what was happening. That distinction must be made. Under the stress of an emergency, the one administering Baptism may not articulate the trinitarian formula with precision. Very few are the pastors who have not on occasion put words in the wrong order in the celebration or

---

in the latter's *Pastoraltheologie*: "'For this reason [the denial of the Trinity] the purported Baptism of all preachers of anti-trinitarian communions can be acknowledged as valid as little as a Baptism in sport and mockery, and those who have received such spurious Baptism are still to be baptized'" (ibid., 123). This quote appeared originally in C. F. W. Walther, *Americanische-lutherische Pastoraltheologie*, 2d ed. (St. Louis: Druckerei der Synode von Missouri, 1875), which provides a fuller discussion of the issue of an invalid Baptism, with citations from the Confessions and Lutheran dogmaticians (120–24).

29. SC IV.2; Tappert, 348; *BKS*, 515.

distribution of the Holy Communion. Concern for verbal precision as a factor affecting whether or not a Baptism has taken place comes from the failure to see that any sacrament has its life within the community of believers. Sacraments are not formulas that individuals make valid by the correct mixture of element and rite.

The story is told that St. Augustine saw some children baptizing their playmates with the water of the sea and declared that a Baptism had really taken place. Even if the right words were used, no Baptism took place. That opinion which insists that a sacramental action takes place in every case in which the proper formula is used verges on trusting in the magical! On the other hand, if in a formal or private setting a pastor or layperson administers Baptism and misspeaks the words, a Baptism has indeed taken place.

CHURCH AS THE LOCATION OF THE SACRAMENTS

Since emergency Baptisms have become rarer under modern conditions, the sacrament is usually held in the presence of the worshiping congregation. Luther's 1523 rite for Baptism assumes in the prayers that a congregation of some sort will be present. Though Baptism in the early church was administered away from the ordinary place for worship, the baptized were expected to join the congregation in celebrating and receiving the Eucharist.[30] Sacraments are not only the marks of the church, but they give the church her form. The church emerges from Baptism as a child emerges from the womb of its mother. On that account, they should not be performed or administered apart from the church. Baptisms away from the church are exceptions, in the cases of real emergencies. The earliest post-apostolic practice indicates that Baptisms were administered on Saturday night before Easter to symbolize the death and resurrection of Christ, whose saving events were accomplished for the believer in this Baptism. Baptizing on Holy Saturday may have been in vogue already during apostolic times (Rom 6:5–6). Since Baptism remains an initiation into the church and is coterminous with the life of the church, it should take place ordinarily where the church gathers. The administration of Baptism need not be restricted to the regular worship of the congregation, however. Philip baptizes the Ethiopian eunuch (Acts 8:38) in what can only be considered a private ceremony. Baptistries were constructed for the sole purpose of administering this sacrament, and did not have provisions for eucharistic worship.

---

30. See J. G. Davies, *The Architectural Setting of Baptism* (London: Barrie & Rockliff, 1962), 165.

THE MINISTERS OF BAPTISM

The ordinary ministers of Baptism are the ordained pastors of the church, since in their roles they are Christ's representatives in the congregations. We do not insist on this simply as a matter of good order, as we would hardly be different from Calvin if this were our sole reason. The fourth gospel refers to Jesus' baptizing activities (Jn 3:22), but quickly adds the corrective that "Jesus himself did not baptize, but only his disciples" (Jn 4:2). C. H. Dodd and Raymond Brown claim that the inconsistency points to multiple authorship.[31] A more probable solution is offered by John A. T. Robinson, who sees John adding his own self-corrective: Jesus' disciples did the baptizing for Him, and He did not actually pour water on anyone.[32] Jesus had given His disciples a command to baptize prior to the dominical command of Mt 28:19.[33] Similarly in the feeding of the five thousand, the disciples and not Jesus were the distributors of the miraculously multiplied bread (Jn 6:11–13). John's comment about Jesus not personally baptizing anyone has theological significance: Baptism's efficacy does not depend on whether Jesus Himself carried it out. In fact, He did not! At the founding of the church, the apostles understood themselves not only as ministers of the Word (Lk 1:2), but also as administrators of the sacraments.[34] Those baptized after the ascension are not at a disadvantage in benefiting from the salvation which Jesus accomplished and promises to give His church in Baptism. It is still carried out by those who stand in the place of Jesus. Historical proximity to Jesus guarantees nothing. Christ's proximity in Baptism guarantees everything. For Luther, it brings the entire Christ and the Holy Spirit (LC IV.41). The Lutheran understanding of Baptism taking place within the context of the church should not be confused with Calvin's insistence that a valid Baptism can be administered only by the recognized ministers of the church within the regular services. For the Lutherans, the congregation at worship is the manifestation of the *una sancta*, the church which Christ has redeemed. The congregation as an incorporated society does not add anything to the Baptism.

---

31. C. H. Dodd, *Historical Tradition in the Fourth Gospel* (Cambridge and New York: Cambridge University Press, 1963), 285–86; Raymond E. Brown, *The Gospel According to John XIII–XXI*, The Anchor Bible, vol. 29, no. 1 (Garden City, NY: Doubleday, 1987), 164.

32. Another example of self-correction is Paul's remembering whom he had baptized. The one who said that he was not sent to baptize did quite a bit of baptizing (1 Cor 1:14–17), and gave the church its most developed baptismal theology.

33. Robinson, *Priority of John*, 184.

34. Note also that, in the feeding of the five thousand, the disciples and not Jesus distribute the miraculously multiplied bread to the crowds (Mt 14:19; also Jn 6:12). Already in these actions they prepare for their role as the sacramental ministers which they would have after the resurrection of Jesus.

Baptism belongs to the church as the body of Christ and not as an association of believers.[35]

Calvin's requirement that only ministers baptize and his prohibition against emergency Baptism provides a key to understanding his theology. Baptism only confirms believers' children in their previous condition as participants in the covenant, and thus there is no need for it.[36] Ultimately, sacraments are extraneous in giving grace. Pieper notes that for the Calvinists Baptism has no power to convey grace.[37] For them a lay-administered Baptism is an affront to the divine command. By breaking the regulations of circumcision or Baptism, "great injury is done to the covenant of God."[38] It is essential for Calvin that the ordinances of God be kept. He says the most dreadful things about Zipporah as a breaker of the Law in circumcising her son when her husband, Moses, refused to do so. From our point of view, she acted commendably. For Luther, circumcision, as Baptism, was seen as an act of grace for children and not as an expression of the Law.[39] Who performed either rite was of secondary importance. Where no pastor can be found to baptize children, then the parents have no other choice than to do it themselves. Calvin also sees circumcision and Baptism in the same light, but for him they are both laws—not commands with promises, but laws which must be obeyed.[40] Hear Calvin: "The last thing intended by Zipporah was to perform a service to God."[41] According to him, Baptism by women is a sin greater than Zipporah's! Our comment is that women who baptize infants in such circumstances do a service to God, the children, and the church—and Calvin is the greater sinner!

BAPTISMS ADMINISTERED BY UNREGENERATE CLERGY AND IMPOSTORS

Questions regarding the validity of Baptism may be raised when this sacrament is administered by an impostor, an unregenerate pastor,

---

35. The rite of administering Baptism does not belong any one individual. On that account lay-administered emergency Baptisms are ratified or confirmed by the pastor in whose stead the layperson was acting. This confirmation is performed not by any clergyman but by the regular pastor of the congregation of which the baptized has become a member. In the Roman church, designated laypeople may administer Baptism (*Catechism of the Catholic Church*, para. 903). The rite of Confirmation, which is also seen as an initiatory sacrament, can be administered only by the bishop.

36. Calvin, *Institutes* IV.XV.20–22.

37. Pieper, *Christian Dogmatics* 3:279–80.

38. Calvin, *Institutes* IV.XV.22. Calvin takes the same attitude toward the administration of the Lord's Supper. Lutherans may agree with him regarding who may administer the Lord's Supper, but hardly for the reasons he offers (ibid., 20).

39. *AE* 3:102–3.

40. Calvin, *Institutes* IV.XV.20–22.

41. Ibid., 22.

or a layperson. Each one of these questions must be answered separately.

In an established church situation, charlatans posing as clergy may be a remote possibility. This is more likely to happen in missionary or frontier situations, where people are not acquainted with the church's ministers. The New Testament knows of false apostles and prophets, people who pretend to be authorized church leaders, claiming to speak with Christ's authority, but who are not. The same situation was not unknown on the American frontier, when for their own financial gain men claiming to be "preachers" went from family to family or even congregation to congregation to preach and administer the sacraments. To the report that someone was casting out demons in His name, Jesus responded to His disciples that he should be left alone (Mk 9:38), although he is not received among the followers of Jesus. The lack of an actual authorization of such impostors does not invalidate their ministry. Should such impostors be discovered within the church, they should, however, be removed and a warning circulated among the congregations.

The Baptisms administered by pastors later found to be unregenerate should not be questioned. Just as the validity and effectiveness of Baptism does not depend on the ordination of the one who does the baptizing, neither does it depend on his faith. "The sacraments are efficacious even if the priests who administer them are wicked men" (AC VIII.2).[42] This is not to say that congregations will not be led into despair and confusion when their pastor is discovered to be an unbeliever; but Baptism, as the preached Word, has an objective reality that does not depend upon either the faith of the pastor or that of those who hear the Word and receive the Baptism. Lutherans reject Baptist notions that Baptism is something that the baptized person does and that the one baptizing contributes something of himself to the act. Lutherans see Baptism as an objective reality worked entirely by God.

For this same reason, Baptism, which is ordinarily to be administered by a called pastor, may in an emergency be administered by a layperson. Christian nurses have legitimately and rightfully taken it upon themselves to baptize infants born critically ill, even when there is no explicit authorization or knowledge by the child's family. In many hospitals, especially Roman Catholic ones, the nurses may actually be required to do this. An implied authorization exists in these cases. Protocol has no meaning in life-and-death situations. Similar are emergency medical procedures performed on children when the parents are not present to give legal authorization. In times of war and exile, Christian

---

42. Grane remarks, "Here the reformers stand together with the church of the papacy against the enthusiasts, all of whom were 'Donatists'" (*Augsburg Confession*, 101).

laypersons are not only required to preach the Gospel, but also to administer Baptism to those who believe.[43]

A seemingly more difficult problem may arise when a known non-Christian performs an emergency Baptism at the request of the family or another Christian. However, such Baptisms by non-Christians are as valid as if they had been performed in the church by the pastor. These also are Baptisms, since the one who is baptizing has been authorized by a person who is a member of the church. Strange as it may seem, in these cases even the avowed unbeliever serves as a "minister" of the Gospel. Baptisms performed under emergency situations or by the laity, regardless of the situation, should be confirmed in church not because they are not efficacious, but to show that the church recognizes the one baptized as part of its fellowship, and so the baptized may know that the church has received him.[44] A parallel and somewhat similar situation may be found in the early church, where the apostles Peter and John confirmed by the laying on of hands those who had been baptized by Philip, commonly called the deacon (Acts 8:14–18). In all probability this Philip was not a layman and did not belong to the order of deacons, which was established only later in the post-apostolic church. He was a minister but not an apostle, but he was carrying out the apostolic functions of preaching and administering the sacraments. By their laying hands on those whom Philip baptized, the apostles recognized that his baptizing activities were on the same level as those of the apostles who were chosen by Jesus before His resurrection. Ratifying a lay Baptism administered in church by the laying on of hands serves a similar function in recognizing a validly administered Baptism. This matter is discussed elsewhere under the absolute necessity of Baptism.

David Bartlett calls attention, with obvious pleasure, to a minister who allows church members to serve as sponsors who then take turns

---

43. Calvin inveighs against emergency Baptisms. Should he concede their validity and their necessity, he would be attributing to them a saving efficacy. This he cannot and does not do (*Institutes* IV.XVI.20).

44. Ratifying a lay-administered Baptism requires investigation into the situation under which it was administered and the formula which was used. The following was told of a recent consecration of a bishop in Nebraska. At a reception following the bishop's consecration, a nun said she was the one who baptized him in the hospital. Apparently this was the first time she had given precise details. She relayed to a stunned and then perhaps also amused audience that she baptized the bishop "in the name of Jesus, Mary, and Joseph," a phrase of popular piety among Roman Catholics. Upon this revelation, the attending bishops whisked the honoree into a back room and administered Baptism, Confirmation, and Ordination and then consecrated him as bishop. As amusing as this story is, it does point out the seriousness of inquiry into Baptisms which are not administered by the pastor in the ordinary way. The bishop in question was not the first to receive a plethora of sacraments on one day. St. Ambrose, the teacher of St. Augustine and writer of the well-known Christmas hymn "Savior of the Nations, Come," was baptized, ordained, and consecrated as bishop, all on one day.

The Baptismal Formula

administering the rite of Baptism.[45] He also mentions without censure a similar practice for Holy Communion, and raises the question of whether this is anarchy or the blowing of the Spirit. Such suggestions may not merit a response, but they are found in a book published by a Lutheran publishing house with a foreword by a Jesuit priest. Without knowing more details, it cannot be said with certainty when a sectarian situation, which clearly this is, evolves into one of apostasy. If such a situation is anarchy and not the blowing of the Spirit, then it is more than likely that the church is not present there. In these kinds of cases, each pastor will make a determined effort to take all the circumstances into consideration and to consult with his brothers in the ministry in making a determination of whether a Baptism has really taken place.

---

45. *Ministry*, 192.

6

ADMINISTRATION OF BAPTISM

Even though there is no debate about the use of Baptism, nevertheless Baptist groups historically have insisted that a valid Baptism must be by immersion.[1] Fortunately this issue has become less prominent, since some Baptist groups are no longer insisting on "re-Baptism" by immersion for those who come into their fellowship from paedobaptist groups, but such tolerance is hardly widespread.[2] The discussion is almost made moot, since those groups insisting on Baptism by immersion are caught in the contradiction that Baptism is not necessary for salvation.[3] Even without Baptism and with only a confession of faith or a decision for Christ, "believers" can enjoy the benefits of that community's fellowship, including participation in their version of the Lord's Supper. At best, Baptism is a commandment which Christians obey to show the depth and loyalty of their faith. Basic to their understanding is that Baptism is primarily an act of the believer and not of God. At the heart of the Baptist argument is that the Greek words from which the English words "baptism" and "baptize" are taken denote immersion. While these words may include the idea of immersion, they mean simply to wash with water.[4]

A controversy over this meaning arose during the Reformation when the Anabaptists insisted that immersion was the only proper way to administer Baptism. Any other form did not qualify as Baptism. Another factor in their doctrine of Baptism is the necessity of an oral confession of faith, which obviously precludes the baptizing of infants. Baptism by immersion has become synonymous with "believers' Baptism," though this was hardly the case at least up to the Reformation. Those baptized as infants, even if it had been by immersion, were re-

---

1. Grenz, *Community of God*, 689–91.
2. Henry C. Thiessen, a Baptist, is not willing to make this an issue (*Lectures in Systematic Theology*, 321). A plea for tolerance is made by Donald Bridge and David Phypers, *The Water That Divides* (Downers Grove, IL: InterVarsity Press, 1977).
3. Typical is the position taken by Wayne Grudem: "While we recognize that Jesus commanded baptism (Matt. 28:19), as did the apostles (Acts 2:38), we should not say that it is *necessary* for salvation" (*Systematic Theology*, 981).
4. One dictionary gives this definition: "A ceremonial immersion in water, or application of water" (*New Century Dictionary of the English Language*, s.v. "baptize"). Another lists as its first definition the following: "To dip or immerse in water or to pour, sprinkle water upon, as a religious rite" (*Webster's Collegiate Dictionary*, 5th ed., s.v. "baptize"). The Greek means to immerse or dip in water.

quired to be rebaptized in order to be saved. From the practice of rebaptizing, these groups were called Anabaptists, which means literally "those baptizing again."[5] Modern Baptists are not descended theologically from the Anabaptists, who were often Arian in their Christology, but they share their characteristic practices in insisting on immersion and "believers' Baptism." While strict Baptists deny any saving efficacy to the act of Baptism itself, as do most Reformed, they insist that it be administered in the one particular way of complete immersion.[6] Immersion is a divinely mandated rite symbolizing Christ's death and resurrection and the believer's response. It is not God's gracious act upon believers (Gospel), they contend, but a fulfilling of a requirement (Law). Ordinarily, the issue of how water is administered belongs more properly to practical theology. However, since the Anabaptists and now traditional Baptists see all forms of Baptism other than immersion as contrary to the divine command or less than fully desirable, it becomes an issue for dogmatic theology. Since Baptist denominations constitute the major Protestant group in North America, their insistence on immersion cannot be sidestepped. With Lutherans, Roman Catholics, Episcopalians, Presbyterians, and Methodists all baptizing infants without insisting on immersion, the opportunity for conflict is always present. In nearly all cases the Eastern Orthodox baptize by immersion, but they do not insist that this is the only form.[7] Matters are exacerbated with the Lutheran insistence on the regenerating power of Baptism, which the

---

5. See FC, Ep. and SD XII for the Lutheran response to these aberrations (Tappert, 632–36; 498–500; BKS, 822–27; 1091–1100).

6. Consider the case of the influential Baptist theologian Augustus Strong. His *Systematic Theology* has a tightly organized discussion of Baptism in twenty-nine pages (931–59). Pages 933 through 959 are devoted to immersion and a refutation of infant Baptism. A less strident position is taken by Stanley J. Grenz: since Baptism is to be defined as a public declaration of inward faith, adult Baptism is superior to baptizing infants who have no faith (*Community of God*, 685–91). Immersion of adults should be a standardized form of Baptism (ibid., 689). Arguments for modes of Baptism other than immersion are presented, but without specifically being condemned (ibid., 690–91). Grenz also lists Baptist groups not practicing immersion. For Grudem, Baptism's value lies in its symbolism. Immersion has more symbolic value than pouring or sprinkling (*Systematic Theology*, 967–69).

7. The Eastern Orthodox baptize by a triple immersion. We agree with Meyendorff that "'drowning' cannot be meaningfully signified other than through immersion" (*Byzantine Theology*, 194). However, washing as a metaphor for Baptism may suggest that immersion is not the only acceptable form of Baptism. Immersion was practiced by the Reformation Lutherans and is implied by Luther in the Small Catechism's description of the signification of Baptism as the dying of the old man and the rising of the new man. Nicholas Cabasilas, a fourteenth-century Eastern Orthodox father, anticipates Luther by saying that "the water destroys the one life, but shows forth the other; it drowns the old man and brings forth the new" (ibid.). At the time the Eastern Orthodox considered triple immersion so necessary that some did not recognize the Western Baptism administered by sprinkling (ibid.). In insisting on a particular form, such Eastern Orthodox theologians are closer to Baptists on this point.

Administration of Baptism

Baptists deny. Reformed denominations practicing infant Baptism agree with the Baptists in denying that Baptism regenerates, and thus accommodation among these groups is possible. In spite of differences over the practice of Baptism, limited fellowship can be practiced among them. Tragically, many Christians baptized as infants are persuaded by Baptist arguments to doubt their own salvation and are baptized again. Pentecostal groups also practice immersion, though a water Baptism is not as significant for them as the waterless "Baptism in the Spirit."

The Greek word from which baptizing is derived, βαπτίζω, means to use water, and thus the sacrament called by this name can be administered in the ways water is commonly used: dipping, washing, pouring, immersing. Immersing means to plunge under liquid, and in a sense several uses of water on objects or persons, especially drenching, loosely fit this definition.[8] Taking a bath or shower has the same results. Baptist ministers are photographed holding their hands over the mouths and the noses of the baptismal candidates and plunging them into the water, often huge pools in their churches. Certain groups go further and baptize in lakes, rivers, bays, and oceans. Their insistence on total immersion seems unnecessarily rigid. Are persons whose arm or other body part was not submerged in the water really baptized? Immersion eliminates the physically infirm and the critically ill from being baptized. Jesus' ministry was directed specifically to such incapacitated persons. They would hardly be excluded from that ministry which now operates through the water of Baptism. Water is universally available wherever there is life, but in some wilderness areas sufficient water for immersion may not be found. As Baptism is universally intended, the insistence upon immersion, which requires an amount of water not readily available in some places, hardly serves Baptism's purpose of incorporating all people into Christ. Baptism depends upon the Word of Christ together with water, and not upon the amount of water applied. Neither the Word as the Gospel nor the water can be understood in quantitative terms. Making immersion a requirement can hardly be right! Again, the issue is moot for Baptists, since Baptism, even in the preferred form of immersion, is not necessary for salvation.

Until the Reformation, infants were baptized by immersion, and the custom persists among the Eastern Orthodox. With the priest holding the infant in one hand and copiously pouring water over him or her, immersion is really a drenching. The Lutherans might find that immer-

---

8. The Greek word to baptize, βαπτίζω, means washing, and in some cases seems to mean ceremonial washing (Johannes P. Louw and Eugene A. Nida, *Greek-English Lexicon of the New Testament*, 2 vols. [New York: United Bible Societies, 1988], 1:536). In some but not all contexts this involves dipping. When the word is used in a Christian context, it means "to employ water in a religious ceremony designed to symbolize purification and initiation on the basis of repentance" (ibid.).

sion may be preferable to other forms of Baptism for certain theological, historical, and even exegetical reasons, but we completely reject that Baptism's validity or value depends on the amount of water used or on its administration in one particular form. Baptism by immersion most characteristically distinguishes Baptist churches from others. Significantly, in the Baptist teaching, Baptism is an act of the believer and not of God, and so it is related to their definition of justifying faith as decision. Placing the initiative with the believer is clearly synergistic. A reintroduction of immersion into Lutheran congregations, especially for adults, might be interpreted to mean that we concede that the Baptists were right in insisting that without an immersion no Baptism has taken place, or that immersion is the preferred mode! This would be an issue especially where the Baptists comprise the dominant religion, as in certain parts of the United States. Also, avoiding confusion is important. If several forms of Baptism were permitted to be practiced side by side, some people might use the form of their Baptism, immersion or pouring, as an opportunity to claim superiority over others. Something like this happened in Corinth, where the congregation divided itself on the basis of who had baptized members (1 Cor 1:10–16)! Since the Baptists err in denying to children original sin and their baptismal regeneration, Lutherans have good reason to avoid giving the impression that their insistence on immersion is right. Such an impression might be given if baptismal pools were constructed in our churches and immersion made an option. Baptizing infants by immersion would not present the same problems, since Baptists do not baptize them.

It is not surprising that Baptist theologians and ministers devote much of their biblical labors to demonstrating that the original Greek words for baptizing require immersing. Pieper provides a succinct and clear refutation of this false opinion which is so fundamental to their position: Pharisees baptized or washed eating instruments, including tables (Mk 7:3–4; Lk 11:38)![9] Plates and utensils were immersed; tables were completely washed, but not carried to pools to be submerged each time they ate. Images of Pharisees carrying tables for baptizing in pools is a bit of Pieper's humor which should settle the issue once and for all.

Lutherans continued the practice of the ancient and medieval church in completely immersing infants. Pictures of Baptisms from the Reformation show pastors lifting babies dripping wet from ample fonts and drying them with towels. This custom has fallen into disuse among Lutherans, most Protestants, and some Roman Catholics, and the large fonts of medieval churches have been replaced by bowls. In some of the older Lutheran churches the large fonts remain. In Eastern Orthodox

---

9. *Christian Dogmatics* 3:256–57, n. 8.

churches, the priests prepare for the showering experience of immersing the infants by wearing aprons. Baptists use the Eastern Orthodox practice to defend their practice of immersion, but of course do not recognize the validity of their baptizing infants.[10] Baptists seem to be unaware that the Lutheran Reformation practice of immersing infants was the same as the Eastern Orthodox practice. References by Baptists to sixteenth-century Lutherans baptizing by sprinkling are uninformed. While Eastern Orthodox churches practice Baptism by immersion, they do not generally rebaptize those who were baptized in other ways.[11]

Paul does connect Baptism with the death, burial, and resurrection of Christ (Rom 6:3–4), and immersion does suggest drowning, death, and a return to life. This imagery of being saved from drowning is common in the Psalms and in the Book of Jonah (2:1–10), and its use in Romans 6 in connection with burial with Christ may suggest that immersion was commonly practiced in that church. For Karl Barth, immersion indicated "a threat of death and a deliverance to life."[12] Anyone foundering around in deep water knows the sensation of drowning and death. Luther includes the idea of drowning in his "Flood Prayer" to describe the fate of Pharaoh and by extension our sinful nature.[13] His Small Catechism compares drowning to the death of the sinful self, followed by a resurrection: "It signifies that the old Adam in us, together with all sins and evil lusts, should be drowned by daily sorrow and repentance and be put to death, and that the new man should come forth daily and rise up, cleansed and righteous, to live forever in God's presence."[14] Luther immersed infants in Baptism, and he saw this as a sign of the child actually dying and rising with Christ. True, Baptists see immersion as symbolic of these events, but for them Baptism is not actually the drowning of the sinful self as it is in Lutheran theology.[15]

---

10. Strong, *Systematic Theology*, 937–38. See also Grenz, *Community of God*, 689.

11. Note can be made here of the Rites of Christian Initiation for Adults, which are at the core of a liturgical movement in the Roman Catholic Church setting specific steps for catechizing adults. Baptizing of these catechumens is often by immersion. Similar rites are now being considered for use in other churches, including Lutheran ones. Since these rites have not assumed specific form, it is too early to determine how they would be incorporated into Lutheran baptismal liturgies and whether they would involve immersion. No doctrinal objection could be raised to baptizing by immersion as long as it is clearly stated that no special grace is attached to this form. Since this movement is concerned with adult catechumens, great care must be taken to avoid the impression that adult Baptism is superior to that of infant Baptism. It is our position, as discussed below, that Baptism is intended primarily for infants. Every Baptism, including that of adults, is in a very real sense infant Baptism.

12. *The Teaching of the Church Regarding Baptism*, trans. Ernest A. Payne (London: SCM Press, 1948), 11.

13. *AE* 53:97, 107.

14. SC IV.12; Tappert, 349; *BKS*, 516.

15. Strong, *Systematic Theology*, 941; Grenz, *Community of God*, 689.

Administration of Baptism

Our discussion on the mode of Baptism need not be limited to determining the meaning of the Greek word from which our word "Baptism" is derived. In the gospel of John, for example, the simple word "water" is used for Baptism (Jn 3:5, 20:34; compare 1 Jn 5:6–8). Salvation is dependent on birth through the water, but nothing is said of its application. The cognate of the Greek word *louo* (λούω), "washing," is also used for this sacrament. Titus 3:5–6 is carried over by Luther into his Small Catechism, where Baptism is called "the washing of regeneration."[16] Similar references can be found in Heb 9:19, Eph 5:26, and especially Acts 22:16, where it is used with the word for baptize: "Be baptized, and wash away your sins." In Greek grammar this construction involving the word "and" is called the epexegetical *kai* (και). Both baptizing and washing refer to the same act. If the Greek word βαπτίζω suggests submersion—a point we do not grant in each instance—other words suggest washing. Consider Heb 10:22: ". . . with our hearts sprinkled clean from an evil conscience and our bodies washed with pure water." Though baptizing by washing is clear, a weaker case can be made for sprinkling. A modest application of water, which may be necessary in the Baptism of premature infants, is a form of washing. Washing is a form of immersion. In washing the feet of Peter with a bowl, Jesus surrounded those feet with water. They may have been immersed in the bowl. A discussion on how much water is used and how to apply it is neither theologically edifying nor constructive, but our people must be prepared to answer errors of those Baptists who cause them to doubt their salvation because they have not been immersed. Water is as necessary for Baptism as is the Word of God, but the quantity of the water or how it is applied has nothing to do with whether or not it is a sacrament.[17] Similarly, a long baptismal service is no more valuable than a shorter one. Unproven is that immersion was the only form used in the New Testament.

Baptisms by the disciples of John and Jesus in the Jordan may have entailed vast quantities of water, but nothing is said of the manner of Baptism of the three thousand who were baptized on Pentecost in Jerusalem (Acts 2:41). This was followed shortly by others, bringing the total baptized to five thousand (Acts 4:4). Since this number included only adult males (ἀριθμὸς τῶν ἀνδρῶν [ὡς] χιλιάδες πέντε), the number must have been significantly more. They could hardly have been baptized in a river, since none exists in Jerusalem. Whether such large pools as Bethesda (Jn 5:2) or Siloam (Jn 9:7) were available to the apostles for baptizing is purely speculative, even though there is good reason to hold that they were later used for this purpose. In Philippi the jailer is

---

16. SC IV.10; Tappert, 349; *BKS*, 516.
17. See Pieper, *Christian Dogmatics* 3:256, n. 7.

baptized in his home (Acts 16:33). Important men gathered at the public baths which had pools for immersion, but most homes did not have the space for such luxuries. It seems as if the same kind of "washing" which the jailer used to heal the wounds of Paul and his companions was used in Paul's baptizing the jailer. "[The jailer] washed [*louo*; ἔλουσεν] their wounds, and he was baptized at once, with all his family" (Acts 16:33). Even in the case of Baptisms in the Jordan River, the question of the water's depth is an issue. Such baptizing in the Jordan began with John and his disciples, and may have continued for several years after the death of Jesus. Thus, the period was at least four years, perhaps much longer.[18] There is no assurance that the river in all places was deep enough at all times for immersion. When the river was not at flood stage, immersion would be difficult at best. Rivers in Asia Minor and Greece, where Lydia and her household may have been baptized (Acts 16:13–15), are often wide and shallow meandering streams.[19] Raging torrents of flooding rivers would hardly serve for Baptisms. Roman baths which separated men and women provided enough water for immersing, but such publicly owned institutions could hardly have been used for a ritual of a religion which was considered illicit until the beginning of the fourth century.

Such church fathers as Tertullian, Cyprian, and Cyril of Jerusalem were alert to the baptismal imagery in the pericope of Jesus washing the disciples' feet in Jn 13:1–11, the first of the farewell discourses of the upper room. Commenting on Jn 15:3, Augustine notes the similarity to footwashing and describes Baptism in terms which would become characteristic of Lutheran theology.[20] Many but certainly not all scholars have followed suit.[21] Since the gospel of John has other references to

---

18. Acts 19:3 suggests that "the baptism of John" continued as a separate rite performed by his disciples even after Paul had established Christianity in Asia Minor.

19. The word "meander" is derived from the ancient Greek name for the Meander River in Asia Minor, which flows into the Aegean Sea. Such rivers, without a consistent course or flow of water, could hardly be depended upon to provide a fitting and safe place for Baptisms at any time of the year.

20. "Why does He not say, Ye are clean through baptism wherewith ye have been washed, but 'through the word which I have spoken unto you,' save only that in the water also it is the word that cleaneth? Take away the word, and the water is neither more nor less than water. The word is added to the element, and there results the Sacrament, in itself also a kind of visible word" (Philip Schaff, ed., *Nicene and Post-Nicene Fathers* [1886; reprint, Peabody, MA: Hendrickson, 1995], 7:344).

21. Raymond E. Brown has an extensive discussion on the use of baptismal terminology in the footwashing episode (*Gospel According to John* 2:565–67). He notes, "The verb 'to bathe,' *louein*, and its cognates are standard NT vocabulary for Baptism" (ibid., 566). This does not mean that other interpretations are not possible, but the suggestion is certainly there. Rudolf Bultmann also weighs the pros and cons of the baptismal interpretation of footwashing, especially in regard to the practices of the gnostic sects who insisted on rebaptism through immersion. Though speculative on certain points, he notes correctly, "The representation of Baptism as footwashing is due

Administration of Baptism

Baptism, this interpretation is not crucial. This pericope may prove useful in questioning immersion as the necessary form of Baptism, since only Peter's feet and not his entire body is to be washed. According to the account, Jesus approaches the disciples with a basin of water and a towel to wash their feet. When Peter refuses (Jn 13:5–8a), Jesus tells him that without footwashing he can have no part of Him and thus will be deprived of eternal life. Peter responds by insisting on having his head and hands washed also (Jn 13:8b–9). Jesus replies that washing the feet cleanses the whole body (Jn 13:10a–b). Attention is then switched to Judas, who, though he apparently has had his feet washed, remains unclean (Jn 13:10c–11). Clearly this is not a discourse on bodily hygiene, and it certainly goes beyond an ancient world hospitality lesson on the value of footwashing. This lesson has ethical implications about humility for Christians, but the water applied by Jesus to the feet or any other part of the body is not an ordinary water, because it has a supernatural effect. Washing one part of Peter's body has the same effect as washing the whole body (Jn 13:10). Though Judas is washed by Jesus, he remains unclean throughout his whole being (Jn 13:10c–11), and, worse, he is in league with Satan (Jn 13:27). Application of the water by itself does not guarantee that its recipients will be saved. Defenders of the baptismal interpretation point out that such terms as water, wash, basin, towel, clean, being part of Jesus, feet, and head are associated with the theology and practice of Baptism.[22] This interpretation is not foolproof, and others have been offered.[23] Even a non-baptismal interpretation of footwashing does not entirely exclude any thought of Baptism. The Greek word λελουμένος, "the one who is washed" (Jn 13:10), can

---

to the ancient Church baptismal rite, whereby the catechumen only stood in water up to his ankles" (*The Gospel of John: A Commentary*, trans. G. R. Beasley-Murray [Philadelphia: Westminster Press, 1971], 469, n. 2). It is also difficult to dispute his conclusion: "That is to say: 1.) whoever becomes clean through My word only needs Baptism and no further washing; and 2.) in Baptism only the feet need to be washed; there is no need for total immersion" (ibid.).

22. Another prominent defender of the baptismal interpretation was John A. T. Robinson ("The One Baptism," *Scottish Journal of Theology* 6 [1953]: 257–74). Also see his "The Significance of the Foot-Washing," in *Neotestamentica et Patristica: Eine Freundesgabe Herrn Professor Dr. Oscar Cullmann zu seinem 60. Geburtstag überreicht*, Supplements to the New Testament, vol. 6 (Leiden: E. J. Brill, 1962), 144–47.

23. John Christopher Thomas provides a useful overview of the options, but sees footwashing as a separate liturgical rite (*Footwashing in John 13 and the Johannine Community* [Sheffield: Sheffield Academic Press, 1991]). He provides a bibliography of those holding to a baptismal reference in this pericope (ibid., 13–14). Oscar Cullmann (*Early Christian Worship* [Philadelphia: Westminster Press, 1953; Bristol, IN: Wyndham Hall Press, 1953]) and A. J. B. Higgins (*The Lord's Supper in the New Testament* [reprint, Chicago: Henry Regnery, 1952]) saw the footwashing as a reference to the Lord's Supper. Hans Urs von Balthasar ("The Holy Church and the Eucharistic Sacrifice," *Communion* 12 [Summer 1985]: 139–45) went further and saw it as a lesson on the meaning of the church's sacrifice of the mass.

refer to one who is already baptized.[24] The evangelist has already informed his readers that Peter and presumably the other disciples had been baptized by John the Baptist (Jn 1:35, 41–42). Since the gospel of John makes a point that Jesus personally baptized no one (4:2), it seems unlikely that Jesus in washing their feet is offering Baptism to his disciples. Whatever the underlying significance of this ritual may have been,[25] it sets forth the principle that God's supernatural activity in water does not depend on the amount used or the manner of its application.

Archaeology provides evidence that is inconclusive but informative. No frescoes show ministers plunging believers into the water, holding their hands over their noses. Just as there are large baptismal tanks in some excavated churches, there is other evidence that the candidate for Baptism stood in a shallow pool and had water poured over his head. It does seem certain that the church in the early centuries, including the apostolic period, was accustomed to using more water than is ordinarily used today. Large baptismal fonts in the earliest medieval churches clearly show that, in immersing infants, the church maintained the custom of a generous use of water in the baptismal rite. A second-century fresco in the Catacomb of St. Calixtus in Rome shows John assisting Jesus out of the water, and another from the third century shows a child standing in water and having water poured over his head. Other frescoes and paintings derived from them depict Jesus standing in the water up to His waist. Roman bathtubs were used for Baptisms but were hardly large enough for complete submersion, except in the case of infants. Similarly, early baptistries were no more than three feet deep.[26] It seems unlikely that these allowed for immersion in each case, again except in the case of children.

A good case can be made for administering Baptism by having the candidate stand in running water and having the priest or deacon pour water over the head. The Didache (vii:3) specifically requires the officiant to "pour water three times on the head 'in the name of the Father and of the Son and of the Holy Spirit.'" Nothing is said of immersion. While standing in water is preferable, it is only an option. The Church of St. Clement in Rome has water running through the subterranean basement which would have allowed the candidates to stand in the water

---

24. This Greek word is used for Baptism in Acts 22:16 and Ti 3:5, and presumably in 1 Cor 6:11, Eph 5:26, and Heb 10:22.

25. Another interpretation sees footwashing as a rite by which the disciples were placed into the apostolic ministry for which they had been called. See Jerome H. Neyrey, "The Footwashing in John 13:6–11: Transformation Ritual or Ceremony?" in *The Social Word of the First Christians: Essays in Honor of Wayne A. Meeks*, ed. L. Michael White and O. Larry Yarborough (Minneapolis: Fortress Press, 1995), 198–213.

26. See Henry F. Brown, *Baptism through the Centuries* (Mountain View, CA: Pacific Press Publishing Association, 1965), 43–72.

and have the officiant pour water on their heads. It seems as if a variety of ways of baptizing was used, of which immersion was only one.[27] Immersion did not imply in each case total submersion. Based on traditional practice, an argument can be made for immersing infants even in cases in which immersing adults is found impractical, for example, because of a lack of water or infirmities of age, physical disability, or sickness. Just as the celebration of the Lord's Supper does not depend on determining the kind of grapes used for the wine at the Last Supper, so Baptism does not depend on replicating the exact mode used in the New Testament, especially if it can be shown that several modes may have been used. Should we feel compelled to duplicate the past accurately, then candidates should be baptized without their clothes. The correlation of the stripping of Jesus before crucifixion was prefigured in his stripping for Baptism. Baptists have not gone this far, though such a complete removal of the clothes is as historically and theologically defensible a custom as immersion. Infants were baptized without their clothes by Lutheran pastors during the Reformation, as babies still are in the Eastern Orthodox Church.

Each form of applying the water of Baptism has a symbolic meaning. Most artwork showing water being poured has it directed to the candidate's head, where man's physical, mental, and spiritual powers are focused symbolically. Similarly, Christ is the head and the church is His body. Ancient paintings show the candidates, including Jesus, standing in water of a variety of depths and having water poured on their heads. These pictures combined the ideas of Baptism as an immersing (drowning) and a washing, thus reflecting New Testament language. Baptism both kills and cleans. The old man is freed from his sins (justification) and rises to a new life of good works in Christ (sanctification). He lives in righteousness and purity before God forever (Luther).

A word should be said about how many times the water should be poured on the baptized. In the Didache the threefold pouring corresponded with the Holy Trinity, and thus this custom has the support of antiquity. The threefold pouring also reflects the three days and nights in which Christ was in the grave. Since Baptism is burial with Christ (immersion in His death by water), this symbolism is attractive and theologically defensible. Yet, as we do not insist on immersion, we cannot require that the water be applied three times. Symbolic references in making the sign of the cross in Baptism and applying water three times, either to signify the Trinity or the three days and nights in which Christ was in the grave, are a proclamation of what we believe about Baptism and of what is actually happening to the candidate (child).

---

27. Louw and Nida, *Greek-English Lexicon* 1:538.

Immersion is a powerful symbol of death and resurrection, but it seems unlikely that many parents would be convinced that their infant children should be baptized in that way. Baptists correctly see the symbolism of death and resurrection implied in immersion, but, sadly, do not believe that Baptism actually accomplishes what it symbolizes.[28]

---

28. A final note about the word "Baptism," the interpretation of which is so critical to the Baptists' insistence on immersion: the word is not native to the English language, but came into our speech from the Greek through the Latin and Norman-French. It is not, strictly speaking, a translation, but rather a transliteration of the Greek word *baptisma* (βάπτισμα). Though the word Baptism has been taken over into languages other than English, with some languages a translation is not possible, since it would have no recognizable meaning. The linguistic scholars Louw and Nida say the meaning of the Greek word *baptisma* does not necessarily carry the meaning of immersion. "In some languages, for example, one may employ an expression such as 'to enter the water' or 'to undergo the ritual involving water.' Such expressions do not necessarily imply the quantity of water nor the particular means by which water is applied" (ibid.).

7

BAPTISM AND THE HOLY SPIRIT

In the early church Baptism was seen as Christ's working in His church through the Holy Spirit. The connection between Christ and the Spirit is based on the prior inner trinitarian reality (*opera ad intra*) that the Spirit is related to the Father through the Son, and that the Father operates toward the world first through Christ and then in Christ through the Spirit. He who is sent by Christ first proceeds from the Father and the Son: *qui ex patre filioque procedit*. This dogmatic distinction becomes necessary in defining the Baptism of the Spirit, if we feel compelled to use this phrase, as nothing else but a Baptism in the name of the Father and of the Son and of the Holy Spirit. In Reformed and Baptist theologies the Baptism of the Holy Spirit,[1] or the inner Baptism, refers to an inner experience not equated with what is called water Baptism, that is, trinitarian Baptism. Baptism in Lutheran theology is both an affirmation and revelation of the Holy Trinity whom Christ reveals: "No one knows the Father except the Son and any one to whom the Son chooses to reveal him" (Mt 11:27). This prior understanding of the Father's relationship to the Son and the revelation through Him comes to completion in Baptism in the name of the Father and of the Son and of the Holy Spirit, and lets this Baptism be understood as the Baptism of the Holy Spirit. Through the Spirit given in Baptism, the Son chooses to reveal the Father. The Spirit's action in the water of Baptism is not merely noetic but salvific. In Reformed theology, including Calvin's, the saving activity is attributed to the Spirit and not to the Word which functions noetically; that is, it informs but does not give salvation.

For Luther, the Spirit works through water Baptism in which, as the Spirit of Christ, "he calls, gathers, enlightens, and sanctifies the whole Christian church on earth and preserves it in union with Jesus Christ in the one true faith."[2] In this way the inner-trinitarian mystery is revealed to and embraces the baptized. The Spirit brings the church to Christ, who presents her to His Father. Though the New Testament can speak

---

1. Anthony A. Hoekema, a Reformed opponent of the charismatic view of Baptism in the Spirit, notes the phrase is not biblical and restricts its meaning to the outpouring of the Holy Spirit in His fullness on Pentecost. He finds no sacramental reference in the phrase (*Holy Spirit Baptism* [Grand Rapids, MI: William B. Eerdmans, 1972], 15–18). Calvin had the same interpretation (*Institutes* IV.XV.8).

2. SC II.3; Tappert, 345; *BKS*, 512.

of faith and confession being created by the Father (Mt 16:17) or by Jesus (Mt 11:27; Acts 2:47), the church is seen as the Spirit's creation through Baptism. The Apostles' Creed places belief in the church in the article on the Holy Spirit: *credo in spiritum sanctum, sanctam ecclesiam catholicam*. Historically, inclusion in the church implies Baptism.[3] Without Baptism, membership in the church is impossible.[4] The Nicene Creed puts the article on Baptism, "I acknowledge one Baptism for the remission of sins," after its confession "in one holy catholic and apostolic church." Belonging to the articles of faith is that the remission of sins is given through Baptism: *confiteor unum Baptisma in remissionem peccatorum*. Whether or not the earliest Christians confessed their faith in the Spirit as they did in God and in the Lord Jesus (1 Cor 8:6), they were aware that this confession was worked by the Holy Spirit (1 Cor 12:3)[5] and this confession granted entrance to Baptism for the forgiveness of sins (Acts 2:32). Luther calls the Holy Spirit the Sanctifier, because sanctification "is nothing else than to bring us to the Lord Christ to receive this blessing, which we could not obtain by ourselves."[6] The Spirit's sanctification of the baptized involves, effects, and requires conversion, faith, and regeneration. Baptism is so complete that the additional rites of the Roman system with their particular graces to improve or perfect the Christian life are not required. The forgiveness which the Holy Spirit gives "is granted through the holy sacraments."[7] Baptism with or of the Holy Spirit in the New Testament is the application of water in the name of the Trinity, as Jesus commanded.

Assigning the Spirit to the Baptism established by Christ does not mean that the Holy Spirit was not at work before Christ's coming. Already present in the ministry of John the Baptist was this necessary interrelationship between faith, confession, Baptism, and the Holy Spirit, which is characteristic of confessional Lutheran theology. The New Testament is clear in saying that Jesus and not John would baptize with the Spirit (Mt 3:11; Jn 1:33; Acts 1:5). Before the crucifixion, the Spirit was present and active in the baptisms of John and Jesus. But after Jesus' resurrection, the Spirit will accomplish things not done before. Consider that John is "filled with the Holy Spirit, even from his mother's womb" (Lk 1:15), and is fully qualified among the prophets through

---

3. J. N. D. Kelly, *Early Christian Creeds*, 152–66.

4. Baptists also define the church as the community of the baptized, but see Baptism not as an act of grace creating the church but of those individuals who have made a declaration of their faith by immersion (Grenz, *Community of God*, 685–89).

5. Beasley-Murray, in the tradition of Calvin, sees water as the symbol of the Holy Spirit, but properly sees the Spirit as God's agent for bringing the believer into the body of Christ (*Baptism*, 164).

6. LC II.39; Tappert, 415–16; *BKS*, 654.

7. LC II.54; Tappert, 417; *BKS*, 658.

whom the Spirit speaks. Jesus' baptism by John is the occasion for the descending of the Holy Spirit to perform the messianic tasks (Mt 3:16; Jn 1:32), and in turn Jesus gives the same Holy Spirit through Baptism to the church (Mt 27:50; Acts 1:5, 2:38). Thus, John's baptism can hardly be an empty ceremony or understood only in a penitential sense of moral introspection,[8] because the Holy Spirit equips Jesus (Τότε ὁ Ἰησοῦς ἀνήχθη εἰς τὴν ἔρημον ὑπὸ τοῦ πνεύματος πειρασθῆναι ὑπὸ τοῦ διαβόλου; Mt 4:1).[9] Jesus receives the Spirit at John's baptism, and after His life, death, and resurrection gives that Spirit to the church in Baptism. In receiving John's baptism, Christ transforms it into the Baptism of the Holy Spirit. Jesus thereby establishes a continuity between the baptism of John and the one He gives the church.[10] Any understanding of the

---

8. The only difference which Calvin finds in the two baptisms is that Jesus in His person is superior to John. Otherwise they are fundamentally the same. Since Baptism is not really a sacrament for Calvin but only a pledge of the baptized and a promise, which gives a person a moment on which to reflect later in life, there are no real differences. Baptism involves mortification, realizing one is a sinner. Calvin's faulty interpretation of John's baptism is determinative for his understanding of Christian Baptism (*Institutes* IV.XV.6–9). The efficacy of circumcision is hardly different. Like the baptisms of John and Jesus, it includes recipients in the external community of the redeemed. Luther also uses circumcision in his definition of Baptism, but for him both rites are God's gracious activity given in faith (*AE* 3:103, 110, 143–44).

9. See Mt 3:16–4:1; Mk 1:10–12; Lk 3:21–23; Jn 1:33.

10. Recent agendas of The Lutheran Church—Missouri Synod make no use of any of the four pericopes of John's baptizing Jesus. This fact may indicate that the connection between John's baptism and Christian Baptism appeared to the revisers of these liturgies to be strained or tangential at best. It may reflect an unresolved post-Reformation debate on the connection between John's baptism and the one mandated by Christ. Luther also does not use these pericopes in his rites of Baptism, but his "Flood Prayer" in his two orders of Baptism (1523 and 1526, *AE* 53:97 and 107) not only makes the connection, but sees John's baptizing of Jesus as the consecration of the water for Baptism: "[God] through the baptism of thy dear Child, our Lord Jesus Christ, hast consecrated and set apart the Jordan and all water as a salutary flood and a rich and full washing away of sins." Bryan D. Spinks notes that the Western church adapted the baptismal liturgy for adults to children and that the Reformers presupposed the candidates would be infants ("Luther's Timely Theology of Unilateral Baptism," *Lutheran Quarterly* 9 [Spring 1995]: 25). This is evident in Luther's rites, with the inclusion of Mk 10:13–16 as the solitary pericope. In the Eastern church the typical pericope initiating the rite of Baptism was Mark's account of John's baptizing Jesus, which reflects the fact that this church makes no distinction between the Baptism of adults and that of infants. Luther connected John's baptism and Christian Baptism in his hymn "To Jordan When Our Lord Had Gone" ("To Jordan Came the Christ, Our Lord"): "Also God's Son himself here stands / In all his manhood tender; / The Holy Spirit on him descends, / In dove's appearance hidden, / That not a doubt should ever rise / That, when we are baptized, / All the three persons do baptize; / And so, here recognized, / Will make their dwelling with us" (*AE* 53:300–301).

It also cannot be overlooked that frescoes and icons of John's baptism of Jesus in the Jordan flourished in early Christianity and indicated the importance of this event. A second-century fresco in the Catacomb of St. Calixtus is the earliest known representation of Jesus being baptized by John (Brown, *Baptism through the Centuries*, 43). Brown provides fifth-century representations in Ravenna (ibid., 55–56). The new order of Sundays

Baptism of the Holy Spirit must take into consideration that this Spirit given to Jesus at His baptism is responsible for bringing Jesus to His temptation by Satan and hence to His whole work of salvation. The Spirit resides permanently in Jesus: "'He on whom you see the Spirit descend and *remain*, this is he who baptizes with the Holy Spirit'" (Jn 1:33; emphasis added). He is not only a full participant in Jesus' humiliation and exaltation, but equips Him to endure it (Heb 9:14).

The Spirit's participation in the life and death of Jesus lays the foundation for the Christian's own dying and rising in Baptism. Since the Christian is made one with Christ in Baptism, there is only one Baptism for Christ and the church. In John's baptism of Jesus, the entire church was baptized with Him and received the Spirit. Luther's "Flood Prayer" attaches the church's redemption to John's baptism of Jesus: ". . . who through the baptism of thy dear Child, our Lord Jesus Christ, hast consecrated and set apart the Jordan and all water as a salutary flood and a rich and full washing away of sins."[11] Paul put Spirit, church, and Baptism together: "There is one body [the church] and one Spirit [the Holy Spirit], just as you were called to the one hope that belongs to your call, one Lord [Jesus, the Son of God], one faith [*fides quae*], one baptism, one God and Father of us all, who is above all and through all and in all" (Eph 4:4–6). Baptism in, by, or through the Spirit belongs necessarily to the definition of trinitarian Baptism in Mt 28:19.[12] As noted on the use of the divine name apart from the administration of Baptism itself, the usual order of the Trinity is reversed so that the Spirit is in the first place, followed by the Son and then the Father. The reversed order reflects how the believer encounters the Trinity.

Baptism as the Spirit's vehicle originates in Jesus' death, and so the Spirit working in Baptism incorporates the baptized into that death (see the excursus entitled "Living Water," p. 116). In His death Jesus gives the Holy Spirit (Mt 27:50, literally, "He released the Spirit" [ἀφῆκεν τὸ πνεῦμα]; Jn 19:30, literally, "He handed over the Spirit" [παρέδωκεν τὸ πνεῦμα]), and so His death defines Baptism in the Holy Spirit as a death to sin for the Christian. Baptism comes from the cross and brings the

---

after Epiphany in *Lutheran Worship* calls the first Sunday "The Baptism of Our Lord," and the Three-Year Series provides for pericopes from the synoptic gospels describing this event (Mt 3:13–17; Mk 1:4–11; Lk 3:15, 21–22). Thus the preacher has occasion to make the connection between the two baptisms. In future revisions of the agenda it would be better to return to the older custom of reading one of these pericopes for Baptism. John's gospel has no specific reference to this baptism but makes the clear connection between the Spirit given Jesus and His giving of the same Spirit: "He on whom you see the Spirit descend and remain, this is he who baptizes with the Holy Spirit" (Jn 1:33). Luther's reference to John's baptism in his "Flood Prayer" reflects many early church liturgies.

11. *AE* 53:107.
12. So also Beasley-Murray, *Baptism*, 199–200.

baptized to the cross. Through participation in the conception of Jesus, His Baptism, His life and death, the Spirit was christologically defined, that is, the Spirit of the Son became the Spirit of Christ. Participation of the Spirit in the life of Jesus is the teaching of all four gospels. Hence New Testament references to the Spirit include the Spirit of Jesus or Christ. This matter can be approached dogmatically, since the Athanasian Creed states that the humanity was brought by the incarnation into the Godhead (the Deity). Now the Spirit comes not only from the Son of God, but from the Son of God who became flesh. He is not simply the Spirit of the LORD or of God, but of Jesus Christ. Being baptized in the name of Jesus means more than the divine legalization of a sacred rite, which of course it is. It means that the baptized is taken by the Holy Spirit into Jesus, through whom he is presented to God. Hence Baptism in the name of Jesus is also called the Baptism of the Holy Spirit. The promise that Jesus will baptize with the Holy Spirit and with fire means that His Baptism will be defined by His cross and death in a sense that John's baptism was not. The Holy Spirit is, in Baptism, the divine fire establishing and confirming faith. As Luther says in the Small Catechism, the Spirit's work is nothing else than bringing us to faith.

As noted above, only the Baptism instituted by Jesus may properly be called Baptism in the Holy Spirit, but this does not mean the Holy Spirit was absent from John's baptism. Those who received that baptism did not of their own doing confess their sins and come to faith in the Coming One. They were not synergists in any sense of the word! Such a position would only be a form of dispensationalism, which means that different rules for salvation are in place in different periods. The Spirit who proceeds from the Father and the Son in eternity could give God's gracious benefits as defined by the cross only after He had assisted Jesus in that death. So the cross is the defining moment for the Trinity in the context of humanity's salvation. Here we come to know God as the Father of Jesus and we are given the Spirit. Thus it is proper to speak of a Baptism of the Holy Spirit only in reference to that Baptism accomplished after the death and resurrection of Jesus, but never with the suggestion that the Spirit was not fully responsible for all the acts of salvation before that. The Spirit's person is revealed and His work is defined and given in Jesus' death and resurrection as two events constituting one act in which God redeems and justifies the world. Pentecost is the formal conferral by Christ of the Holy Spirit on His church: "And behold, I send the promise of my Father upon you" (Lk 24:49; also Acts 1:5, 2:4). Placing the Baptism in the name of the Triune God and of Jesus and of the Holy Spirit in opposition to each other is allowed neither by our doctrine of the Trinity nor by our understanding of the person and work of Christ. Though the New Testament can speak of Jesus giving the Spirit in His death, as we have shown, or immediately after the resurrection (Jn 20:22), to avoid confusion and to conform with New Testament usage, the term "Baptism of the Holy Spirit" should be reserved for the Spirit's activity after the ascension.

This term has become problematic because the neo-Pentecostals and charismatics distinguish the Baptism of the Holy Spirit from "water Baptism," which is seen as the inferior of the two. This invalid distinction first became an issue in the Reformation, when the Anabaptists claimed for themselves a special Baptism in the Holy Spirit.[13] Lutherans strongly opposed the Anabaptists and insisted on attaching the person and work of the Spirit to the Word and specifically to Baptism (AC II.2). Unlike the Son who can be known in the person of Jesus, the Spirit is known chiefly in His work, and He works through the water of Baptism. In distinguishing between inner and outer Baptisms, one with the Spirit and the other with water, Zwingli's position was not different from that of the Anabaptists, who were indebted to him. For the sake of his own social, political, and ecclesiological views he had to find biblical reasons for maintaining infant Baptism, but like the Anabaptists, he denied any saving value to the act of Baptism.[14] For both the Anabaptists and Zwingli, sins were not forgiven in Baptism.[15] Even today there is a difference only in degree and not in substance between the neo-Pentecostal or charismatic Baptism in the Spirit and the Reformed inner Baptism. Clearly the Reformed object to the outrageous expressions attached to the inner experience by charismatics,[16] but they also locate the certainty of salvation not in water Baptism but within the individual. Calvin distinguishes between an inward Baptism and the outward rite without separating them. His is a Nestorian sacramentalism, because Baptism indicates that the Spirit is at work, but is itself not the Spirit's means. Whether the Spirit works at the same time as Baptism depends on whether the baptized has been elected.[17] For Calvin, the Holy Spirit does not tie Himself down to "vessels and vehicles," and Baptism cannot confer the Holy Spirit, who works faith directly.[18] Baptism in the Spirit has its origin in the divine election, and not in the rite of water.[19]

---

13. Trigg, *Baptism*, 211.
14. Ibid.
15. Gäbler, *Zwingli*, 128.
16. See Hoekema, *Holy Spirit Baptism*, 15–18.
17. "Calvin insists upon the distinction between the administration of the water and the operation of the Spirit, but does not permit a dissociation of the two.... Thus the unity of the inward and outward events is not fundamental, but is contingent upon the divine election.... But that outward baptism and inward regeneration are indissolubly linked for Luther there can be no doubt. This unity is a function of that between water and word" (Trigg, *Baptism*, 220).
18. *Institutes* IV.XIV.17.
19. For a discussion of differences between Calvin and Luther, see Trigg, *Baptism*, 217–19.

Modern Baptists see Baptism in the Spirit simply as another term for conversion, and see no necessary connection between it and water Baptism, which can be viewed as an initiation ceremony into the local congregation or an opportunity to demonstrate good faith.[20] Pentecostals go further and attribute such miraculous signs as speaking in tongues, healings, and sometimes snake handling to Baptism in the Holy Spirit.[21] Similar are those charismatics who maintain membership in Lutheran, Anglican, or Roman Catholic churches, all with a sacramental view of Baptism. For them Baptism in the Holy Spirit raises to a higher level what originally and sacramentally happened in water Baptism, which in most cases was administered to them as children. Baptismal regeneration is confirmed by the additional charismatic experience.[22] This experience takes the place of Baptism for the certainty of salvation. Charismatics can also be members of Reformed churches which practice infant Baptism, but they have no need to correlate their later experiences with the water Baptism which had only symbolic significance.

Like the Pentecostals, these charismatics use their peculiar interpretations of the book of Acts to distinguish the Baptism of the Holy Spirit from water Baptism. The evidence, however, does not support their claims. In some cases miraculous signs of the Holy Spirit are given along with Baptism, as on Pentecost (Acts 2:38), while in other cases such signs are given before Baptism, as with the household of Cornelius (Acts 10:47). In this case, as with the disciples at Ephesus (Acts 19:5–6), there is a miraculous speaking of foreign languages, a sign to *others* that the newly baptized have been received fully into the church: "And the believers from among the circumcised who came with Peter were amazed, because the gift of the Holy Spirit had been poured out even on the Gentiles . . . 'Can any one forbid water for baptizing these people who have received the Holy Spirit just as we have?'" (Acts 10:45, 47). Speaking in tongues in Acts does not give the assurance of salvation to those who are being baptized, but it is a sign to other Christians that believers seeking Baptism or the newly baptized stand within the church. Baptism grants the certainty of salvation to believers (1 Cor 6:11).

Those holding that a Baptism in the Holy Spirit is accompanied with miraculous signs, especially speaking in unknown languages or tongues, advance their arguments by equating the phenomena in Acts with that of 1 Corinthians 14. Such a conclusion does not take into account any number of clear differences between them, and therefore they should not be equated. The Corinthian tongue-speaking is capable of a

---

20. Grenz, *Community of God*, 550–51; 709–14.
21. See ibid., 545–50, for an evaluation of their position.
22. See Theodore R. Jungkuntz, *Confirmation and the Charismata* (Lanham, MD: University Press, 1983), 91–92.

psychological explanation as an altered state of consciousness, common even among ancient pagans and contemporary non-Christian groups, such as Mormons and Jehovah's Witnesses. There is no suggestion that such abnormal and sometimes disruptive behavior was in any sense comparable to what happened in Acts. If the Spirit is connected to tongue-speaking, it is only in the sense that this was happening in a congregation which had been called together by the Spirit. It was not in fulfillment of anything Jesus promised.

Paul's thanksgiving for his tongue-speaking ability which surpasses that of his readers (1 Cor 14:18) has all the marks of irony, of which he was a master, especially in the Corinthian correspondence. He no more spoke in tongues than he considered himself an inferior apostle (2 Cor 12:11)! His claim to speak in tongues is contradicted by his stated preference to speak five words in a known tongue than ten thousand in an unknown one. Did Paul really expect that someone would count? Paul could and did use the arguments of the opponents against themselves. He did not baptize the dead, but he cited this practice to prove his case for the resurrection, as previously discussed. His request for interpreters was intended to put the tongue-speakers out of existence (1 Cor 14:26–28). The Spirit converts through intelligible words and never through babbling (1 Cor 14:20–25).[23] Putting a higher value on five intelligible words than ten thousand unintelligible ones (1 Cor 14:19) is simply a polite way of saying that the Holy Spirit does not work through garble. The Word causing the element to become a sacrament is not a magical, secret Word, but the Gospel, that is, the proclamation of the death and resurrection of Jesus. While acknowledging that tongue-speakers experience a heightened sense of well-being, Paul claims that they are not speaking this word of salvation to themselves or anyone else (1 Cor 14:5), and hence it is hardly more than an exercise in self-absorption! This is not the sanctifying work of the Spirit, who as the Spirit of Christ makes us to share in His humility and not in a feeling of satisfaction with ourselves. Tongue-speaking is not taking up the cross of Jesus. In congregations, tongue-speakers can present a practical problem for pastors who seek to prevent them from disturbing the liturgy of the church. Rarely does speaking in tongues remain simply a practical problem, however. It becomes a grave theological problem when the tongue-speakers claim that this is a Baptism in the Holy Spirit which indicates an advanced stage of sanctification. The problem is compounded when they invite and urge others to have the same experience. The true and only Baptism in the Holy Spirit is the Baptism of which Jesus speaks: "With the baptism with which I am baptized, you

---

23. David P. Scaer, "An Essay for Lutheran Pastors on the Charismatic Movement," *Springfielder* 37 (March 1974): 210–23.

will be baptized" (Mk 10:39). Baptism of the Holy Spirit is sharing in the death of Jesus!

A difficulty in locating the giving of the Spirit in connection with Baptism may come from a desire for a precise chronological order of the events connected with Baptism. As with many Christian mysteries, we are able to look at the same act from different perspectives, all of which are true but which still must be taken together. For example, we can say that the Gospel converts, the pastor converts, the Holy Spirit converts. Or consider that conversion, belief, and regeneration all refer to one act, but each term may be used to describe a particular aspect thereof. In the Large Catechism, Luther places all these activities under the general category of sanctification: "Therefore to sanctify is nothing else than to bring us to the Lord Christ to receive this blessing, which we could not obtain by ourselves."[24]

Baptism in the name of Jesus or the Trinity *is* baptizing in the Holy Spirit. So the New Testament can speak of the Spirit being given before, during, or after Baptism. Locating one time for the Spirit's action does not rule out other times. The Spirit brings the believer to Baptism, works on him in Baptism, and renews him after Baptism. Concerning infant Baptism, Lutherans may commonly attach the activity of the Holy Spirit solely to the pouring of the water. This is hardly right! Water does not activate the Word, but the Word activates the water. The water of Baptism is in the midst of the entire proclamation of the Word which comes to a pinnacle in the reciting of the name of God: Father-Son-Spirit. Still the Spirit is attached to the entire service of the Word which surrounds Baptism, and not to certain words to the exclusion of others. That would be magic! Where the Word is, there the Holy Spirit must be present! *Ubi est Verbum, ibi est Spiritum Sanctum.* The Spirit's activity makes use of a wide range of words. What would be implied about the Spirit's inspiration and working through the Word if the situation were otherwise?

Consider the Spirit's activity in the life of Jesus. He was conceived by the Spirit before Baptism; He was designated as God's Son by the Spirit in Baptism; He was led by the Spirit after Baptism; He offered Himself to God by the Spirit in death, which was for Him a Baptism (Lk 12:50); and He was raised by the Spirit. All this correlates with the Spirit's activity in the Christian life. This activity can be pinpointed to the moment of Baptism, but nevertheless comprehends everything in the Christian life. For the Christian, death will be a real "Baptism," just as Baptism was itself a real death.

That the Spirit is given *during and after* Baptism is only a logical consequence of one's inclusion in Christ, who gives the Spirit. This does

---

24. LC II.39; Tappert, 415–16; *BKS*, 654.

not mean that the Spirit was not already at work before the act itself. Use of chrism (oil) in Baptism, especially on infants in the Eastern Orthodox and Luther's 1523 liturgies, only symbolizes the giving of the Spirit at Baptism and does not indicate that He was not present at the recitation of the name of God in which He is included.[25] The rite for Baptism in *Lutheran Worship* is quite specific in attributing regeneration to Baptism and the Spirit as one act,[26] but it lacks a specific reference to the giving of the Spirit. Luther's rite, which required an exorcism to make room for the Holy Spirit, is clearer on this point and suggests that the Spirit is given *before* Baptism.[27] In his Large Catechism Luther attaches the giving of the Spirit to Baptism: "In Baptism we are given the grace, Spirit, and power to suppress the old man so that the new may come forth and grow strong."[28] Our position is that the entire activity is the Spirit's, and we leave it to Him how and when He works (Jn 3:8). The rite of Baptism is itself an *epiklesis*, that is, it is an effectual prayer for the bestowal of the Holy Spirit on the baptized.

The development of confirmation in the Middle Ages allowed for a bestowal of the Spirit after Baptism, and thus it came to be seen as a sacrament in its own right with a special grace. A special grace was inherent in John Wesley's "second blessing," from which more recent Pentecostal and charismatic ideas about a Baptism of the Holy Spirit developed.[29] A special Baptism in the Spirit becomes a problem where a trinitarian Baptism with water falls into disuse.

As different as Roman Catholicism and Methodism are on the surface, both traditions point to a fuller giving of the Spirit *after* Baptism. In the Reformation, Luther recognized that both the *Schwärmer* and the Roman Catholics were distinguishing the giving of the Spirit from Baptism.[30] While Roman Catholicism correctly sees Baptism as a "new birth

---

25. "And I anoint thee with the oil of salvation in Jesus Christ our Lord" (*AE* 53:100).

26. "Almighty God, the Father of our Lord Jesus Christ, who has given you the new birth of water and of the Spirit and has forgiven you all your sins, strengthen you with his grace to life everlasting" (*Lutheran Worship*, 203).

27. "Depart thou unclean spirit and make room for the Holy Spirit" (*AE* 53:96 and 107). This phrase is present in both the 1523 and 1526 orders of Baptism and fell into disuse during the eighteenth-century Enlightenment.

28. LC IV.76; Tappert, 445–46; *BKS*, 706.

29. Consider Grenz's analysis: "America had become fertile soil for the teachings of John Wesley, the founder of the Methodists. Wesleyans drew from their leader the idea of a 'second blessing,' a definable moment of grace after conversion which decisively breaks the stranglehold that sin otherwise exercises even over a believer's life" (*Community of God*, 542).

30. "Luther's opinion of the baptismal theology of some of his opponents is already clear. He attacks a whole spectrum of errors. In their different ways the *Schwärmer* and the papists are guilty of separating what should be indissolubly joined: the water and the word of baptism. The papists deny that the benefits of baptism are only to be received in faith, while the *Täufer* make baptism dependent upon faith. Rome negates the abiding

in the Holy Spirit"[31] and complete as an act of initiation into the church, Confirmation and Penance are needed to provide grace for life. Lutheran theology recognizes a place for the Holy Spirit in these other rites, but Baptism remains foundational for them. In distinction to the Lutheran, Roman Catholic, and Eastern Orthodox views, Reformed theology understands individual faith or commitment as the inner Baptism or Baptism of the Holy Spirit. Since the Baptism of the Holy Spirit involves a human response, the phrase is a misnomer. Calvin does see an objectivity in Baptism as divine pledge, but still sees the real Baptism as the internal working of the Spirit in the elect. One scholar's assessment of Luther's opponents adequately sums up their position: "Its place at the end of the process of salvation places *baptism on the side of human response*, not on the side of the divine initiative. An individual's baptism seals the covenant pledge of faith, testifies to that faith before others, and commits him or her to live according to the new creation."[32]

Confessional Lutheran theology does not allow for a distinction between what non-Lutherans call water Baptism and an internal Baptism, whether or not it is called "Baptism in the Holy Spirit" or inner Baptism. Faith, which is the content of confession (Rom 10:9) and is antecedent to Baptism, is created by the Holy Spirit (1 Cor 12:3). The preaching of the Gospel, the teaching of the Christian doctrine, the confession of faith, and the application of water in the name of the Triune God constitute one act of the Holy Spirit. On that account the Holy Spirit can be said to be given before Baptism, as with Cornelius; during Baptism, as with those who were converted at Pentecost; or after Baptism, as with the Samaritans baptized by Philip. Baptism and the Word are congruent and corresponding realities, with Baptism deriving its life and substance from the Word and the Word coming to full and permanent expression in Baptism: "Therefore Baptism remains forever."[33] Not only is the Spirit present and active in the act of Baptism, but He is the one who awakens faith through the preaching of the Gospel, leads the believer through his catechetical training, evokes his confession at Baptism, incorporates the believer into Christ by Baptism, and becomes the determining factor for the rest of his life.

It might be falsely concluded from a reading of Article II of the Augsburg Confession, in reference to the necessity of regeneration through Baptism and the Holy Spirit (*renascuntur per baptismum et spiritum sanctum*), that Baptism and the giving of the Holy Spirit can be

---

power of baptism in its turning to 'second planks.' Many are guilty of despising baptism, and in one way or another seeking salvation and knowledge of God in a self-chosen religion or piety of their own" (Trigg, *Baptism*, 207–8).

31. *Catechism of the Catholic Church*, para. 1262.
32. Trigg, *Baptism*, 211; emphasis added.
33. LC IV.77; Tappert, 446; BKS, 706.

divided into two separate "Baptisms." Note here that the reference is not to two regenerations but one. Charismatic Lutherans may see here two "regenerations," one with the water and the other an internal experience often accompanied by tongue-speaking. To this we again reply that regeneration is one act, not two, and does not allow for a Baptism of the Holy Spirit after Baptism. A later experience, no matter how authentic, cannot be called a Baptism in any sense. The church does not attempt to authenticate internal personal experience, and therefore places no value on it. Paul neither relies on his personal experiences (2 Cor 12:1–10) nor makes them the subject of his proclamation (1 Cor 15:3–4). Whatever that experience may or may not be, even if it is faith, it is not a Baptism of the Holy Spirit: "Nevertheless I cannot build on the fact that I believe and many people are praying for me."[34] The church relies solely on the confession of faith made at Baptism and discounts all other claims of the Spirit's working. Baptism is neither faith (Baptists) nor the experience or obedience of faith (charismatics and Calvin, respectively). Lutherans too often fall into the Reformed pattern of looking for true signs of the Spirit's working in personal works of piety (which even unbelievers can do), and not in Baptism. Compare Luther: "Baptism promises and brings . . . the entire Christ, and the Holy Spirit with his gifts."[35]

Article V.2 of the Augsburg Confession could not be more clear in claiming that the Spirit is given in the sacraments to create faith (*Nam per verbum et sacramenta tamquam per instrumenta donatur spiritus sanctus, qui fidem efficit*).[36] Even when an unbeliever receives Baptism and is later converted, he is not rebaptized. The first Baptism remains the Baptism of the Holy Spirit. Immersion in water one hundred times grants nothing![37] Luther argues that unbelief no more destroys Baptism than it can destroy Christ: "Therefore only presumptuous and stupid persons draw the conclusion that where there is no true faith, there can be no true Baptism. Likewise I might argue, 'If I have no faith, then Christ is nothing.'"[38]

The Spirit can give people as gifts to the church, e.g. apostles and pastors, and He can give gifts to individuals (Eph 4:8), but this activity of the Spirit manifests itself only in certain individuals and cannot be identified as the Baptism of the Holy Spirit, which is promised to all who are baptized.[39] The presence of such gifts in no way guarantees

---

34. LC IV.56; Tappert, 443–44; *BKS*, 702.
35. LC IV.41; Tappert, 441–42; *BKS*, 699.
36. Tappert, 31; *BKS*, 58.
37. LC IV.77–79; Tappert, 446; *BKS*, 706.
38. LC IV.58; Tappert, 444; *BKS*, 702.
39. *Spiritual Gifts*, A Report of the Commission on Theology and Church Relations of The Lutheran Church–Missouri Synod, September 1994, 29–30.

salvation, and can never be used as a measure of God's grace to believers or as a barometer of their level of commitment to God. Judas is listed as an apostle (Mt 10:2), an office which serves as a foundation for the church (Eph 2:20). Possession of this office as a gift to him from Jesus did not in any way point to the working of saving grace in his life or his level of commitment and personal holiness. Whatever these gifts of the Spirit may be, they cannot be called a Baptism of the Spirit, nor do they in any way assure those who possess them that they are believers or holy. Baptism, and not individual gifts of the Spirit, is the assurance and sign of salvation. Luther can speak of Baptism giving "victory over death and the devil, forgiveness of sin, God's grace, the entire Christ, and the Holy Spirit with his gifts."[40] Here Luther is not referring to unusual or ecstatic gifts or even church offices, but to different perspectives of salvation all available in Baptism. Only in this light does his cry *baptizatus sum*—"But I am baptized!"—have meaning.

The Reformed move quickly from water Baptism to the inner Baptism or Baptism of the Holy Spirit. Roman Catholics properly see Baptism as regenerative, but move to Confirmation and Penance to find grace for living.[41] Charismatics may allow for Baptism even of infants, but take their focus off Baptism and put it on their spectacular gifts. Calvin and Barth stress Baptism as a pledge of obedience. So also does the Lima document, which the World Council of Churches adopted.[42] Now popular among some Roman Catholics and Protestants, including Barth and some Lutherans, is making Baptism the foundation of the ministry, as discussed in the excursus following chapter 4. These positions are not identical and each has its own unique problems, but they all fail to see what great benefits Baptism gives, and in some cases attempt to make up for this deficiency with their own additions.

In the Apology Melanchthon specifically says that the Holy Spirit is given in Baptism: "That God does approve the Baptism of little children [*parvulorum*] is shown by the fact that *God gives the Holy Spirit* to those who were baptized this way" (i.e., as infants).[43] Here the equation is clear: *the Baptism of infants is the Baptism of the Holy Spirit*. If we must speak of a Baptism in the Holy Spirit, then let it be infant Baptism. The giving of the Spirit in Baptism corresponds to the presence of faith

---

40. LC IV.41; Tappert, 441–42; BKS, 699.
41. See LC IV.77–82; Tappert, 446; BKS, 706–7.
42. "Baptism is both God's gift and our human response to that gift" (*Baptism, Eucharist, and Ministry* [Geneva: World Council of Churches, 1982], 8). Barth as well as the Baptists could live with this.
43. Ap. IX.3; Tappert, 178; BKS, 247; emphasis added. Leif Grane astutely observes that the Anabaptist idea that the Spirit worked outside of Baptism compelled Luther to speak less of the Spirit's activity in Baptism. Baptism for the Anabaptists was the mark of those who were already filled with the Spirit, and from this reasoning they denied Baptism to infants (*Augsburg Confession*, 110).

worked by the Spirit in Baptism. The New Testament simply does not know of a Baptism administered where faith is known to be absent. Unbelievers are not baptized. Lutherans have no quarrel with Baptists who insist that Baptism be given in faith, but disagree with their view that faith constitutes Baptism. Baptism is and remains entirely God's work. The Baptist distinction between their Baptism as "believers' Baptism" and ours as paedobaptism (infant Baptism) can be entirely misleading. Lutherans do not baptize confessed or known unbelievers, into which category baptized infants do not belong. Infant Baptism is not only believers' Baptism, but the highest form of believers' Baptism. This idea is developed more fully in chapter 10, on infant faith.

Luther's argument must be followed carefully. Without faith Baptism is inoperative, even in children: "Without faith Baptism is of no use."[44] For the sake of argument he says that if infants did not believe, their Baptism would be valid (LC IV.55).[45] This is a contrary-to-fact sentence, because he is careful to say as part of his argument that they do believe: "As we said, even if infants did not believe—which, however, is not the case, as we have proved—still their Baptism would be valid and no one should rebaptize them."[46] So important is faith for receiving Baptism, that if Luther were convinced that children did not believe, he would no longer baptize them.[47] Luther makes it clear in the Large Catechism that Baptism lasts forever, even where faith fails or was never present to begin with. The Baptism of a hypocrite or unbeliever is as valid as the Baptism of a believer.[48] Still, without faith Baptism does not reach its intended purpose of placing the baptized into the death and resurrection of Christ.

---

44. LC IV.34; Tappert, 440; *BKS*, 697.
45. Tappert, 443; *BKS*, 702.
46. Ibid.
47. References to Luther's Lenten Sermons of 1525 are taken from Gottfried Hoffmann, "Baptism and the Faith of Children," in *A Lively Legacy: Essays in Honor of Robert Preus*, ed. Kurt E. Marquart, John R. Stephenson, and Bjarne W. Teigen (Fort Wayne, IN: Concordia Theological Seminary, 1985), 82.
48. LC IV.54; Tappert, 443; *BKS*, 702.

Excursus

LIVING WATER: WATER AND THE SPIRIT

Foundational for the Holy Spirit's activity in Baptism is His creative activity with water in Gn 1:2: "and the Spirit of God was moving over the face of the waters." This relationship between Spirit and water plays a part in at least three places in the gospel of John. An explicit connection is found in Jn 3:5: "Unless one is born of water and the Spirit . . ." A second is found in Jesus' logion, "He who believes in me, as the scripture has said, 'Out of his heart shall flow rivers of living water'" (Jn 7:38). After this, John interprets "rivers of living water" as Jesus' own reference to the giving of the Holy Spirit: "Now this he said about the Spirit, which those who believed in him were to receive; for as yet the Spirit had not been given, because Jesus was not yet glorified" (Jn 7:39). The third reference is in the crucifixion of Jesus: He gives up His (Holy) Spirit (Jn 19:30), and after the thrust of the soldier's spear, water with blood flows out of the victim's side (Jn 19:34).

Identification of water with the Spirit in Jn 7:38–39 invites further attention. Apart from its interpretation, the hearers of the fourth gospel would have expected that the evangelist would provide a fulfillment of this prophecy within the body of the gospel itself. Though some commentators see the prophecy "out of his belly will come rivers of living water" as a reference to believers, Joel Marcus argues convincingly that the words refer back to Jesus.[1] In this view the prophecy was fulfilled when the soldier's spear lanced his side, "and at once there came out blood and water" (Jn 19:34). In the prophecy of the living waters (Jn 7:38) and John's description of the crucifixion scene (Jn 19:30, 34), Spirit and water occupy pivotal positions. The living waters pericope promises that only after Jesus has been glorified will the Spirit be given (Jn 7:38–39). Jesus hands over the Holy Spirit (Jn 19:30), and immediately after the spear lances His side, out come the blood and the water (Jn 19:34). For John, Jesus' death is the hour of his glorification (Jn 17:1; compare Jn 21:15). The hour of glorification, the giving of the Spirit, and the bestowal of the sacraments constitute for John a single event.

Jesus says that the waters flowing from the belly will happen in accord with the Scripture (Jn 7:38), though no particular scripture is

---

[1]. "Rivers of Living Water From Jesus' Belly (John 7:38)," *Journal of Biblical Literature* 117 (Summer 1998): 328–30.

designated. Locating the particular Old Testament passage to which Jesus refers may provide other clues in interpreting this passage. Joel Marcus provides a compelling argument that Jesus was referring to Is 12:3, "With joy you will draw water from the wells of salvation."[2] He notes that Jesus spoke these words at the feast of Tabernacles (Jn 7:2), during which a water libation took place: "In this ceremony, water was drawn from the Siloam stream to the south of Jerusalem, carried up to the Temple in a joyful procession, and poured out on the altar."[3] Rabbinical literature uses Is 12:3 to show that water was symbolic of the Holy Spirit.[4] The drawing out of the water was a drawing out of the Holy Spirit: "Joshua ben Levi said: Why is [the Temple courtyard] called 'the Place of Water-drawing'? Because from it they draw out the Holy Spirit, as it is said, 'With joy you will draw water from the wells of salvation' [Isa 12:3]."[5] So it seems that Jesus took advantage of this festival to point to Himself as the living water, and used an Old Testament prophecy which was associated with this celebration. Jesus customarily took institutions and festivals, like Temple, priesthood, and Passover, and saw their ultimate reference in Himself. So He interpreted the water ceremony of the feast of Tabernacles in regard to Himself. Another argument offered by Marcus for connecting Is 12:3 with Jesus is the similarity of the name 'Jesus' with הַיְשׁוּעָה, the Hebrew word for salvation "in the wells of salvation."[6] Not only is this hypothesis attractive in itself, but it furthers the line of thought introduced in Jn 4:4–15, where Jesus encountered the woman at Jacob's well and identified Himself as living water (Jn 4:10–14). In both the pericopes of the woman at the well in Samaria and at the feast of Tabernacles, Jesus presented Himself as the Well from which salvation shall come. The culmination of these water pericopes comes in the water pouring out of the side of Jesus, who in accord with His own prophecy gives the church in His death the Holy Spirit.

Ancient interpreters and some modern ones understand the water flowing from the side of Jesus as Baptism.[7] In retelling these circumstances surrounding the death of Jesus, the Fourth Evangelist places himself under oath: "He who saw it has borne witness—his testimony is true, and he knows that he tells the truth—that you also may believe" (Jn 19:35). At the end of his gospel, he uses a similar oath to confirm the veracity of his message (Jn 21:24). John wants to be accepted as a reliable witness, not only in regard to his historical testimony but in regard

---

2. Ibid., 328.
3. Ibid.
4. Ibid.
5. Ibid., 329.
6. Ibid.
7. See Brown, *Gospel of John* 1:320–24.

Excursus

to the greater mystery of the incarnation which is able to awaken faith in Jesus as the Christ, the Son of God (Jn 20:30–31). For the evangelist the pouring out of the water and blood is more than just an extraordinary physical occurrence, but like the totality of his written testimony, this event following the giving of the Spirit and the death of Jesus has heavenly meaning. Within the context of this gospel, the meaning is sacramental.

Johann Gerhard adopted this ancient sacramental view of Christ's death. This great Lutheran dogmatician made a distinction between the institution of the sacraments and what he called the publication of their institution. He placed the declaration of Baptism in Mt 28:16–20, but its origin belonged to Christ's death. It can be noted that John does not include a specific institution of Baptism, as Matthew does, but his gospel is rich in baptismal imagery and implications. Such a distinction between an event and its publication, as Gerhard makes regarding the sacraments, is not uncommon. American independence was enacted by the Continental Congress on July 2, 1776, but the declaration was made on July 4, and it is on this day that the nation's founding is commemorated. Gerhard approvingly quotes Thomas Aquinas that "the church of Christ is said to have been made through the sacraments which flowed from the side of Christ as he was hanging on the cross," but "the publication of this event can be made by somebody else."[8] It is not contradictory to find the church's origin in Christ's death, the Holy Spirit, and the sacraments. Christ in His death provides the water of Baptism, in which the Holy Spirit by creating and confirming faith gives birth to the church.

---

8. *Loci Theologici* 4:148 (locus 18, para. 26).

Excursus

A CASE IN PASTORAL PRACTICE

Like the Eastern Orthodox today, the early post-apostolic church did not have separate services for the Baptism of infants. When parents had finished three years of catechetical preparation, they and their children were baptized together on the eve of Easter. Baptizing infants is clearly in view in this passage from Tertullian: "First you should baptize the little ones. All who can speak for themselves, should speak. But for those who cannot speak, their parents should speak, or another who belongs to their family. Then baptize the grown men, lastly the women."[1]

Jeremias, who among modern scholars has made the most vigorous historical defense for infant Baptism, uses the *Apostolic Tradition* of Hippolytus and Tertullian's *De Baptismo* (*Treatise on Baptism*) (both from ca. AD 200) to support his view that already in the apostolic period entire households were baptized, including the children. At issue here is not whether infants were baptized—they clearly were—but that their Baptism was reserved for Easter. Adult catechumens and their children were baptized together. Reserving Easter as the time for administering Baptism is not entirely without New Testament support, since Baptism was seen as the death (burial) and resurrection of the baptized. Following St. Augustine's successful refutation of the Pelagian denial of original sin, Baptism was usually administered to infants soon after birth. When nearly all of Europe had become Christian, children could hardly be baptized with their parents, who had long since received Baptism. Baptizing entire families thus had become the exception, and infants were baptized separately. This natural development of baptizing infants soon after birth was then reinforced by St. Augustine's definition of original sin. The saving necessity of Baptism for children was more carefully articulated, and centuries later became prominent in the Lutheran understanding (AC II). Original sin was only one reason for infant Baptism; inclusion in Christ's redemption was another. Children not only are being saved from something evil, they are being included in something supremely good.[2] The promise of salvation in Baptism negates the evil which awaits all mankind.

---

1. Joachim Jeremias, *The Origins of Infant Baptism: A Further Study in Reply to Kurt Aland*, trans. Dorothea M. Barton (London: SCM Press; Naperville, IL: Allensons, 1963), 28–29.

2. The Eastern church sees Baptism as its entrance into a new life and anticipatory of

Excursus

In order to be redeemed from original sin and obtain Christ's salvation, children should be baptized as soon as possible. Infant mortality is greatly reduced by modern technologies, but in ancient and some contemporary societies, infant survival is rarer than infant mortality. Even with medical advantages there is no certainty that children will not die before, during, or right after birth. Today, with abortion so widely practiced throughout the world, the number of children not reaching full term may, in terms of the percentage of the total population, be greater than in the ancient and medieval world. We are hardly the first to raise the question of baptismal necessity in these cases. The Lutheran Confessions do not address this issue. Their concern is the Anabaptist denial of Baptism as a necessary sacrament for children, and not that some children whose parents have every intention to have them baptized nevertheless die without Baptism. Luther addresses this issue in his *Lectures on Genesis* in connection with boys who die before circumcision and girls, for whom the rite was not intended: such children are saved. Since God is by nature merciful, He will not let their condition be worse because they were unable to obtain circumcision in the Old Testament or Baptism in the New Testament.[3]

Luther is not alone in allowing for the salvation of unbaptized infants, but his arguments should not be confused with those of the Reformed or Roman Catholics. For Calvin, children's claim to salvation is through a natural inheritance from their parents.[4] Contemporary Roman Catholicism allows "us to hope that there is a way of salvation for children who have died without Baptism."[5] Such hope seems to be no more than raising the possibility of salvation to a higher degree of probability. Luther's hope for the salvation of such children is certain: children of Christian parents who die without Baptism *are saved by faith*.[6]

Some of these issues touch as well on the discussion of infant faith which may exist before Baptism, or in this case before and apart from circumcision. Luther is clear on how he understands the necessity of Baptism in regard to the unbaptized. His argument is consistent with his grasp of justification by grace through faith, of which Abraham is the clearest example. Abraham's descendants, both girls and uncircumcised boys, are, like him, justified through faith. God justifies sinners by

---

future glories. This contrasts with the Roman church, which sees Baptism as eradicating original sin but not later actual sins. In Lutheran as in Roman Catholic theology, original sin makes Baptism necessary, but its doctrine also resembles the Eastern Orthodox view that it remains effective throughout life and into eternity. See Meyendorff, *Byzantine Theology*, 192–95.

3. *AE* 3:103.
4. *Institutes* IV.XV.20–22.
5. *Catechism of the Catholic Church*, para. 1261.
6. *AE* 3:103.

A Case in Pastoral Practice

grace, a justification received through faith alone. Luther understands the benefits of circumcision not in terms of becoming a member of the society of Israel, a chief argument for Zwingli, the Enlightenment theologians, and Schleiermacher, but in terms of faith which infants have before and apart from circumcision and Baptism. Condemned are not those who die without Baptism, but those who refuse them Baptism![7]

Some parents have no concern about having their children baptized. Others whose children die without Baptism suffer unnecessarily. Some suggest that children, even those not in immediate danger of death, be baptized in the delivery room right after birth. This means that a pastor should be present or called soon thereafter, and that Baptisms will no longer *ordinarily* be administered in the church. Praiseworthy as this concern for children is, it may be motivated by a groveling posture toward a God who penalizes the unbaptized (Law!). As late as the last century, children were carried by their fathers on the day of birth or the day after to church for Baptism. Some of these children may have been baptized by those in attendance, if death seemed imminent. In other cases death did not seem imminent, and they still died. Even now any number of scenarios are possible. In one case, a Caesarean operation would have saved the life of a stillborn child. What about the child who dies in an automobile accident on the way to church? Or before the service or before its completion? Such questions may seem trite, but they are real concerns for parents burdened by the erroneous view that Baptism is a legal requirement for salvation. Such parents should be told that Baptism belongs to the proclamation of the Word from which it takes its life. Basic to Lutheran theology is St. Augustine's principle that the Gospel gives shape and form to this sacrament. *Accedat verbum ad elementum et fit sacramentum.*[8] The Word, which shapes the sacrament, has its existence prior to its formation of the sacrament. It is effective for salvation apart from the elements.

Children are no less capable of believing this Gospel than adults. If we take the words of Jesus seriously, they are even more capable of faith than their parents. This the world cannot understand. To take a page

---

7. Luther's discussion is profitable for those concerned with the fate of the unbaptized (ibid., 101–7). In commenting on this section, Trigg says, "It is those adults who have contempt for circumcision or baptism who are surely damned" (*Baptism*, 41). A question was posed to Thomas Hopko at the 1992 Symposium on the Lutheran Confessions at Concordia Theological Seminary, Fort Wayne, Indiana, about the fate of children baptized with the modalistic formula "Creator-Redeemer-Sanctifier." Hopko, a leading Eastern Orthodox theologian in the United States, responded in Luther-like fashion: "I have no doubt about the salvation of such children, but I do about those who administer that kind of Baptism." Reconsider Luther: "Adults . . . who despise Baptism are surely damned" (*AE* 3:103).

8. SA III.v.1; Tappert, 310; *BKS*, 449–50.

Excursus

from Luther and adjust it, a boy who died on the seventh day, before circumcision could be administered, was as surely saved as the boy on whom this rite had been performed. Children can believe before, in, and after Baptism. A funeral service for an unbaptized infant will be substantially the same as for a baptized one. These circumstances are tragedies, but not obstacles to God's grace in Christ Jesus. Those who grieve in the face of the death of such children lack the certainty which Baptism gives, but they do not lack the certainty of God's promise. Perhaps we have spent an inordinate amount of space on this issue, but fewer issues demand a more theologically informed and sensitive approach from the pastor. This discussion is expanded in chapter 11, on Baptism's necessity and its exceptions. Some pastors may find the following paragraphs from Luther's *Lectures on Genesis* of some value in handling the deaths of unbaptized children in their parishes.

> But here another question arises. If the uncircumcised males of the Jews were lost, what is one to conclude about infants who died before the eighth day? What about the other sex, the girls? Likewise, what about our own infants, either those who are stillborn or those who die shortly after birth, before they are baptized?
>
> Concerning infants who died before the eighth day the answer is easy, just as it is easy to give an answer about our own infants who die before Baptism. For these do not sin against the covenant of circumcision or Baptism. Since the Law commands them to be baptized on the eighth day, could God condemn those who die before the eighth day?
>
> Accordingly, the souls of those infants must be left to the will of the Heavenly Father, whom we know to be merciful. Furthermore, what Paul says in a gentle manner about "those whose sins were not like the transgression of Adam" (Rom. 5:14) and about Jacob and Esau—"though they were born and had nothing good or bad" (Rom. 9:11)—holds true in their case too.
>
> Even though infants bring with them inborn sin, which we call original sin, it is nevertheless important that they have committed no sin against the Law. Since God is by nature merciful, He will not let their condition be worse because they were unable to obtain circumcision in the Old Testament or Baptism in the New Testament.
>
> With regard to girls among the Jews the answer is easy. For because this sign was prescribed only for the male sex, it does not pertain to girls. Nevertheless, since the girls are Abraham's descendants, they are not excluded from Abraham's righteousness; they attain it through faith. But those adults who despised circumcision or who despise Baptism are surely damned.[9]

Funeral liturgies for the baptized and unbaptized children should not be so obsessed with the terrors from which they have been saved, but should portray the glories which these children are enjoying and

---

9. *AE* 3:103.

which Baptism conveys on all believers.[10] The following prayer from the *Book of Common Prayer* would serve these purposes.

> O Merciful Father, whose face the angels of thy little ones do always behold in heaven; Grant us steadfastly to believe that this thy child hath been taken into the safe keeping of thine eternal love; through Jesus Christ our Lord. *Amen.*[11]

---

10. Consider the following from Theodoret of Cyprus: "If the only meaning of baptism were the remission of sins, why would we baptize newborn children who have not yet tasted of sin? But the mystery of baptism is not limited to this; it is the promise of greater and more perfect gifts. In it are the promises of future delights; it is the type of the future resurrection, a communion with the master's Passion, a participation in His Resurrection, a mantle of salvation, a tunic of gladness, a garment of light, or rather it is light itself" (quoted from Meyendorff, *Byzantine Theology*, 194). Theodoret's position is similar to Luther's, that newborn children have committed no actual sin.

11. *Book of Common Prayer*, 340.

8

INFANT BAPTISM: AN HISTORICAL DEBATE WITH THEOLOGICAL IMPLICATIONS

The issue of baptizing infants, which was the first issue to divide opponents of the papacy in the Reformation, was revived in Protestant German territorial churches in the 1950s and 1960s. This debate had practical consequences because approximately forty pastors in the territorial churches, some of which were Lutheran, were ready to dispense with baptizing their own children, and others were ready to give up the practice in their churches entirely.[1] Since the Enlightenment, nearly all German Protestant theologians have denied the *fides infantium*, Luther's doctrine that children could believe. This denial, fundamental to the Baptist position, inevitably leads to dispensing with infant Baptism, unless other considerations are introduced in favor of the practice. This more recent conflict over infant Baptism was waged on dogmatical and exegetical fronts. Karl Barth had earlier expressed reservations about infant Baptism, but reserved a wholesale rejection of the practice for the last volume of his *Church Dogmatics* (vol. 4/4), which appeared in German in 1967. Barth claimed that he was persuaded by the exegetical arguments offered by his son, Markus Barth; however, even before he arrived at out-and-out rejection, it was obvious that his theology of the encounter would have difficulty tolerating the inclusion of children, especially infants. His theology of the encounter (German, *Begegnung*) consisted of the divine 'I' or 'Thou' [German, *ich/du*] confronting or meeting the human 'I'. The moment of the encounter between the divine you [German, *du*] and the human 'I' was the moment of revelation. Without the participation of the human 'I', there was no revelation. While Barth began his theological development in protest to Schleiermacher's concept of consciousness [German, *Bewußtsein*] as the source of revelation, his view was just as subjective. Infants were no more capable of attaining to Barth's encounter with God than they were to Schleiermacher's consciousness of the divine.

---

1. Hoffmann, "Baptism," 79. Wilhelm Oesch speaks of one hundred pastors in the Rhineland who announced support of the practice of adult Baptism only ("Abschluss des Barthischen Lebenswerk," *Solus Christus Sola Scriptura*, ed. Dieter Oesch [Gr. Oesingen: Lutherische Buchhandlung, 1996], 235). See chapter 12, on Karl Barth, for a description of his encounter theology and its influence on the movement away from infant Baptism.

Infant Baptism: An Historical Debate

At the same time an exegetical and historical debate about the origins of infant Baptism arose between two widely recognized New Testament scholars in Europe. It began with two books by Joachim Jeremias published in 1938 and 1949.[2] In 1958 his *Infant Baptism in the First Four Centuries* appeared.[3] Kurt Aland responded in 1961 with what later appeared in English as *Did the Early Church Baptize Infants?*[4] As implied in the titles, Jeremias took the affirmative position and Aland the negative. In 1962 Jeremias replied to Aland with the book that would be translated as *The Origins of Infant Baptism*.[5] Aland published a collection of essays in 1971 in which he compared his position with that of Karl Barth, from whom he distanced himself.[6] The potential importance of this debate is seen in that the great and perhaps leading Baptist exegetical scholar and theologian G. R. Beasley-Murray translated Aland's reply to Jeremias. Beasley-Murray's *Baptism in the New Testament* is the classical defense of adult or believers' Baptism. Each side of the question saw in the historical discussion evidence for its own position. This debate did not address the theological propriety of whether infants should be baptized, but whether the custom was historically demonstrable in the apostolic and post-apostolic churches. Neither combatant proposed abolishing the practice altogether, and even Barth never proposed rebaptizing. Aland's last word was that abolition of infant Baptism could have terrible consequences and he moved to defend it on the basis of original sin,[7] the argument of the Augsburg Confession (Article II). The problem with historical debates is that what may be considered hard-core objective evidence is often capable of multiple interpretations. Objections to infant Baptism have been theological and not historical ones. Historical evidence is generally mustered to support prior convictions, not the other way around.[8] As the question of the history of

---

2. *Hat die älteste Christenheit die Kindertaufe geübt?* (Göttingen: Vandenhoeck & Ruprecht, 1938) and *Hat die Urkirche die Kindertaufe geübt?* (Göttingen: Vandenhoeck & Ruprecht, 1949).

3. *Die Kindertaufe in den ersten vier Jahrhunderten*, which appeared in English under the title *Infant Baptism in the First Four Centuries*, trans. David Cairns (Philadelphia: Westminster Press, 1958).

4. *Die Säuglingstaufe im Neuen Testament und in der Alten Kirche: Eine Antwort an Joachim Jeremias* (München: Chr. Kaiser, 1961) which was translated into English by G. R. Beasley-Murray (Philadelphia: Westminster Press, 1963).

5. German, *Nochmals: Die Anfänge der Kindertaufe* (München: Chr. Kaiser, 1962).

6. *Taufe und Kindertaufe* (Gütersloh: Gerhard Mohn, 1971).

7. Ibid., 81. Dale Moody expresses astonishment that Aland defends infant Baptism after he presents what he considers conclusive historical evidence against this practice in the early church (*Baptism: Foundation for Christian Unity* [Philadelphia: Westminster Press, 1968], 158). Moody presents an overview of the debate (127–61).

8. So also Hermann Sasse: "If we must answer yes with the greatest probability to the historical question, whether the church of the apostolic age knew and practiced infant baptism, we have still in no way decided the theological question, whether it is right to baptize infants" (*We Confess the Sacraments*, trans. Norman Nagel [St. Louis: Concordia Publishing House, 1985], 39). This chapter is a translation of Sasse's "Letter

Infant Baptism: An Historical Debate

Jesus cannot be ignored in formulating Christology, so the debate over infant Baptism cannot ignore the historical evidences.

At the center of the debate were the Greek words *oikos* (οἶκος, house) and *oikia* (οἰκία, household), especially in Acts. Only this New Testament book gives an historical, chronological account of the early church. Regardless of how fragmentary it might be, the text provides a unique look into the ministries of Peter, John, James (the Lord's brother), Stephen, Philip (commonly called the deacon), and Paul. This is not to say that historical facts about the early church cannot be gleaned from the epistles as well, but these are not offered in the neat, orderly form of Acts.

Acts, as a record of the church's origins, is chiefly an account of how the church spread from Jerusalem through Samaria and Antioch into Asia Minor, Greece, and finally Rome. In these missionary endeavors, Baptism is presented as the rite of initiation: first the Gospel is preached, people confess their sins and Jesus as Lord and Christ, and they are then admitted into fellowship through Baptism. This pattern follows the pre-Easter baptizing practices of John and Jesus. Significantly different is that this preaching and baptizing in Acts often takes place in households. John's baptism and presumably that of Jesus took place in the Jordan, but other places, unspecified, are also mentioned (Jn 3:26, 4:1). Peter preaches to the household of Cornelius and baptizes them (Acts 10). Paul does the same with the household of Lydia (Acts 16:15) and the jailer at Philippi (Acts 16:27–34). At Corinth Paul baptizes the household of a certain Crispus, who seems to be the first one there to believe and to be baptized (Acts 18:8). The baptizing of entire households is corroborated from 1 Corinthians, where Paul claims to have baptized the household of Stephanus (1 Cor 1:16). The Crispus of 1 Cor 1:14, who is baptized, and of Acts 18:8, who is the ruler of a synagogue, seems to be the same person. A household in the ancient world more closely resembled an extended family than a nuclear family. Along with Crispus, Paul mentions that he baptized a certain Gaius (1 Cor 1:14). Then follows the reference to the household of Stephanus (1 Cor 1:15). If this Crispus is the same one mentioned in Acts 18:8, then Paul intends inclusion of his whole household. Of course the same would be true for Gaius, though his household is not mentioned either. Together with his household, Stephanus and two other men believe. Individuals were baptized, as in the case of the Ethiopian eunuch (Acts 8:27–39), but the apostolic ministry often focused on entire households.

Since Crispus is identified as the ruler of a synagogue in Acts 18:8, it is difficult to avoid the conclusion that his household formed the nucleus

---

to Lutheran Pastors, No. 4, March 1949" and was written before Aland's reply.

of that synagogue. This raises the possibility that his children belonged to the synagogue, which would provide ancillary evidence for including children in the church and their being baptized. Synagogues came to prominence after the fall of Jerusalem in AD 70, but they were the centers of Jewish life and provided the setting for the ministries of Jesus (Mt 9:35; Lk 4:16, 4:44) and Paul (Acts 13:5, 13:14, 14:1, 17:1, 17:10, 18:4, 18:8, 18:18, 19:8). Most scholars place the origins of the synagogue in Babylon, where the Jews were deprived of Temple worship. Archeologists have recently uncovered a synagogue in Jericho which dates between 50 and 70 BC. An older view that the synagogues as separate buildings originated no earlier than the first century must be readjusted. References to synagogues in the first century may be to gatherings of people or the buildings where these gatherings took place.[9] These gatherings may at one time have taken place outdoors, but large private homes and separate buildings for this purpose were used in the first century. Even after synagogues were constructed, homes were used for synagogue gatherings.[10] A certain Titus Justus, who is described as a worshiper of God, owned a house next door to a synagogue, whose ruler was Crispus (Acts 18:7–8). Along with the family of Crispus, probably other inhabitants of the city, including Titus Justus, were members of this synagogue.[11] The implication is that believing Corinthians had heard Paul in the synagogue or household of Crispus.

The full development of the synagogue as the place of worship may have happened only after the destruction of Jerusalem: "Until the destruction of the Temple, synagogues were places for reading the Bible and for sermons, and there is no evidence that they were used for communal prayer."[12] These assemblies may have served as courts and for other purposes, most likely social ones. At the time of the destruction of the Temple, 394 synagogues existed in Jerusalem alone.[13] These gatherings or synagogues served as the base for the preaching of Jesus and became the nucleus for Christian synagogues, that is, churches (Jas 2:22). We can only speculate about the size of these synagogue gatherings. Perhaps they had ordinarily a membership of fifty to about one hun-

---

9. For an overview of the rise of synagogues as separate buildings, see essays collected by Joseph Gutmann, ed., *Ancient Synagogues: The State of Research* (Chico, CA: Scholars Press, 1981).

10. *Anchor Bible Dictionary* (New York: Doubleday, 1992), 6:251–63, esp. 255 s.v. "Synagogue," by Rachel Hachlile.

11. "And he left there and went to the house of a man named Titus Justus, a worshiper of God; his house was next door to the synagogue. Crispus, the ruler of the synagogue, believed in the Lord, together with all his household; and many of the Corinthians hearing Paul believed and were baptized" (Acts 18:7–8).

12. R. J. Zwi Werblowsky and Geoffrey Wigoder, eds., *The Oxford Dictionary of the Jewish Religion* (New York: Oxford University Press, 1997), s.v. "Synagogue."

13. Ibid.

dred (Acts 1:15), depending on the size of the house or building where they gathered. The Great Synagogue in Alexandria was so large that the flag was waved to tell those who were in the back of the room that the prayer had concluded.[14]

The household of Crispus, which had served as a synagogue, became after his conversion a setting for a church. Acts 19:8–9 reports that Paul preached in the synagogue for three months and then took the disciples, that is, the believers, out to form his own gathering. As the core of Paul's churches were made up of synagogue participants and in some cases entire synagogues, these Jews were acquainted with the public reading of the Bible and sermons (Acts 13:15), which were also essential to Christian worship (1 Tm 4:13). Inclusion of children in the synagogue of Crispus is quite plausible, since they were already members of his household. There are other evidences that children were part of synagogue procedures. One scholar says, "Children were occasionally called 'rulers of the synagogue,' which may mean that the title was hereditary."[15] Such titled children were most certainly included in synagogues. If this practice was in vogue in the first century, the children of Crispus would have been so titled. When some synagogues were transformed into churches, as seems the case with Crispus in Corinth, children would have maintained their place in these assemblies. The only other possibility is that these children were excommunicated from these synagogues when they were formed into churches, which is highly unlikely.

A synagogue may be in view in Paul's claim that his understudy and apostolic associate had known the Holy Scriptures since infancy (ἀπὸ βρέφους τὰ ἱερὰ γράμματα οἶδας; 2 Tm 3:15). "The sacred writings" or "the Holy Scriptures" is a clear reference to the entire Old Testament, and not simply certain parts. These scrolls were so costly that it is improbable and nearly impossible that the ordinary people had copies in their homes. Private ownership of biblical documents was the prerogative of the titled wealthy, such as the "minister of Candace the queen of the Ethiopians, [who was] in charge of all her treasure" (Acts 8:27). Apart from the issue of whether or not Timothy's mother or grandmother had the means to purchase scrolls for family possessions, it is unlikely that women would have been given the responsibility of reading them even to their own children. Timothy's Greek and presumably unbelieving father (Acts 16:1) would hardly have performed this sacred Jewish obligation. Home Bible study is a modern phenomenon which became religiously fashionable first with seventeenth-century Pietism. Biblical scrolls were, however, the treasured possession of the

---

14. Ibid.
15. Claudia J. Seizer, "Rulers of the Synagogue," in *Anchor Bible Dictionary* 6:841–42.

synagogues, which were more the centers of Jewish life in the Diaspora where they had originated.[16] So there seems to be no other reasonable possibility than that Timothy, uncircumcised as he was, had heard the Holy Scriptures read in the synagogue where he was taken by his mother and grandmother soon after birth. Biblical scrolls in the practices of both the synagogue and the church were for public reading. Since the pious Jewish boy Timothy was instructed in the sacred writings already in infancy, his inclusion in the synagogue seems highly probable.

Another evidence for the inclusion of children in synagogue and church is that Timothy had acquired faith through his mother and grandmother (2 Tm 1:4–5). Paul's preaching of Christ to Timothy built on the foundation which had been placed there in infancy. So it seems highly likely that Jewish synagogues which accepted Jesus as the Christ, as in the case of Crispus's synagogue, would have brought their children with them when these assemblies called themselves churches. Additional research may expand our knowledge of the structures of first-century synagogues, but the evidence at hand strongly suggests that children, even infants, were members. Timothy, who was obligated by Paul to attend to the public reading of the Scriptures as pastor and bishop (1 Tm 4:13), had begun his training for this sacred duty as an infant (2 Tm 3:15).

Jeremias's and Aland's debate was not about whether such households served as churches, but whether children were included in them.[17] This debate is important, not because the practice of infant Baptism is necessarily derived from recorded apostolic customs, but because a negative finding would lend support to those opposing it. Aland's arguments were important for Baptists, even though he himself, to their dismay, was not persuaded by them to give up baptizing children. Theological convictions overcame his own historical conclusions. An argument from silence is not conclusive, but cannot be dismissed simply because it does not support our conclusions. Demonstrating that only adults in these households were baptized would support the view that infants were not and still should not be baptized. It must be granted that the New Testament does not say in so many words that infants were baptized. But this same argument could be used in regard to women receiving Holy Communion: there is no New Testament reference. Consider that it is frequently claimed that Jesus never says "I am the Son of God," but He obviously did (Mt 27:43). We are not looking for an ex-

---

16. Werblowsky and Wigoder, *Oxford Dictionary*, s.v. "Synagogue."

17. Consider that Dale Moody's reference sheepishly points out that "house" in 1 Sm 22:16 mentions "oxen, asses and sheep" along with men, children, and sucklings (*Baptism*, 128, n. 62). Appreciating Moody's humor, it can be pointed out that the New Testament households were urban. If the New Testament were written to a rural audience, we can assume that the barnyard animals would have been exempted from the Baptism.

cuse to discredit historical arguments, but must insist that all parties to the dispute use them in the same way.

It is not surprising that the book of Acts should recount how adults heard the Gospel and were baptized, since Acts is an account of the missionary church, how the church was planted in the Roman Empire, and not how life developed in these congregations. Absence of the mention of children is not an unusual phenomenon. Unless a gathering is specifically for children, they are not mentioned. This is more so of infants. Without denying their legal rights, they simply are rarely factors in public affairs and so are not included in historical reports. Where they are mentioned, they are not distinguished from adults. Great men in the ancient world are often reported to have had marvelous childhoods, but these are clearly later and imaginary reflections. More informative and detailed about an established, matured church are the Pauline epistles. They are not missionary documents but treatises on how Christians should act and what they should believe. Quite naturally, accounts of the church's later developments, especially in the post-apostolic period, provide explicit historical detail about baptizing infants. This does not mean that Acts and the rest of the New Testament do not make mention of children at all. Perhaps an analogy from our own history would not be inappropriate. History records that the first citizens of the United States were the signers of the Declaration of Independence and soldiers in the War for American Independence. Though children are not mentioned as citizens, they obviously were. Today, citizenship is conferred in the overwhelming majority of cases by birth and not by an open act of allegiance. This analogy is not offered as a conclusive argument, but only as an illustration of how children are included in groups other than the church.

In his sermon on Pentecost, which culminates in the Baptism of three thousand, Peter asserts that the promise of the forgiveness of sins in Baptism and the giving of the Holy Spirit are for the hearers and their children (Acts 2:39). While this assertion contains the promise that the church will survive for generations (Mt 16:18), it includes the children of those who were present in the promise. "Children" refers to more than those not yet at the point of maturity, but it certainly includes them. This passage also serves as the Magna Carta for the rest of Acts. The promise made to those baptized on the first Pentecost applies to all those recorded in Acts as being baptized. The promise including their children is given to them also. Thus, by the end of the first century the church is literally everywhere. Peter and Paul were examples in their ministries of what all the apostles and their successors were doing. Nothing is said of the ministry of nine of the twelve apostles originally present in Jerusalem. But what was done in Acts was done countless times by these apostles throughout the Roman Empire. Peter's minis-

Infant Baptism: An Historical Debate

try, for example, is much more extensive than what is reported in Acts. After his release from prison, with the exception of the council of Jerusalem (Acts 15:8), he disappears (Acts 12:17), but this hardly means that his ministry came to an end. Sound evidence exists that he went to Rome.[18] Only a fraction of Peter's and Paul's careers is preserved in Acts. These comparatively few episodes were characteristic of countless apostolic practices in Persia and North Africa. What was happening in the churches mentioned in Acts was happening everywhere the apostles went: "And they went forth and preached everywhere" (Mk 16:20). Even if this passage does not belong to the original Mark, it is descriptive of what happened. This preaching everywhere included preaching in households and baptizing them.

Households of the ancient world were self-contained social units including the father, the mother, their children, the servants and slaves and their children, and anyone else who might be attached to them for business or agricultural reasons. In size, some approximated small villages. The argument for baptizing infants centers on whether there were any present in the households of Cornelius, Lydia, or the jailer in Philippi. As with most historical arguments, absolute certainty remains elusive, but possibility and even degrees of probability can be shown. The *possibility* that any or all of these households contained children cannot be denied, since children are by definition part of the households of the ancient world. It is highly probable that children were in all of these households. Pieper advances this argument.[19] Even if the head of the household was childless, his servants were not. A childless household would have been the exception. That the three households mentioned in Acts were all childless is highly improbable.

First Corinthians also speaks of baptizing households. While Paul says he baptized only the household of Stephanas, by clear implication he also baptized the households of Gaius and Crispus. Then add the households which Paul is grateful to God not to have baptized himself, but which had been baptized (1 Cor 1:14). This had to be a significant number for him to be so thankful! Beyond these add the hundreds, yes thousands, of households in which the apostles preached and which were formed into churches. Not only did the great majority doubtless include children, but indeed, the one without children would have been rare! The ancient world, unlike the modern one, did not know of detached single persons living by themselves, but all, master and slave, husband and wife, adult and child, widowed parents, were embraced within the family or household unit. Persons were encouraged to marry

---

18. John Wenham, *Redating Matthew, Mark and Luke* (Downers Grove, IL: InterVarsity Press, 1992), 146–72. The chapter is entitled "The Date of Peter's Going to Rome."
19. Pieper, *Christian Dogmatics* 3:277–78.

and have children at a much younger age than is customary now. There is enough evidence to suggest that these household structures were not eradicated but embraced within the church (cf. Gal 3:28, Eph 5:21–6:9, and 1 Jn 2:12–14). They were practicing churches (1 Cor 16:15, 19).

Minimally it must be said that the New Testament, from a historical perspective, does not categorically rule out the Baptism of infants and children. From the laws of historical probability, the arguments lean with a vengeance in the opposite direction. The historical conclusion is that from the very beginning, children and infants were baptized. We are faced with substantiating one of two options: either (1) the early church did not baptize infants, but an unknown person later introduced this practice which was foreign to established church custom; or (2) the church from earliest times did baptize children. The former option has more problems, because no report exists of any disruption accompanying its introduction. It is reasonable to think that someone would have objected to the introduction of what would have been immediately recognized as a non-apostolic custom. Customs were important. Removing circumcision from the list of required customs almost split the church. Arguments against infant Baptism cannot explain why there is no record of objections raised against its introduction. Historical arguments by themselves are inconclusive, but such evidence cannot be used selectively by the opponents of infant Baptism to prove their position, while other evidence detrimental to their position is ignored.[20]

Another demonstration for infant Baptism is that the New Testament includes infants in the church. These are not chiefly historical but exegetical arguments, because they depend on how the texts are read.[21] Our Confessions argue the matter theologically, and it is introduced as a corollary to the doctrine of original sin: "All men who are propagated according to nature are born in sin," with the only solution provided by a rebirth (*renascantur*) through "Baptism and the Holy Spirit" (AC II.1, 2).[22] At the start of the Reformation, infant Baptism was virtually the only form of Baptism practiced. The meaning can be only that infants born with sin (*nascantur cum peccato*) require for salvation the rebirth of Baptism and the Holy Spirit (*renascuntur per baptismum et spiritum sanc-*

---

20. Grudem's chief argument against including children in households is that, with the exception of Lydia, those baptized are described as believing or doing something (*Systematic Theology*, 978). The household of the jailer at Philippi heard the Word and received it with joy. Also, the household of Stephanas devoted themselves to the service of the saints. Since for Grudem children, especially infants, cannot believe, they are excluded. Their exclusion is a dogmatic and not an historical conclusion. His definition of faith, "I Must Decide to Depend on Jesus to Save Me Personally" (ibid., 710, a chapter heading), is not the biblical definition, but has the strong aroma of synergism.

21. For a summary of the issues involved, see Moody, *Baptism*, 127–61.

22. Tappert, 29; *BKS*, 53.

tum). All those who are born must be reborn through Baptism to obtain salvation. Baptism is not only a privilege for infants as those who have been redeemed by Christ, but it was seen as a necessity for salvation, as discussed above.

Prominent in the Lutheran presentation of infant Baptism is the universal command to baptize the nations recorded in Mt 28:19, which is taken to include children as well as adults (Ap. IX.2).[23] The equally universal dimensions of the atonement embracing all people are essential to the universality of the command to baptize. Thus, the command to baptize does not hang suspended as a divine, sovereign fiat demanding blind obedience from the church, but is a necessary conclusion of the atonement by which Christ has embraced children.

The Lutheran Confessions do not pursue this line of reasoning explicitly, but it is suggested by their outline of theology. Immediately following the Augsburg Confession's article on original sin, which includes children in its scope, comes the article on Christ, "who was born of the virgin Mary, truly suffered, was crucified, dead, and buried, that he might reconcile the Father to us and be a sacrifice not only for original sin but also for all actual sins of men."[24] Christ has ascended on high to give the Holy Spirit to bestow the blessings earned by His saving acts on those who believe (AC III.4). Only those stand forgiven before God (*coram Deo*) who are justified for Christ's sake through faith (*iustificentur propter Christum per fidem*).[25] Article V speaks of the divine establishment of the ministry so that through the Word and sacraments the Holy Spirit may be given to create the faith needed for justification to be received. Article IX speaks specifically about baptizing children in order that they might be received into God's grace (*pueri ... per baptismum oblati Deo recipiuntur in gratiam Dei*).[26] This article, which speaks for the first time specifically to the Baptism of infants, only makes explicit what was already implicit in Articles II through V. Children are included in original sin (AC II), are embraced in the work of Christ (AC III), and need faith to stand before God as justified (AC IV), which can take place only through the ministry which offers grace through the sacraments (AC V). The argument is complete even before and without a separate article on Baptism. Though the Augsburg Confession does not address infant faith (*fides infantium*), it is the only conclusion possible. Children, like everyone else, are embraced in both the original sin of Adam and

---

23. "From Luther's point of view the command to administer baptism found at the end of the Gospel of St. Matthew puts an end to any debate about the sense or nonsense of baptizing children" (Oberman, *Luther*, 229).
24. AC III.2, 3; Tappert, 29–30; *BKS*, 54.
25. AC IV.1; Tappert, 30; *BKS*, 56.
26. AC IX.2; Tappert, 33; *BKS*, 63.

the atoning work of Christ. To be justified, they too need the faith which can be created only by the Holy Spirit, who works through the means of grace; and of these means, Baptism marks the regeneration of the person dead in sin. As valuable as the historical arguments for infant Baptism are, as shown above, the Lutheran Confessions' chief argument for it comes from their understanding of the universality of sin and grace: the theological principles of Law and Gospel are as applicable to children as they are to anyone else.

9

THE BIBLICAL SUPPORT FOR INFANT BAPTISM

The historical argument for infant Baptism based on the *oikos* (οἶκος) formula suggests a high probability that this was already being practiced by the apostles. By itself, any argument based on probability is not conclusive and hence cannot provide the support for that dogmatical certainty necessary to require its acceptance for salvation. Since inclusion in the church was dependent on Baptism, the case for infant Baptism can be advanced by showing from certain New Testament passages that children were included in the command to baptize, and are themselves also addressed in passages related to Baptism. The synoptic gospels, the Johannine writings, and the Pauline epistles will be surveyed to identify support for infant Baptism.

THE SYNOPTIC GOSPELS

The Lutheran Confessions deduce the Baptism of infants from Mt 28:19, where the disciples are commanded to baptize all the nations, including children.[1] The use of this passage invites examination of the matter of infant Baptism in the light of other parts of this gospel. Following the command to baptize is the command to teach *all* things. Matthew is clearly referring to the words of Jesus which he recorded. Among these necessary teachings of Jesus is that children should have *the* prominent place in the kingdom of the heavens. Strategically placed between Jesus' second (Mt 17:22, 23) and third (Mt 20:17–28) announcements of His death and resurrection are the two pericopes of the children (Mt 18:1–4 and 19:13–15), with the entry into Jerusalem recorded in chapter 21. The placement of the pericopes of the children within Jesus' prediction of His death and entry into Jerusalem makes it clear that Matthew intends his readers to see the children as those whom Jesus has included in His work of the world's atonement. The children are among the "many" for whom the Son of Man gives His life as a ransom (Mt 20:28).

The question is whether the pericopes, which hold up the child as an example for those entering the kingdom (Mt 18:1–4) and which record His blessing of them (Mt 19:13–15), have anything to do with Baptism

---

1. "Just as salvation is there offered to all, so Baptism is offered to all—men, women, children, and infants" (Ap. IX.2–3; Tappert, 178; *BKS*, 247).

The Biblical Support for Infant Baptism

at all. The question has liturgical importance, since the parallel to Matthew 19 in Mk 10:13–16 is ordinarily the gospel read in Lutheran and other Western rites of infant Baptism. Many, including some Lutherans, hold that the pericopes have no reference to Baptism and that their liturgical usage is awkward, or at best an accommodation to provide an appropriate reading from the gospels.[2] This inability or unwillingness to make a connection between the pericopes of the children and the command to baptize often results from a failure to consider the gospels as self-contained theological treatises. They are not random collections of historical events, but are *theologies* about Jesus. To regard the gospels as a collection of historical anecdotes would tend to support the Baptist position that there is no evidence that Jesus baptized children. Many Lutherans adopt this same approach, and are content with theological arguments from the universality of sin and salvation and the deduction from Mt 28:19. The command to teach all things requires that *all* the prior material determine who should be baptized and instructed.

Take, for example, the pericopes of the two centurions, the one with the stricken servant (Mt 8:5–13) and the other at the cross (Mt 27:51–54). When the reader comes to the gospel's end, he already knows who those Gentiles are who are to be baptized. In both cases the centurions have fulfilled the baptismal requirement of making a confession of faith. They are examples of candidates for Baptism. In the case of the first centurion, there is no reason to assume that he did not receive the pre-resurrection baptism of John or Jesus. Similarly, the pericopes of the children inform the baptismal command. Children are included in the kingdom, hence they are entitled to Baptism and indeed must be baptized. Regin Prenter supports this line of reasoning: "When Jesus says that the kingdom of God belongs to little children, there can be no doubt about his including them in that congregation of tax collectors and sinners who through repentance and faith are gathered about the Son of Man."[3]

So far our argument of their inclusion in the kingdom by Baptism is by inference, but it can be supported by the specific details of the pericopes themselves. In Mt 18:1–5 children not only are allowed into the kingdom and seen as members, but are understood as exemplary for others. Pieper comments on Mt 18:6, stating that children have faith and are not future but present members of the church.[4] Their place in the kingdom is more certain than that of adults: "Unless you turn and become like children . . ." (Mt 18:3). This pericope initiated by the ques-

---

2. Such Baptist theologians as Beasley-Murray (*Baptism in the New Testament*) and Grenz (*Community of God*) pay them no heed in their arguments against infant Baptism.
3. *Creation and Redemption*, 471.
4. *Christian Dogmatics* 3:277.

tion "Who is the greatest in the kingdom of heaven?" is paralleled by the one initiated by the request of the mother of James and John to give them seats "one at your right hand and one at your left, in your kingdom" (Mt 20:21). Both deal with the most prominent positions in the kingdom. In the first, Mt 18:1–5, Jesus resolves the difficulty by putting a child in their midst and admonishing them to become like him or her (Mt 18:4), and in the second they are instructed to follow the servanthood of Jesus who gave His life as a ransom (Mt 20:26–28).

Baptism is not incidental to these pericopes. Matthew has made it clear at the beginning of his gospel that Baptism is required for inclusion in the kingdom. In both the ministries of John the Baptist (Mt 3:1–6) and Jesus (Mt 4:17), preparation for the kingdom which is coming with Jesus involves confessing and being baptized. Suddenly the baptism of John is not an incidental historical question, because quite evidently those whom Matthew lists as coming to Jesus and being found acceptable by Him are those who confess and are baptized. The argument for infant Baptism is virtually proven.

Matthew even addresses the conversion or repentance of children (Mt 18:3)! This is the important issue raised by the opponents of infant Baptism who claim that children are not capable of contrition and faith. They "have not yet developed to the point of making moral choices" and therefore "do not fall under the eternal condemnation of a righteous God."[5] This is how they interpret Matthew 18. Clearly the Baptist position on faith as moral decision is nothing less than Pelagian, and excusing children from divine judgment is modified universalism! Others hold to the same view of Baptism and see children as incapable of faith, but baptize them nevertheless. Luther considered this position to be dogmatically intolerable. Baptism must never be administered where it is certain that faith is impossible or simply not present. Lutherans do not contest the Baptist argument that faith must be present for Baptism;[6] they contest the Baptist definition of faith and assert that children can have faith.

The pericopes involving Jesus are striking because they contrast those whom the early Christians knew as apostles (Mt 10:1–2, 28:16–20) with children who are held up as examples of conversion. Apostles are entrusted with "the faith," *fides quae*, of the church, and the children believe it, *fides qua*! Even for the apostles themselves the only solution is to

---

5. Grenz, *Community of God*, 271.
6. The Baptist theologian Dale Moody recognizes this: "Individual faith has been the concern of both Lutherans and Baptists" (*Baptism*, 298). Luther, Lutheran orthodoxy, and now only confessional-minded Lutherans see faith as a prerequisite for Baptism, a view rarely supported by Lutheran theologians since the eighteenth-century Enlightenment.

The Biblical Support for Infant Baptism

become like the believing children. Unless they do, they will have no part in Jesus. Their faith must become that of infants, *fides infantium*. Here the counterargument, that infants cannot believe, is that the Greek word for child, *paidion* (παιδίον), refers to an older child who has sufficient consciousness to confess his sins. This argument cannot stand, since the children (*paidas*, παῖδας) slaughtered by Herod have not reached their second year or birthday (Mt 2:16). Since the Jews quite appropriately considered the actual day of birth to be the first birthday, the first year anniversary of birth was the second. The massacred children had not begun their second year of life. In our popular reckoning our "birth day" is not our first birthday. While it is impossible to determine the age of the child whom Jesus placed in the disciples' midst (Mt 18:2), the children (*paidia*, παιδία) of Mt 19:13, at least in Matthew's usage, included infants. The child of Mt 18:2 presumably was standing and could easily have been a one-year-old.

In Mt 19:13–15 the disciples are incensed that children (*paidia*, παιδία) are being brought to Jesus for a blessing. Here Luke more precisely identifies them as infants (*brefe*, βρέφη; 18:15), children who have just been born. Again Jesus refers to their place in the kingdom, and says that nothing should prevent their admittance into it. All three synoptic evangelists conclude with Jesus' blessing them by laying His hands on them (Mt 19:13, 15; Mk 10:13, 16; Lk 18:15). It simply will not do to suggest that this blessing by hands was inconsequential. Matthew and Mark each included two references to the hands and Jesus' touch. Through the hands a blessing was given which included them in the kingdom. In Acts the laying on of hands is part of the Baptism and the occasion for the giving of the Holy Spirit (Acts 8:17). Certainly Jesus' laying His hands on the children was not *the* Pentecost of the Holy Spirit which came only after Christ's death (Mt 27:50) and resurrection, but the One who had received the Spirit in His Baptism (Mt 3:16) was working faith in those children *by that same Spirit* in Himself (Mt 18:6). God's kingdom which Jesus brings comes with the Spirit of God (Mt 12:28). The laying on of the hands of Jesus does not simply display His fondness for children, and is no empty liturgical gesture. One could use Lutheran sacramental terminology in saying that the Word was attached to those hands, but these were the hands of the eternal Word of the Father who works only through the Holy Spirit. The image here was of infant Baptism.

Joachim Jeremias, a professor with chairs both in Basel and Paris, took another approach to these pericopes. He focused on the words "do not prevent them" (Mt 19:14; Mk 10:14; Lk 18:16; my translation), as the word prevent or forbid (*koluein*, κωλύειν) was used in connection with the Baptism of the Ethiopian eunuch: "What is to prevent my being baptized?" (Acts 8:36). This Acts passage was seen by Cullmann as part of the oldest Baptism ritual.[7] Peter uses this phrase again with regard to the baptizing of the household of Cornelius: "Can anyone forbid water for baptizing these people who have received the Holy Spirit just as we have?" (Acts 10:47). The argument is not as tenuous as it might first seem. The Christians for whom the gospels were first intended understood them in the light of their own liturgical experiences, which included a recognition of Baptism as necessary for entering the church. Congregations would have heard the liturgical leader ask whether any impediment stood in the way of the catechumens receiving Baptism. Jesus' words that children should not be forbidden from coming to Him (Mt 19:14) would have been understood in the context of their Baptism. In both pericopes (Mt 19:14 and Mk 10:14) not only are children prominent, but these children belong to the kingdom. All four gospels contain accounts of John preaching that Baptism is necessary to enter the kingdom. In the non-sacramental environment of Protestant societies it may be hard to accept that the early Christian churches were formed by Baptism (Mt 28:19). Understanding that children may and must be baptized can come only from realizing that Baptism permeated early Christian consciousness.

For the rite of infant Baptism Lutherans use Mk 10:13–16 as the gospel reading, and not its parallels, Mt 19:13–15 and Lk 18:15–17. Matthew 18:1–14 provides a more thorough discussion of children's place in the kingdom, and Luke (18:15) uses the more precise term infants (*brefe*, βρέφη). Mark, however, offers the most graphic presentation of the actual blessing: "And [Jesus] taking them up in His arms gave them an intense blessing [*kateulogei* (κατευλόγει) and not merely *eulogei* (ευλόγει)] by placing His hands on them" (Mk 10:16; my translation). Though Mark does not use the word for infants in describing the children, it clearly seems implied by Jesus' taking them up in His arms. The word for blessing, *eulogei* (ευλόγει), is used in Jesus' blessing of the bread in the Supper (Mk 14:22). Paul also has a eucharistic usage for the word: "The cup of blessing which we bless, is it not the communion of the blood of Christ?" (1 Cor 10:16 KJV). Add to this that Jesus is greeted with "Blessed is he who comes in the name of the Lord!" (εὐλογημένος ὁ ἐρχόμενος ἐν ὀνόματι κυρίου; Mt 21:9). Thus, the word "bless" has both a christological and a sacramental significance. To this we add that what is sacramental is inherently christological. Children are brought into the arena of the sacraments, where Christ Himself embraces them with salvation.

All three evangelists include the reference to receiving the child in Christ's name as in fact receiving Him (Mt 18:5; Mk 9:37; Lk 9:48), which

---

7. *Christian Baptism in the New Testament*, trans. J. K. S. Reid, Studies in Biblical Theology, no. 1 (London: SCM Press, 1950), 71–80.

also suggests Baptism. In the book of Acts, Baptism was "in the name of the Lord Jesus." The evangelists look upon children as members of a baptized community of believers, that is, the church. Matthew alone has the warning against offending the little ones who believe in Him: being tossed into the Mediterranean with a millstone around one's neck would be a better fate for such offenders (Mt 18:6). Such a phrase may be taken literally or as hyperbole, but it is more likely a reference to excommunication from the Christian community. The parable of the lost sheep (Mt 18:10–14) is introduced by another warning not to despise "these little ones . . . [whose] angels always behold the face of [Jesus'] Father." Matthew reinforces the high place of children in the response of Jesus to the chief priests and the scribes. They have become incensed that children are singing His praises on His entry into Jerusalem (Mt 21:14–16); Jesus responds, "Have you never read, 'Out of the mouths of babes and sucklings thou hast brought perfect praise'?" Matthew's strong attention to children, whether these pericopes are taken separately or collectively, proves that for Jesus and the early church, children were regarded as participants in Jesus' kingdom work and thus entitled to Baptism. It cannot be overlooked that all three synoptic evangelists include both of these pericopes of children. Combined there are six references to their participation in the kingdom. We can only speculate whether some in the first century denied children a place in the church. There were concerns about how the Gentiles should be incorporated. Matthew's sharp rebukes against those who stand in the way of children and Mark's graphic description of Jesus and the children may suggest that the Anabaptists were not the first to raise doubts about the status of children. Luther went so far as to deny salvation to those who had contempt for baptizing children.[8] Jesus did the same (Mt 18:5–9).

A word should be said about whether Jesus Himself baptized the children. The identical descriptions of the ministries of John and Jesus (Mt 3:2 and 4:17) imply that Jesus also baptized, though the synoptic gospels have no explicit reference to this activity. The fourth gospel makes Jesus' baptizing ministry explicit, but adds that the disciples and not Jesus did the actual baptizing (Jn 4:1–2). But that aside, the gospels do not inform us about who precisely was baptized, and it is only an assumption to conclude that therefore only adults were baptized and not children. The Jews, in the tradition of the Old Testament, included children in all their religious festivals, including the all-important festival of the Passover, and thus it seems probable that they were not excluded from the baptism of John, which for them had eschatological significance in the announcement of the last times. Infant boys were

---

8. Trigg, *Baptism*, 41; *AE* 3:103.

included by circumcision in Israel as God's redeemed and redemptive community. If they were included in the redemptive liturgical rites of the Passover, they would hardly have been excluded from the consummation of God's redemptive work in the day of judgment. Of course, Luther argues in just this way.[9]

The inclusiveness of Mt 28:19, which is basic to the confessional presentation of infant Baptism, is not an isolated reference but only continues the universality of John's baptism: "All Judea and all the region about the Jordan" came to John to be baptized (Mt 3:5, 6).[10] Matthew has a penchant for the word "all," and his "all nations [or Gentiles]" of 28:19 is already suggested in Mt 3:5–6 with "all the region about the Jordan." Jesus' mission to extend His kingdom was already beginning with the baptism of John. "All the nations" to whom Baptism is given will stand before God in judgment (Mt 25:32). Certainly here there is no distinction in regard to ethnicity, race, or age! It is far too simple to conclude that John or Jesus, that is, His disciples, did not baptize children. The evidence, in fact, points in just the opposite direction. In baptizing the children in the households, mentioned in Acts, the apostles were probably continuing a practice used by them as the disciples of Jesus before His crucifixion.

JOHANNINE WRITINGS

John rarely offers precise parallels to the synoptic gospels, and, expectedly, he has no pericopes about the children. Absence of clear parallels to the synoptic pericopes is not surprising. The Fourth Evangelist is more likely to substitute new material for that found in the synoptics, if indeed he used them. His Nicodemus pericope (Jn 3:1–15, especially v. 4, with the query about the possibility of an old man going

---

9. *AE* 3:103.

10. Commenting on Mt 28:19, Davies and Allison make this observation: "Matthew, despite his insistence on upholding the Jewish law, never mentions circumcision. That he expected Jewish Christians to circumcise their male children is plausible; but he evidently did not think such necessary for Gentiles. Perhaps his belief in baptism explains this. Had baptism come to replace circumcision as the ritual of entry for his church? Certainly this was so for the author of Colossians; see 2:11–12" (*Matthew* 3:685). We may dispute whether Matthew insisted on the keeping of the law for Jewish Christians; however, these scholars have provided a prima facie case for infant Baptism. If Baptism became "the ritual of entry for his church" in the place of circumcision, even if it were only for Gentiles, then at least the male infants would have been baptized. If Matthew had a Jewish Christian congregation with only a few Gentiles, then the absence of any mention of circumcision is even more mystifying. There is no reason to conclude that circumcision had no real meaning for Matthew. It may have been practiced, but hardly required or even encouraged. Perhaps the argument can be taken further: that John's baptism had already begun to take the place of circumcision. This possibility is suggested by the Baptist's warning that descent from Abraham, which was marked by circumcision, is no longer the guarantee of salvation (Mt 3:9).

back into his mother's womb to obtain the rebirth necessary for entrance into the kingdom of God) can be taken as a parallel to the synoptic accounts of the children. Whether or not this was the evangelist's intention, scholars note similarities.[11] Certainly the current Lutheran rite of infant Baptism makes a connection by including both texts. In both cases, conversion involves becoming as little children, even though in the case of John the example is more extreme, going beyond childhood to the time before birth. Lutherans traditionally have used Jn 3:5 to demonstrate the necessity of rebirth through Baptism, and from that have concluded the necessity of infant Baptism. Certainly the language of AC II.2, *renascuntur per baptismum et spiritum sanctum*, seems to be that of Jn 3:5, "born of water and the Spirit." The thematic goal both for the synoptic gospels' pericopes on the children and for John's Nicodemus account is how one enters the kingdom. The disciples must become like children, and Nicodemus must be born again. In a sense, the Nicodemus account is more radical in its demand for rebirth. Though he misinterprets "birth from on high" (my translation) as an actual birth from his mother—this is the theological and literary genius of the account—Nicodemus does recognize that Jesus is asking something truly revolutionary of him. He must become a different person, something which he either does not understand or does not want. This, according to Jesus, happens in Baptism. It is no wonder that the Baptists, as did Calvin, attempt to remove any reference to Baptism from Jn 3:5.

There is a similarity between Nicodemus entering his mother's womb for the second time and Paul's understanding that the Christian becomes a new man in Christ. In the New Testament the imagery of both birth and death is used for Baptism. John holds, as we have discussed, that Nicodemus must undergo a new or different kind of birth, one from on high. Paul speaks of Baptism as a burial with Christ and a subsequent resurrection to a new life (Rom 6:4). While John uses the language of birth in describing Baptism and Paul uses the language of death and resurrection, a fundamental structure is common to both themes: the one who undergoes Baptism becomes a new person in Christ. Nicodemus's birth from on high requires that what he was previously must be put to death. After Baptism he will not be the same person, but will be "resurrected" as a different person. His flesh prevents him from accepting the birth from on high. Paul's resurrection language in describing Baptism brings him to a like conclusion: the baptized will experience a life which he has not known before. Resurrection through Baptism is in every sense a birth to a new life (ἵνα ὥσπερ ἠγέρθη Χριστὸς ἐκ νεκρῶν διὰ τῆς δόξης τοῦ πατρός, οὕτως καὶ ἡμεῖς ἐν καινότητι ζωῆς

---

11. See Brown, *Gospel According to John* 2:143–44.

περιπατήσωμεν; Rom 6:4). The similarity does not end here. Paul makes the Christian's experience in Baptism analogous to Christ's death and resurrection. John makes the Christian's being born from on high in Baptism analogous to Christ's birth (generation) from God. This analogy is suggested, even evident, in Jn 1:13, where Christians are said to be born from God: οἳ οὐκ ἐξ αἱμάτων οὐδὲ ἐκ θελήματος σαρκὸς οὐδὲ ἐκ θελήματος ἀνδρὸς ἀλλ᾽ ἐκ θεοῦ ἐγεννήθησαν. Variant readings and the patristic evidence favor the singular over the plural, and so make this verse a reference to the virgin birth of Christ, who is born from God without the aid of a human father. Raymond Brown opposes this interpretation on the grounds that texts tend to move in a christological direction over the course of time, though he acknowledges that the logic of the opening prologue (Jn 1:1–14) favors this view: the Word which was with God from the beginning is made flesh.[12] On the other hand, a reference to the conversion of Christians in Jn 1:13 would be strangely out of place.

Though this argument cannot be resolved here, either set of variants indicates that very early in the church, perhaps during the evangelist's own lifetime, the correlation between Christ's incarnation and Christian regeneration through Baptism was recognized. John 1:13 and the Nicodemus pericope (Jn 3:1–10) share a common thought-pattern and vocabulary. The Jewish leader does not grasp what it means to be born from on high (γεννηθῆναι ἄνωθεν; Jn 3:7), which is also called being born from the water and the Spirit (γεννηθῇ ἐξ ὕδατος καὶ πνεύματος; Jn 3:5). Christians are born from God (Jn 1:13), if the plural is the correct reading. If Paul can speak of Christians being buried and raised with Christ, John speaks of Christians being born in Baptism by the Spirit with the same vocabulary of Christ being born from above into this world (ἐγὼ εἰς τοῦτο γεγέννημαι καὶ εἰς τοῦτο ἐλήλυθα εἰς τὸν κόσμον; Jn 18:37). It would seem very strange that the evangelist's use of birth language in describing Jesus' entry into the world and Christians' regeneration from above and through water and the Spirit should exclude the smallest of children, who are closest to the experience of birth. Christ's own infancy, His coming into the world from God, may provide the strongest support for baptizing infants, though this theme is rarely made central to the discussion.[13]

John in his first letter addresses the congregation as his children (*teknia*, τεκνία). This term may suggest any or all of three options: he is an old man; he established the congregation and hence has a special relationship to it (Jn 2:1, 12, 28); or that as an elder (*presbyteros*,

---
12. For a fuller discussion of this topic, see ibid. 1:10–13.
13. See Judith M. Lieu, "The Mother of the Son," *Journal of Biblical Literature* 117 (Spring 1998): 75–76.

πρεσβύτερος), he is like a father to the members of the congregation (2 Jn 1; 3 Jn 1). There is no suggestion that the members have not reached the age of majority. John does, however, divide his children (*teknia*, i.e., the congregation; 1 Jn 2:12) into three groups: fathers, young men, and children, *paidia* (1 Jn 2:12–14). Three age categories are evident: those who are older, those still in the prime of life, and children, among whom infants would be included. The theme of this pericope concerning victory (1 Jn 2:13) reappears in the pericope on Baptism (1 Jn 5:4). Jesus as God's Son now comes to the church in the water (i.e., Baptism; 1 Jn 5:5–6): "This is he who came by water and blood, Jesus Christ." Another reference to Baptism appears in the previous section, where John specifically addresses the children (*paidia*): "[Their] sins have been forgiven *through his name*" (1 Jn 2:12; my translation).[14] In these pericopes the language, like that of John's gospel, is clearly sacramental. Baptism was offered in the name of Jesus, and it forgave sins. The children (*paidia*) are included among those whose sins have been forgiven in this way (1 Jn 2:14). They are all said to "know the Father," a knowledge which is given by the Son through the Spirit in Baptism (cf. Mt 11:27).[15]

For John, Baptism and faith are seen as necessary for inclusion in the fellowship of Jesus Christ. The child of God is identified as "every one who believes that Jesus is the Christ" (1 Jn 5:1). Similarly, in classical baptismal terminology, the one who overcomes the world is said to be born of God (1 Jn 5:4). Jesus Christ is now the One who comes to the church through the water of Baptism, the blood of the Lord's Supper, and the testimony of the Holy Spirit in preaching (1 Jn 5:6–8).[16] In 1 John the congregation is addressed as "my little children" (2:1), "little children" (2:12), "children" (2:18), and each individual member as "a child of God" (5:1). Second John speaks of the members as the children of "the elect lady" (v. 1) and "children of [her] elect sister" (v. 13), that is, children of the church. Designating members of the congregation as children expresses their relationship to John, who calls himself an elder (2 Jn 1); this term probably has a double reference, one to his age as an old man and the other to his position as their pastor. It probably also carries with it the idea that he was the one who baptized them, and that in the stead of Christ he was exercising the role of a father to them. In this context he presumed to write a letter to them as his children. (This

---

14. The RSV omits reference to Christ's name. In rendering this translation "your sins are forgiven for his sake" (Γράφω ὑμῖν, τεκνία, ὅτι ἀφέωνται ὑμῖν αἱ ἁμαρτίαι διὰ τὸ ὄνομα αὐτοῦ; 1 Jn 2:12), it obviates any possible reference to Baptism. The KJV preserves the full Greek text: "I write unto you, little children, because your sins are forgiven you for his name's sake."

15. For a discussion of various views on the defensibility of infant Baptism as biblical see Moody, *Baptism*.

16. This exegesis is corroborated by C. H. Dodd, B. F. Westcott, J. A. Findlay, H. Windisch, and E. K. Lee. See Beasley-Murray, *Baptism*, 239–40.

approach is similar to that of Paul, who asserts that he begot the Corinthians as Christians through the Gospel [1 Cor 4:15], though this analogy is diluted in the RSV: "For I became your father in Christ Jesus through the Gospel.") While these Johannine and Pauline references do not *prove* that individuals were baptized as infants, the possibility and even the suggestion in some cases that a Baptism of infants is indicated is quite strong, especially in the case of John, who is writing to a congregation that had been Christian for at least a generation. These were established congregations in which "little children" were regarded as members of equal standing with the others. Both Paul's and John's writings reflect upon and seem to draw upon the words of Jesus that unless His disciples become as little children, they will not enter the kingdom of God. The members of John's and Paul's congregations had a special relationship to them as children to fathers, since the word of the Gospel, which has the power to beget, was active on them through their Baptism.

PAUL'S EPISTLES

Several of Paul's epistles also indicate that infant Baptism was in place in the early church. In Col 2:11 Baptism is called the circumcision made without hands. Here Paul's prime thrust in the comparison of Baptism to circumcision is the removal of the flesh of the old nature (Col 2:11, 13), and not the inclusion of infants in Baptism. The reference to circumcision does suggest, however, that infants were included in the church by Baptism at this time, since the readers, whether Jews or Gentiles, would have understood this as a rite of infancy, required on the eighth day after birth. In Ephesians Paul includes them in his division of the congregation, where he addresses as separate units husbands, wives, children, parents, fathers, masters, and slaves (Eph 5:21–6:9). As part of the church, that is, the bride of Christ, they too have been washed by Baptism (Eph 5:25, 26).

First Corinthians 7:14 recognizes children as members of the congregation at Corinth, but by itself this passage is inconclusive in determining whether they were baptized. Again, Paul is addressing not primarily the status of children in the congregation, but the relationship between believing and unbelieving spouses. The believer should not divorce his unbelieving spouse, since through this union the unbeliever is sanctified, or made holy. Evidence of the salvific significance of the marital relationship is that the children are not unclean but holy. Paul is not referring here to children's moral innocence or internal holiness, but to their status as believers in the church. In conjunction with 1 Cor 6:11, the matter of whether these believing children were baptized is then capable of resolution. According to this earlier passage, the sanctified (those who are already holy) attain this status through a washing "in the name of the Lord Jesus Christ and of the Spirit of our God." The believer can have an influence on the unbelieving spouse simply by remaining in the marriage. This influence can be seen in their children, who have become members of the church through Baptism.

An argument for infant Baptism can also be drawn from Paul's reference to Israel's passing through the sea and under the cloud as a Baptism into Moses: "I want you to know, brethren, that our fathers were all under the cloud, and all passed through the sea, and all were baptized into Moses in the cloud and in the sea" (1 Cor 10:1–2). Here Moses is the salvific figure in whom all Israel was saved by being baptized into the water present in the cloud and the sea. Though Paul speaks of fathers, everyone, including women and the smallest children, passed through the sea and was baptized.

10

INFANT FAITH

Even the opponents of infant Baptism know that the lack of specific reference in the New Testament is not a foolproof argument for their position, and thus they too must argue the matter on theological grounds. The argument used most frequently against the Baptism of infants is the assertion that they are unable to believe, a position which is asserted rather than proven.[1] For Luther, the validity of the Baptism of infants does not rest on their faith, but he nevertheless firmly upheld it: "As we said, even if infants did not believe—which, however, is not the case, as we have proved—still their Baptism would be valid and no one should rebaptize them."[2] On the other hand, Luther said that if he were certain that children did not and could not believe, he would not baptize them.[3] Of course, he would not baptize any professed unbelievers. Luther is aware of the Anabaptist position which denies Baptism to children because they are alleged to be without faith, and responds that they do have faith. Thus, superficially the Lutheran and the Anabaptist position on the necessity of faith in connection with Baptism are the same. Luther, however, does not make faith a part of his definition of Baptism, nor does he understand faith as decision. Faith and Baptism are defined differently by Lutherans and Baptists.[4] Still, Lutherans and Baptists recognize that the New Testament requires faith for Baptism, though the Baptists have no tolerance for Luther's view of infant faith.[5]

---

1. Ultimately Grudem's main argument against baptizing infants is their inability to have faith. Arguments for infant Baptism based on the parallel between Baptism and circumcision and on the baptizing of households carry no weight with him because children do not have faith (*Systematic Theology*, 975–80). It must be noted that the pericopes on the blessing of the children play no role in his argument. He does allow, however, for a dedication ceremony (ibid., 983). Since the child does not differ from animals and inanimate objects in their inability to believe, these also might be included in such a ceremony.

2. LC IV.55; Tappert, 443; *BKS*, 702. For a complete discussion of Luther's views on infant faith see Karl Brinkel, *Die Lehre Luthers von der fides infantium bei der Kindertaufe* (Berlin: Evangelische Verlagsanstalt, 1957). For a reconstruction of Luther's position in the form of a dialog, see Uuras Saarnivaara, *Scriptural Baptism: A Dialog between John Bapstead and Martin Childfont* (New York: Vantage Press, 1953).

3. Hoffmann, "Baptism," 82.

4. Consider Grenz: "Because [it] cannot be an outward expression of faith, infant baptism also loses its value as a day to be remembered" (*Community of God*, 689).

5. Ibid., 688.

Infant Faith

The Lutheran Confessions do not know of any justification of the sinner apart from faith; thus, the Lutherans are consistent in affirming infant faith as a necessary dogmatic corollary of their doctrine of justification. Children have the Holy Spirit in Baptism, and this possession of the Spirit occurs only through faith (LC IV.49–51), though this has been contested by some Lutheran theologians.[6] A biblical argument for infant faith has been made by Lutheran theologians, beginning with Luther, Quenstedt, Walther, and Pieper.[7] John the Baptist leaps for joy in his mother's womb (Lk 1:41).[8] After holding up a child as an example of those who enter the kingdom, Jesus warns against offending "these little ones who believe in me"—that is, they are not to be treated as unbelievers (Mt 18:5). Pieper argues for infant faith apart from his discussion on Baptism,[9] which means that children can be saved apart from Baptism, but never without the Gospel and faith.[10] Luther argued

---

6. Paul Althaus, Sr., *Die Heilsbedeutung der Taufe im Neuen Testament* (Gütersloh: C. Bertelsmann, 1897). He took issue with Luther's concept of infant faith (ibid., 296), but nevertheless could speak of baptismal regeneration (*Taufwiedergeburt*).

7. Recently a defense of infant faith has been made by Hoffmann ("Baptism," 79–95; see especially the biblical arguments, 84–88). A still more recent contribution has been made by Bishop Eero Huovinen of Helsinki: "*Fides Infantium—Fides Infusa*?: A Contribution to the Understanding of the Faith of Children in Luther," *Lutheran Forum* 30 (Winter 1996): 37–42. In responding to Karl Brinkel's *Die Lehre Luthers von der fides infantium*, Huovinen sees infant faith as "poured-in faith by means of the Holy Spirit" (ibid., 40). Such a position is at odds with the view that the child is addressed by the Word of God through which the Holy Spirit works faith. To be sure, this definitely happens in Baptism, but it can happen even before the sacrament is administered.

8. Luther's remarks to the Anabaptists deserve preserving: "Who has made you so sure that baptized children do not believe in the face of what I here prove that they can believe? But if you are not sure, why then are you so bold as to discard the first Baptism, since you do not and cannot know that it is meaningless? What if all children in Baptism not only were able to believe but believed as well as John in his mother's womb? We can hardly deny that the same Christ is present at Baptism and in Baptism, in fact is himself the baptizer, who in those days came in his mother's womb to John. In Baptism he can speak as well through the mouth of the priest as when he spoke through his mother. Since then he is present, speaks, and baptizes, why should not his Word and Baptism call forth spirit and faith in the child as then it produced faith in John? He is the same who speaks and acts then and now" (AE 40:242–43).

9. *Christian Dogmatics* 2:44–49.

10. "The Order of Holy Baptism: The Baptism of Infants (without Sponsors)" in *The Lutheran Agenda* gives the impression that children are saved not by the Gospel but by Baptism: "But since little children are as yet unable to understand the Gospel, faith cannot be worked in them by telling them of Christ. We can never sufficiently thank God, therefore, that He has made Baptism a means whereby He works in little children with His divine grace, turning their hearts to faith, cleansing away their sins, and receiving them into His kingdom" ([St. Louis: Concordia Publishing House, 195–], 8). Open to a similar misinterpretation is the defense of infant Baptism in The Lutheran Church—Missouri Synod's edition of the Small Catechism: "Because Holy Baptism is the *only means* whereby infants, *who, too, must be born again, can ordinarily be regenerated and brought to faith* . . ." ([St. Louis: Concordia Publishing House, 1943], 173; emphasis original). Clarification is needed here. Baptism is as much the sacrament of regeneration for adults as it is for infants. However, if regeneration here simply means coming to faith, which

for infant faith in connection with his discussion on circumcision in his *Lectures on Genesis*, where he concluded that faith can exist before circumcision and Baptism.[11]

The Anabaptist arguments for the denial of infant faith were adopted by the eighteenth-century Rationalists and then by Schleiermacher, who held that children had not come to the first level of "self-consciousness" and so were incapable of a higher level of "God consciousness." Their arguments against infant faith were characteristically those of the Baptists, who denied infant Baptism because of the absence of a conscious decision.[12] The Rationalists and Schleiermacher found infant Baptism useful in maintaining the Christian community, though they preferred it be eliminated. Just how one proves or disproves that children are intellectually incapable of faith or knowledge in general is not addressed; that they have not come to a sufficient level of consciousness is often simply assumed, even by some proponents of infant faith when they compare infant believers to sleeping or mentally retarded adults.[13] Such a comparison is valuable, because it shows that faith does not depend on a certain level of intellectual development, an argument which the Baptists really cannot answer. This argument may itself be faulty, however, as will be shown below.

Many contemporary Lutheran theologians have assumed the Enlightenment view, espoused by Schleiermacher, that children cannot believe, yet still support infant Baptism.[14] For them, faith follows later in life.[15] This solution of prevenient grace was advocated by such con-

---

seems to be the intended and more generally accepted meaning, then Baptism is no more the only means of regeneration for infants than it is for adults. Calling Baptism the "only means" for infants denies they can come to faith apart from Baptism. The remainder of the sentence does allow for infant faith apart from Baptism, by saying that infants by Baptism "can ordinarily be regenerated and brought to faith." Ironically, Mk 10:13–15, which is cited for proof of this position that Baptism is the only means of grace for infants, makes no mention of this sacrament. As we have argued elsewhere, this pericope and its parallels in Matthew and Mark were intended by the evangelists to carry baptismal weight. Claiming that "little children are as yet unable to understand the Gospel" ironically contradicts the demand of Jesus that Christians are to follow their example in entering the kingdom, that is, by believing the Gospel. Though in an American Protestant society regeneration generally is associated only with coming to faith, as noted above, its biblical use also involves Baptism, as we have argued elsewhere.

11. *AE* 3:103.

12. So Grenz: "Infant baptism is performed by necessity in the absence of the participant's conscious faith" (*Community of God*, 687).

13. Pieper, *Christian Dogmatics* 2:449; Hoffmann, "Baptism," 89.

14. So Edmund Schlink, *Ökumenische Dogmatik*, 2nd ed. (Göttingen: Vandenhoeck & Ruprecht, 1985), 489. This influential Lutheran theologian claims that the relationship between Baptism and faith is complex. The faith needed for Baptism is supplied by the church, and self-reflecting faith will come later. He avoids the question in *The Doctrine of Baptism* (160).

15. So Paul Althaus, Jr., "Martin Luther über die Kindertaufe," in *Theologische Literaturzeitung* 12 (1948): 19–31. Concerning Althaus, Dale Moody writes, "He sees

fessional Lutheran scholars as Gustaf Aulen,[16] Paul Althaus, Jr., and Werner Elert.[17] In this view, grace in Baptism has an objectivity which does not require that infants believe at the time of their Baptism.[18] Such a view is common among the Reformed, who baptize infants without asserting that they believe. Calvin in the 1536 edition of his *Institutes* accepts the reality of infant faith.[19] Yet in the 1539 edition he quite clearly denies it. Here he says that infants have the seed of faith and repentance—what this seed is remains undefined—and they are baptized in regard to future repentance and faith.[20] Among recent Lutheran theologians, one happy exception to the denial of infant faith or Baptism offered in regard to future faith is the Danish theologian Regin Prenter, who defends Luther's view against this Baptist intrusion into Lutheran theology.[21] Frederick Dale Brunner, a neo-Evangelical scholar, publicly and happily expresses his agreement with Luther.[22] Pieper discusses infant faith in connection with infant Baptism, and follows Luther in insisting that it be present at the time of Baptism.[23] Still, he insists that faith can exist in infants apart from their Baptism.[24] Infant faith is not

---

infant faith in Luther only as a possibility for the future, not as a reality at the time of infant baptism" (*Baptism*, 120).

16. *The Faith of the Christian Church*, trans. Erich H. Wahlstrom and G. Everett Arden (Philadelphia: Muhlenberg Press, 1948), 379–85.

17. *Der Christliche Glaube*, 449–50. Also Helmut Thielicke, *The Evangelical Faith*, trans. Geoffrey W. Bromiley (Grand Rapids, MI: William B. Eerdmans, 1982). Gottfried Hoffmann makes the same observation about much contemporary Lutheran theology ("Baptism," 83).

18. Moody observes: "Lutheran debate on infant baptism indicates that confusion has arisen out of the conflict between the God-centered theology of Luther and the man-centered theology of Schleiermacher" (*Baptism*, 127).

19. "Therefore, the opinion stands firm, that no men are saved except by faith, whether they be children or adults. For this reason, baptism also rightly applies to infants who possess faith in common with adults" (trans. Ford Lewis Battles; Book IV, p. 101).

20. "I would not rashly affirm that they are endued with the same faith which we experience in ourselves, or have any knowledge at all resembling faith (this I would leave undecided) . . ." (Calvin, *Institutes* IV.XVI.19).

21. "Most of the modern apologetic for infant baptism is ineffective because it usually concedes the Baptist argument that children cannot have faith and then draws the very questionable conclusion that faith and Baptism are not necessarily inseparable. Baptism thus becomes a purely objective offer of salvation, which because it is absolutely objective can be made to anyone at any time. Accordingly, faith becomes a subjective attitude which man can take only after he has attained to a degree of intellectual development and is capable of making a decision. If this viewpoint is united with a view of adult baptism according to which faith must precede baptism, baptism following as a result of self-determining faith, then we have defended infant baptism at the price of our having embraced two entirely different forms of baptism, which have only the name in common. Such an essential difference between infant baptism and adult baptism is utterly foreign both to the New Testament and to Reformation thinking. It is a modern, post-Baptist innovation" (*Creation and Redemption*, 471).

22. *The Christ Book*, 95.

23. *Christian Dogmatics* 3:264–65.

24. Ibid. 3:448–49, "The Faith of Infants."

necessarily dependent on their being baptized. This is very important in the case of children who die without Baptism. Against the idea of baptizing infants on the basis of their future faith, the Baptist theologian Wayne Grudem rightly claims that there is no certainty that they will believe. The Lutheran position is that they do believe at the time of their Baptism.[25]

The allegedly scientifically demonstrated fact that infants are incapable of any cognitive thought is being challenged seriously by recent findings that the child's time in its mother's womb and the first days and weeks after birth are the child's most formative period.[26] An infant can distinguish his mother's voice from others and is capable of emotions. Other studies show that infants, even deaf children, are born with grammatical categories which enable them to learn not one but several languages, and to keep these separate from each other, before they reach the age of one. Many educational programs are based on the hypothesis that the first years are the most important for learning. Now this is not the basis for any argument for infant faith, but it certainly deserves more attention than those widely assumed but unproven claims that infants are without sufficient intellect, consciousness, or will.

Arguments for infant faith can be related to those offered in opposition to abortion. Opponents of abortion generally understand the un-

---

25. Grudem shows that Reformed paedobaptists agree with the Baptists in denying faith to infants and baptismal regeneration: "So the most accurate paedobaptist explanation of what baptism symbolizes is that it symbolizes *probable future regeneration*. It does not cause regeneration, nor does it symbolize actual regeneration; therefore it must be understood as symbolizing a probable regeneration at some time in the future" (*Systematic Theology*, 979). As welcome as this biting criticism is in showing the inconsistency in the Reformed reasoning for administering infant Baptism, Grudem makes no mention of the Lutheran doctrine of infant faith in connection with infant Baptism.

26. See for example Annette Karmiloff-Smith, "Annotation: The Extraordinary Cognitive Journey from Foetus through Infancy," *Journal of Child Psychology and Psychiatry and Allied Disciplines* 6/8 (1995): 1293–1313. Here is a portion of the abstract: "Reviews some of the exciting discoveries that have been made with respect to infant 'knowledge' in a number of areas, focusing on the capacities infants have to process auditory, visual, and cross-modal inputs. By the time they produce their first recognizable words, infants' brains have been actively processing the speech and language in the environment, using cues from prosody, structure, and distributional patterns to construct the particularities of the system underlying their native tongues. Infants often demonstrate surprisingly sophisticated capacities with respect to their cognitive inferences about the object behavior in the physical world, and differentiate these from the intentional and rational interpretations that they attribute to stimuli in the social world. Intermodal processing of input is a capacity that can be demonstrated in very young infants and serves them to make sense of the multiple overlapping environmental stimuli." This should answer a major objection to infant Baptism, that infants lack the capacity to believe. Surely if infant brains can process human language and make sense out of their environment, they can process the divine language which proceeds from the mouth of God and calls to faith. It would be strange to assert that the words of the Holy Spirit lack the efficaciousness which human language has with infants.

born as full and complete human beings with intellect, will, and emotions. Though scientific arguments for establishing the full personhood of the unborn can hardly establish the fact of infant faith, they should remove any prior scientific objections to infant faith based on their alleged lack of intellect and will. Since Baptists do not see infants as complete human beings, to be consistent they should have no reason for opposing abortion. Perhaps the argument should be turned around: since so many of the conservative Baptists are vehemently opposed to abortion, they should assert the full humanity of infants and fetuses, and assert that they are capable of faith and at birth should be baptized.

The question of when infants believe should be addressed, but cannot be answered with precision. Do they believe first when the water is applied with the trinitarian formula, or is faith possible before? As with any action of the Gospel, including the sacraments, precision in regard to time may not be possible. Luther, for example, can assert that infant faith is created by the exorcism, that part of the rite of Baptism which precedes the actual pouring of the water in the name of the Trinity, but he quickly adds that the Word present with the exorcism is no different than the one present in the water.[27] Luther understands the Word in Baptism as the dominical command within the entire rite.[28] Baptism takes place in the community of the baptized, who reaffirm their Baptism as their foundation by gathering "in the name of Jesus" or "in the name of the Father and of the Son and of the Holy Spirit." So Baptism determines the form of the church's liturgy and provides a context for its own administration. It is distinguished from the other forms of the Word of God or the Gospel by the use of water, but it does not on that account become separable or isolated from them. All forms of the Word— the reading of the Scriptures, the liturgy, the hymns, the prayers, the rite of Baptism and its actual administration—have inherent power to convert. The child in, before, or during the rite of Baptism comes under all forms of the Word of God, by which faith is awakened. This Word culminates in the application of the water administered in the name of the Father-Son–Holy Spirit. In Baptism, God "preaches" to the child and he believes. Everything which God is and has is given to the child. This is pure Luther! "In Baptism the voice of the Trinity sounds, and words of Baptism must not be heard or received in any other way."[29]

---

27. *WA* 11:301.26ff. Children receive faith "when they are exorcized through the power of the word" (*per vim verbi, quo exorcisantur*).

28. Trigg sees three distinctions in the meaning of the Word for Luther: (1) the preached Word in distinction from the sacramental Word; (2) the Gospel which unites all forms of the Word; and (3) the Word connected with and commanding Baptism. Baptism has the same content as the Gospel, but has the benefit of being commanded and given with an element (*Baptism*, 70).

29. *AE* 8:145 (*In Baptismo sonat vox Trinitatis, nec aliter audienda aut accipienda sunt*

Appropriately, the ancient church liturgy properly requires of the infant a confession of faith through the sponsors, a renunciation of Satan, and perhaps even the exorcism, as Luther used it, before the Baptism.[30] The child receives the water of Baptism having confessed his faith and renounced Satan. Upon being baptized, he receives the Holy Spirit, who in fact has already been active in the child by creating faith and having him renounce Satan. Thus, no distinction is made in the form of baptizing an infant or an adult![31] We are forced to speak of infant Baptism as a separate topic only because their Baptism is contested and said to be of no value or even harmful.[32]

From God's point of view, all things belonging to the rite of Baptism happen at the same time, but the liturgy expresses them in a logical though not necessarily chronological sequence. As mentioned, Luther can speak of infants receiving faith by the Word of God in the exorcism, while in no way diminishing the power of the Word in the actual administration of the water. Pieper discusses these issues in his *Christian Dogmatics*, in a section entitled "Baptismal Customs."[33] Here he insists again that the child is baptized on the basis of his own faith. Like Luther, Pieper says that we cannot speak with precision about the advent of faith in the child. "The question whence the child acquired a faith of its own is not seriously troublesome for us. . . . Moreover, we know that Baptism as Gospel itself has the power to *work* the faith it calls for."[34] We should no more speak of infant faith as mysterious than we do of the faith of adults. It is hard to avoid the conclusion that in a Baptist environment, the faith of adults as conscious, premeditated decision has become the norm and model from which infant faith deviates. Faith in all cases is beyond psychological explanation. Our arguments about the intellectual and emotional capacities of children are offered *only*

---

verba Baptismi).

30. *AE* 5:99, 107; Pieper, *Christian Dogmatics* 3:282.

31. The Eastern Orthodox make no distinction between the Baptism of infants and that of adults. Chrismation is administered at Baptism, and unlike the rite of confirmation in the Western churches is not delayed to adolescence. See Meyendorff, *Byzantine Theology*, 192–95. A fuller discussion of the relationship of confirmation to Baptism is planned for the volume on the sacraments in Confessional Lutheran Dogmatics.

32. Grenz states the Baptist view thus: "Infant baptism is also harmful because it denies the child the divinely ordained means of declaring conscious and responsible belief in Jesus Christ later in life. And it fosters the separation of conscious faith from baptism, in that baptism occurs before the experience of personal faith in Jesus Christ. Finally Baptists argue that infant baptism is dangerous, because historically the practice has opened the way to a national church which extends the boundaries of the faith community to the political boundaries of the land" (*Community of God*, 688). Obviously Baptists look at faith and confession much differently than Lutherans. Whether infant Baptism is the foundation of a national church is debatable. It certainly is not in North and South America and certain countries in Africa.

33. 3:282–87.

34. Ibid., 285.

because of the Baptists' position of denying Baptism to children for these reasons. Lutheran theology has since the eighteenth century too often capitulated to the Baptist arguments about faith, and even assumed them. The tables should be reversed: *infant faith is the norm for adult faith*. Baptists are aware of this argument, and thus are determined to show that the pericopes of Jesus and the children have reference to their childlike characteristics and not to their faith.

Baptism administered without faith is a misuse of this sacrament, and it would be better to omit it; so concludes Pieper.[35] Luther explicitly says, "Infants hear the Word of God when they are brought to Baptism; therefore they receive faith. This is proven in the case of John the Baptist who rejoiced in the womb when he heard the Word of God."[36] As in the case of John the Baptist, infant faith is created by the preached Word, the Word now accompanying Baptism. In 1 Cor 7:14 the children of a Christian parent are called sanctified. In conjunction with 1 Cor 6:11, it appears this sanctification may have taken place in Baptism or possibly before. There is nothing to suggest that children are incapable of faith before Baptism, or that the Word of God becomes operative only with the use of water. The solution offered by some Lutherans, that God works salvation in infants apart from faith, destroys the article on justification, as Pieper points out.[37]

This matter is discussed in some length in C. F. W. Walther's edition of Baier's *Compendium*. The Lutheran dogmatician Johann Gerhard is cited to show that Christian parents are to have no fear about their stillborn children or those who die before Baptism, because of the prayers of such parents. If it seems that the salvation of such children is made to depend on the piety of the parents, Gerhard adds, the children of "parents who are in part negligent [in their prayers] are received into grace and life by the prayers of the church to God who mercifully hears their prayers."[38] So the Baier-Walther *Compendium* holds that children can believe before or after their birth, and *before* Baptism. Luther's sermons on Rom 10:10 are cited, where four distinctions are made: (1) those who

---

35. Ibid., 267.

36. My translation; *WATr* 3:2904a (*Verbum Dei audiunt infantes, cum adferuntur ad baptismum; ergo fidem concipiunt. Hoc probatur Johannem Baptistam, qui audito verbo Dei saltavit in utero*).

37. *Christian Dogmatics* 3:267: "Many recent Lutherans . . . teach that Baptism communicates psychic (or 'psychophysical') powers and gifts which the baptized do not receive with the hand of faith. This is the Romanizing element in their teaching."

38. *Infantes illos, qui vel in utero materno, vel repentino quodam casu ante baptismi susceptionem extinguuntur, temere damnare nec possumus, nec debemus; quin potius statuimus, preces piorum parentum, vel, si parentes in hac parte negligentes fuerunt, preces ecclesiae ad Deum pro his infantibus fusas clementer exaudiri eosdemque in gratiam et vitam a Deo recipi* (John William Baier, *Compendium Theologicae Positivae*, ed. Carl Ferdinand Wilhelm Walther [St. Louis: Lutheran Concordia Verlag, 1879], 3:466).

believe and are baptized, which is the norm; (2) those who believe and are not baptized; (3) those who do not believe and are baptized; and (4) those who neither believe nor are baptized. Luther says that "whether someone believes and dies unbaptized, he would not therefore be damned, for it would fall into this [second] category, that he believed and, although he desired Baptism, he was overtaken by death, as it can happen with young children who before, or in, or also after their birth, nevertheless through the faith or prayer of their parents or others are offered to Christ and commended to Him, which He receives according to His expressed words, 'Let the children come to Me.'"[39]

Lutherans never argue for the salvation of infants on the basis of their moral innocence, a view they condemned in the Anabaptists (FC SD XII.11), or that their Baptism is only a ratification of a right inherited from their parents, the Reformed position (FC SD XII.13). On one hand, the Confessions do not deviate from the necessity of Word and sacrament (which for Luther is derived from Mk 16:16, "he who believes and is baptized shall be saved"), but still they allow for faith before Baptism. This principle of the Word preceding Baptism is set forth explicitly by Luther: "Even those who have come to faith before they were baptized and those who came to faith in Baptism came to their faith through the external Word which preceded."[40] Cornelius believed ten years before he was baptized (SA III.viii.8). The case of John the Baptist believing while still in his mother's womb is listed as an example of this principle (SA III.viii.7, 12, 13). Luther does not hesitate to use the case of John the Baptist often; thus, dismissing this example as an exceptional case is without warrant. John believes upon hearing the voice of Mary, and thus his faith was created by an external Word of God before he was born (SA III.viii.7–12).[41] God does not act against nature and give

---

39. Ibid., 466–67 (my translation).
40. SA III.viii.7; Tappert, 313; *BKS*, 437.
41. The faith of John the Baptist before his birth is a factor in discussing infant faith. Is Jesus' faith also to be considered? Since by faith sinners are forgiven, discussion of the faith of Jesus, God's sinless Son, may appear awkward. Frederick Dale Brunner says, "Though the Gospels rarely speak of Jesus' faith, perhaps from respect for his unique sonship, nevertheless Jesus' temptation and Gethsemane especially taught us that Jesus did trust God" (*Matthew: A Commentary* [Dallas: Word Publishing, 1990], 1045). At His conception all the divine nature's attributes were communicated to the human nature (*genus maiestaticum*), and in its humiliation that human nature put aside the full use of these divine attributes. God lived among us as a man (*homo factus est*). From conception Jesus as a man trusted God the Father to deliver Him. He heard Jesus' prayers and raised Him from the dead.

Jesus' faith is a factor in Matthew's crucifixion scene. In His sense of abandonment by God, Jesus prays Ps 22:1: "My God, my God, why hast thou forsaken me?" (Mt 27:46). In their taunts, however, His enemies are the first to use Ps 22: "He trusts in God; let God deliver him now, if he desires him; for he said, 'I am the Son of God'" (Mt 27:43). Matthew uses the sarcasm of Christ's adversaries to show they heard His claim to be God's Son and that He trusted God. Their taunts reflect Ps 22:8, "He committed his

faith to creatures who ordinarily do not believe. Luther spoke of the temporal priority of the Word without contradicting his principle that both Word and sacrament bring salvation: "Accordingly, we should and must constantly maintain that God will not deal with us except through his external Word and sacrament. Whatever is attributed to the Spirit apart from such Word and sacrament is of the devil."[42]

The Gospel, called the Word of faith because it creates faith, is effective on children before their Baptism, when, for example, they hear it from Christian parents. As pointed out elsewhere, the same principle is at work in the rite of Baptism itself, where the Word is operative throughout.[43] Whether unborn children are saved, an issue of grave concern in those centuries when stillbirths and infant death were common, is a question that has resurfaced because of the availability of abortion. The position of the Lutheran dogmaticians in not absolutely denying faith to such children could not be more relevant today.[44] Lutherans take some of the arguments to support infant faith before or in Baptism into their debate against abortion. Unborn and born infants are moral creatures accountable to God, redeemed by His Son, and capable of believing the Word through the Spirit's work. Baptism does not establish their status as moral creatures before God (*coram Deo*), but presupposes and confirms it. It is not surprising but completely consistent that confessional Lutherans have been leaders in the anti-abortion movement.

---

cause to the LORD; let him deliver him, let him rescue him, for he delights in him!" Verse 9 refers to the Messiah's trust in God the Father as an infant: "But You are He who took Me out of the womb; You made Me trust while on My mother's breasts" (NKJV). Jesus in trusting in His Father from infancy is the model for Christians (1 Pt 1:21). In Him the *fides infantium* reached perfection.

42. SA III.viii.10; Tappert, 313; BKS, 437. The role of faith in Luther's doctrine of infant Baptism has long been a subject of debate among scholars. An historical overview is presented by Brinkel (*Die Lehre Luthers von der fides infantium*, 9–19). In 1896 Georg Rietschel popularized the view that in his conflict with the Anabaptists, Luther ascribed a secondary role to faith so that it virtually became unnecessary. Brinkel's research depends on Luther's writings from 1517 to 1545 to demonstrate that he held to infant faith throughout his life (ibid., 19–23). Not surprisingly, Rietschel worked to remove from the rite of infant Baptism any suggestion that children had faith. James Atkinson notes that Luther used the blessing of the children to demonstrate infant faith, even though he finds this argument untenable (*Martin Luther*, 192).

43. AE 36:300–301. Luther can speak of the exorcism, the faith and prayers of the congregation, and the act of Baptism itself as creating faith in the infant, since he does not look upon the efficacy of the Word of God or the Gospel in an atomistic way but as one activity.

44. Mention must be made here of Johann Georg Walch, *Faith of Unborn Children*, ed. with annotations by Adam Lebrecht Mueller, trans. Otto Stahlke and ed. David R. Liefeld (St. Paul, MN: Lutherans for Life, 1988). First published in German in 1733, its author was the editor of the Walch edition of Luther's works, later published by Concordia Publishing House, St. Louis. As the title indicates, the work argues for the faith of unborn infants, and is being used by Lutherans in their opposition to abortion.

11

BAPTISM'S NECESSITY AND ITS EXCEPTIONS

Baptism does not belong to what our theologians call the primary fundamental doctrines or to the Gospel proclamation. This means that people can be saved without having a full or correct understanding of Baptism, without even having heard about it or without being baptized, though its absence may damn in certain cases.[1] The doctrine of Baptism is an extension of Christology, apart from which it cannot be understood. In Baptism Christ, that is, His divine and human person and His redemptive work, is present and made available to the believer. Through the one act of Baptism, Christ approaches the believer and the believer approaches Christ. Christ wins salvation for us, and in Baptism He applies His salvation. Apart from Christ the sacraments, including Baptism, have no independent or autonomous existence. The doctrine of Baptism is functioning Christology, because through it Christ acts to give Himself to the believer. Sacraments are more than just divinely mandated rituals which provide the Christian community with external structures; such a view would be nothing else than ceremonial legalism, by which believers attempt to serve the pleasure of God through ritualistic performances.

Luther's "I am baptized!" did not suggest that there was a way to find God other than in Christ, but this phrase expressed his full trust in Him. Baptism and Christ are not two goals competing for the believer's allegiance, but only one. This complete faith in Christ means that one does not seek Him apart from the sacraments, of which Baptism is the first in which the believer meets Him. This necessary connection be-

---

1. Nicholas Hunnius was the first of many seventeenth-century Lutheran theologians to draw a distinction between fundamental and non-fundamental doctrines. He further divided the fundamental doctrines into primary and secondary ones. Robert D. Preus points out that these distinctions, "arbitrarily worked out, tended, regrettably and unintentionally, to obscure the articles of faith" (*The Theology of Post-Reformation Lutheranism*, vol. 1 [St. Louis: Concordia Publishing House, 1970], 147). Pieper places Baptism among the secondary fundamental articles of faith, and so allows for the Gospel to be operative in the lives of children in Reformed denominations. As helpful as the distinction might be, it obscures the fact that where the sacraments are absent, there the presence of Christ is curtailed, and so the church can be neither created nor nourished by the sacraments. Luther does not know of the distinction, and Pieper may be less than fully satisfied with it, as he does not include the word "secondary" in the following sentence: "Hence the doctrines of Baptism and the Lord's Supper are fundamental doctrines" (*Christian Dogmatics* 1:85).

tween Christ and Baptism is alien to most Reformed Protestantism, and it is not surprising that its adherents delay baptizing their children, or in many cases neglect it altogether. Reasons for not baptizing children are varied. Some children are born to non-Christians; some are born to those who oppose or are ignorant of the practice; others are victims of abortion and infanticide; and still others are stillborn or die shortly after birth. If the crime of the ancients was infanticide, the crime of the modern world is widespread abortion. Baptist and Pentecostal churches predominate in North America and are gaining ground in Latin America; correspondingly, children even in large Christian populations remain unbaptized. Where infant Baptism was the normal practice throughout Europe, it is now often neglected, because secularism has increased its grip. Equally destructive is the lingering influence of the atheistic Marxist philosophy in those countries where Communist ideology was politically enforced. Here the majority of populations no longer understand themselves as Christian or have any knowledge of this heritage. Parents not bringing their children to Baptism are likely acting out of ignorance, but this does not detract from the seriousness of this neglect for the children. Abortion is even more serious, because it involves the mother's willful desire to kill a helpless child, the fruit of her own body. Few premeditated crimes require so many accomplices.

In facing moral and theological problems of such proportions, the church makes no distinction in praying for all these children in life and in the hour of their deaths, especially if they lose their lives at the hands of the practitioners of abortion. Christ is the new and last Adam in whom all mankind has its origin, and in His becoming a child (incarnation) He included children in His salvation. Preaching the damnation of such children has no place in the church's proclamation of the Gospel and serves no good purpose. Still, the church must face the issue of the salvation of infants and attempt to provide an answer in its theology. A church which allows, condones, or in some cases even financially supports abortion lives in a condition of self-contradiction when it articulates a theological position on the salvation of unbaptized children. Such groups have already made an implicit admission that children are subhuman or pre-human and so are not entitled to life or salvation. On the other hand, a church which has a fully sacramental understanding of Baptism and still prays for the salvation of all unbaptized children should consistently be opposed to abortion. Abortion first prevents children from being born, and then from being born from on high through Baptism.[2] They are denied both birth and rebirth.

---

2. Two different views about infants have caused a momentary regrouping within the Evangelical Lutheran Church in America. Some of its members have found this church to be in a state of apostasy because it funds abortions. These same theologians

Infants dying without faith and Baptism, outside of the church, must be committed to God, who will judge both the great and the small (Rv 20:12). Pieper writes, "For children of unbelievers we do not venture to hold out such hope [of salvation]. We are entering the field of the unsearchable judgments of God (Rom. 11:33)."[3] Possibly God will not hold accountable the children who die defenselessly by treacherous hands. What Luther says about the uncircumcised in Israel is applicable to aborted children: "Even though infants bring with them inborn sin, which we call original sin, it is nevertheless important that they have committed no sin against the Law. Since God is by nature merciful, He will not let their condition be worse because they were unable to obtain circumcision in the Old Testament or Baptism in the New Testament."[4] The suggestion that all children who die without Baptism are necessarily consigned to damnation is essentially a Christianized form of Manicheanism, which attributes to God good and evil motives at the same time. Consignment to physical death would automatically carry the penalty of eternal death. This is not the Lutheran position.[5] Helpful in addressing the fate of unbaptized children are remarks in Luther's *Lectures on Genesis* on Israelite children who died without circumcision, including all girls.[6] Also worthy of note is the church liturgical and hymnic tradition which understands the children slaughtered by Herod as martyrs.[7] These infant martyrs were hardly all children of believers. On the contrary, their deaths were judgments on their parents, as were the deaths of the firstborn in Egypt.[8] The Lutheran position is thus to be

---

who are opposed to abortion are consistent in supporting not only infant Baptism but also infant communion. See for example James Nuechterlein, "Catholics at Home," and Leonard Klein, "Catholics in Exile," *First Things* 73 (May 1997): 9–10. *Lutheran Forum* devotes an entire issue to infant communion (30 [Winter 1996]).

3. *Christian Dogmatics* 3:278.
4. *AE* 3:103.
5. Moody mentions that some Lutheran theologians offer no hope for the unbaptized (*Baptism*, 161). He does not mention which ones. Certainly these do not include Luther himself, the leading sixteenth- and seventeenth-century dogmaticians, or current Lutheran theologians.
6. *AE* 3:103.
7. December 28 is set aside in the liturgical calendar as The Holy Innocents in honor of the martyred children. The appointed collect suggests not only that these children were believers, but that their deaths pictured Jesus' death: "Almighty God, whose praise on this day was proclaimed by the wicked death of innocent children, giving us thereby a picture of the death of your beloved Son, mortify and destroy in us all that is in conflict with you that we who have been called in faith to be your children may in life and death bear witness to your salvation; through our Lord Jesus Christ . . ." (*Lutheran Worship*, p. 117). Note should also be made of the traditional hymn for this day, "Sweet Flowerets of the Martyr Band," by Aurelius Prudentius Clemens, AD 348–413 (ibid., #188). Consider also Luther's view that "the children were taken straight to heaven as blessed martyrs" (*The Martin Luther Christmas Book*, trans. and arr. Roland H. Bainton [Philadelphia: Muhlenberg Press, 1968], 74).
8. Consider Davies and Allison: "To the extent that the Jewish people are seen as

distinguished from the Calvinist doctrine of election, wherein the children of believers are given special consideration from God which is denied to others.

The matter of Christians whose children are stillborn or who die shortly after birth raises the question of the minister's pastoral obligations to the grieving parents. The Reformed idea classically enunciated by Calvin, that these children by right of birth from Christian parents are already included in the covenant, works from a faulty view of what covenant means. This aberration aside, the children of confessing Christians have an advantage, not through inheritance of birth, but because of contact with the Word. Melanchthon sets forth this position in the Apology: "It is most certain that the promise of salvation also applies to little children. It does not apply to those who are outside of Christ's church, where there is neither Word nor sacrament, because Christ regenerates through Word and sacrament."[9] Such children come under the influence of the Word through their parents, and have been offered to God by the prayers of the congregation. Even before birth, such children hear the Gospel and believe. The case of John the Baptist, as Pieper points out, "establishes no rule for us to follow; yet it proves beyond doubt that it is not above the power of the Holy Ghost to create faith in infants."[10] Luther had no difficulty in using the example of John the Baptist to show that children do believe before they are born. God's Word spoken by an ordinary Christian is no less effective than when the Word is spoken by God's mother. When the Lutheran Confessions assert the necessary connection between Baptism and faith, the meaning is *not* that faith, even for children, is only possible through Baptism.[11] When the Bohemian Brethren asserted that infants should be baptized on the basis of their future faith, a position popular among the Reformed and some Lutherans, Luther insisted that faith had to be present either before or at the time of Baptism.[12]

---

supporters of Herod and therefore seen as sharing his guilt . . . to that extent are they responsible for the slaughter of the infants of Bethlehem, and to that extent they bring judgment upon themselves" (*Matthew* [1:270]).

9. Ap. IX.2; Tappert, 178; BKS, 247.

10. *Christian Dogmatics* 2:448.

11. Addressed in the previous chapter was the status of the "holy children" of 1 Cor 7:14: "For the unbelieving husband is consecrated [ἡγίασται] through his wife, and the unbelieving wife is consecrated through her husband. Otherwise, your children would be unclean, but as it is they are holy." Holy people believe and are baptized. These children, like their parents, were believing members of the baptized community. They may have been waiting for Baptism. For a summary of the debate see Beasley-Murray, who argues that these children do not have their holiness from Baptism (*Baptism*, 192–99). Conceding this point for the sake of argument, their holiness, which is only through faith, existed before and entitled them to Baptism. Thus the Word's action through the believing parent culminated in Baptism, and these components together constituted one action.

12. "Second, as I hear from your messengers, the sacrament of baptism is properly

The importance of Baptism in the plan of salvation is evident by its inclusion in Article II of the Augsburg Confession, which deals with original sin. Eternal damnation is the destiny of those who are not reborn by Baptism and the Holy Spirit: *damnans et afferens nunc quoque aeternam mortem his, qui non renascuntur per baptismum et spiritum sanctum*.[13] This strict view of the necessity of Baptism in the Augsburg Confession seems to be contradicted by positing the salvation of the unbaptized, who in some cases have confessed their faith but in other cases have been unable to do even this. These exceptions, if that is what they truly are, have allowed some to regard Baptism less seriously or not really necessary in any sense. The dying thief to whom Jesus promised salvation is frequently cited (Lk 23:42–43). In the early church, martyred catechumens were considered baptized by their death, "the Baptism by blood." The issue of unbaptized infants is a different problem. Distinctions are made between children of Christians and of non-Christians, though Lutherans do not adopt the Reformed view that the children of Christians have covenant rights through their parents. Roman Catholics traditionally have considered Baptism unconditionally necessary for the salvation of infants, regardless of their parents' faith. Those who died without Baptism were entitled only to the somewhat lesser bliss of the *limbus infantium*, and not heaven itself. Belief in the *limbus infantium* may be less operative in the Roman church today,[14] but this construct was an attempt to reconcile the church's belief in the comparative moral innocence of children with its teaching on the absolute necessity of Baptism. Of greater concern are Baptist denominations, whose members leave their children unbaptized because they believe infants and young children do not meet the requirements for Baptism. Modern-day Baptists are not the lineal descendants of the Reformation Anabaptists, but

---

observed among you. But I am much concerned because you baptize young children on the basis of future faith, which they are supposed to learn when they come to understand, and not on the basis of present faith. For you [the Bohemian Brethren] hold (as they tell me) that the young children do not have faith; nevertheless you baptize them. On this point I have said it would be better not to baptize any children anywhere at all than to baptize them without faith, since in such procedure the sacrament and God's holy name are taken in vain [Ex 20:7], and to me that is a serious matter. For without faith the sacrament should not and cannot be received or if it is received, it works great injury.... I would rather teach that children should not be baptized (as I have said) than that they should be baptized without faith" (*AE* 36:300–301). This section from Luther's "The Adoration of the Sacrament" was also cited in the Baier-Walther *Compendium*, the first dogmatics book of The Lutheran Church—Missouri Synod (3:479–80). Cf. Brinkel: "Dasz der Glaube 'vor oder in der Taufe' dasein müsse, hatte Luther gegenüber den Böhmischen Brüdern gesagt, die kleinen Kinder auf zukünftigen Glauben taufen" (*Die Lehre Luthers von der fides infantium*, 58).

13. AC II.2; Tappert, 29; BKS, 53.
14. The *Catechism of the Catholic Church* makes no mention of the *limbus infantium*, but entrusts them to the mercy of God (para. 1250). Vatican II makes no mention of the *limbus infantium*, but says simply that faith and Baptism are necessary ("Lumen Gentium," 365).

share their absolute opposition to infant Baptism.[15] At the time of the Reformation nearly all Christians were baptized as infants, and the matter of catechumens waiting for Baptism was not a major issue. Our confessions speak of Baptism clearly with infants in mind, though the Large Catechism sees Baptism as the sacrament embracing all of life (IV.41).

Lutheran theology makes a distinction between what is necessary and what is absolutely necessary. Baptism is necessary, but not absolutely so. Luther, commenting on Mk 16:16, "He who believes and is baptized will be saved; but he who does not believe will be condemned," speaks in unequivocal terms: "Moreover, it is solemnly and strictly commanded that we must be baptized or we shall not be saved."[16] This assertion is directed against the Anabaptists, who saw faith without Baptism as sufficient. Luther says emphatically that "without faith Baptism is of no use,"[17] but the emphasis for him is on Baptism's divine origin, which is embraced in a divine command. Opposing Baptism is despising God. Luther does not put Baptism on the same level as faith, and any idea that they are coequal partners in accomplishing salvation must be rejected. Faith is not a meritorious work. Of the words "he who believes," Luther says "that it excludes and rejects all works that we may do with the intention of meriting salvation through them."[18] While faith is necessary, it is not necessary in the sense that it has anything to offer, but only because it takes what is given in Baptism. Faith has no substantive meaning in itself, but its total value is given it by Christ, who is presented to the believer in Baptism. The Reformer spoke against the Zwinglians and Anabaptists who ridiculed Baptism and exalted faith: "Our know-it-alls, the new spirits, assert that faith alone saves and that works and external things contribute nothing to this event."[19] Regardless of the authenticity of the Mark passage, over which most scholars, including confessional Lutheran theologians, have expressed doubts,[20] the necessity of Baptism can easily be drawn from Jn 3:5: "Unless one is born of water and the Spirit, he cannot enter the kingdom of God." Calvin could not bring himself to say that Baptism gave salvation, nor did his interpretation of Jn 3:5 require it.[21] Roman Catholics

---

15. Grenz, *Community of God*, 709–12.
16. LC IV.6; Tappert, 437; BKS, 692.
17. LC IV.34; Tappert, 440; BKS, 697.
18. LC IV.34; Tappert, 440–41; BKS, 697.
19. LC IV.28; Tappert, 440; BKS, 696. Tappert identifies the "know-it-alls" as the Zwinglians or Anabaptists (440, n. 4). Zwingli was indifferent to outward forms (Trigg, *Baptism*, 213).
20. William R. Farmer argues for its authenticity (*Last Twelve Verses*), as discussed previously.
21. *Institutes* IV.XVI.25. So also Beasley-Murray: "For Zwingli, 'whoever makes being a Christian to depend upon the manner or fact of baptism is falling into sacramentalism

allow for exceptions for those dying without Baptism, including a modified form of universalism for Jews and Muslims.[22] Hardly at issue for Lutherans is the fate of unbelievers, whether or not they are baptized. Without faith salvation is impossible. The question is whether the insistence made for Baptism in the Lutheran Confessions allows an exception for unbaptized children, an exception which nearly all Christians make—including Baptists, who do not baptize children!

The Anabaptists' refusal to baptize their own children provided the opportunity for Lutherans to set forth the doctrine that Baptism is necessary. For the Anabaptists, Baptism conferred no grace and children were exempt from the penalties of original sin.[23] Salvation was assured through believing parents. Modern Baptists hold the same views, and so the Lutheran condemnation remains appropriate (FC SD XII.2). As noted, Calvin also saw children's special relationship to their parents as a basis for salvation, but unlike the Baptists he saw this as a reason for baptizing them. His practice was acceptable, but the reason for it was not (FC SD XII.4).[24] Anabaptists, as their name implies, rebaptized those who were baptized as infants. This practice led Luther to insist in the Large Catechism that the first act of Baptism remains forever (LC IV.77), and that multiple immersions counted for nothing and could never replace the validity and effectiveness of the first Baptism (LC IV.78). For Luther, Baptism was God's act, could be performed only once, and was necessary. The Anabaptists saw Baptism as a pledge of faith which could be repeated. Since the Anabaptists promised salvation to infants apart from Baptism, the Augsburg Confession, the Apology, Luther's Large Catechism, and the Formula of Concord all affirm that it "is necessary to baptize children."[25] Baptism is not a *legal* requirement (Law), but it is a *saving* necessity (Gospel).

---

or legalism'" (*Baptism*, 229–30). Trigg points out that Lutherans and Anabaptists come under Zwingli's condemnation (*Baptism,* 213). Anabaptists insist on the manner and Lutherans on the fact of Baptism.

22. *Catechism of the Catholic Church*, para. 839–41.

23. Baptists seem to hold a view of sin and conversion which is essentially Pelagian. Grenz holds that infants "are egocentric and self-absorbed, although at this stage egocentrism does not entail guilt" (*Community of God*, 267). Children are judged to be egocentric, which by any definition is a sin against the First Commandment; however, they are not held morally accountable. So in this view, sin, no less than faith, involves decision. The view that children are capable of actual sin but not faith raises questions about Baptist doctrines of God and man. In addition, ascribing salvation to children without faith transgresses the Reformation principle of *sola fide*.

24. The Reformed have consistently maintained this view that the children through their birth from Christian parents are entitled to Baptism. See for example Geoffrey W. Bromiley, *Children of the Promise* (Grand Rapids, MI: William B. Eerdmans, 1979). He argues that a child with a Christian ancestor is entitled to Baptism, a novel but strained argument. It is arguable that all children might meet this requirement. Their inclusion in God's redemptive love in Jesus provides a preferred certainty.

25. Ap. IX.2; Tappert, 178; *BKS*, 247.

Those who refuse Baptism to children defy God and are accountable to Him (LC IV.6–9). They are themselves condemned: "[Such] erroneous and heretical teaching ... cannot be suffered or tolerated in the churches or in the body politic or in domestic society."[26] The Reformed denied a real sacramental efficacy to Baptism, but at least they obeyed God's command to baptize. Roman Catholics not only obeyed God's command, but attributed to it a limited but nevertheless saving efficacy. The Anabaptists, who prohibited the Baptism of infants entirely, were regarded as completely intolerable; the Confessions and Luther go so far as to say that they are outside the church. In denying emergency Baptism to infants, Calvin falls partially under the condemnation of the Formula of Concord. Among some Baptists, the awareness that children are included in Christ's work of salvation expresses itself in infant dedication ceremonies. This service is an obligation of the parents, but the child is not directly affected by it, so that it cannot be regarded as a substitute for Baptism. The confessional position on the necessity of Baptism still stands against all groups who fail to baptize their children. Equally deplorable are those mainline denominations who are committed to baptizing infants, but whose ministers are indifferent to the practice. Some Lutheran pastors in Germany have neglected to baptize their own children.[27] The Roman Catholic Church shows its seriousness about Baptism by declaring those parents who do not have their children baptized by the age of three months to be in a state of sin. Lutherans have no canon law, but refusing to have one's children baptized is not a matter of indifference, and sooner or later may be one reason, perhaps among others, for excommunication.

The necessity of Baptism, especially for infants, finds prominent support among Lutherans in Jn 3:5.[28] The Lutheran position that Baptism is necessary as a means of salvation and regeneration should be distinguished from that of most Reformed paedobaptists, for whom it is a *necessitas praecepti*, a requirement of the Law. In their view, Baptism fulfills God's law and is not a means through which Christ incorporates believers into Himself.[29] Whereas in Lutheran theology Baptism as Gospel is God's last word, for the Reformed God's final word is Law. For Anabaptists Baptism for adults is necessary as a legal obligation (Law) and not because of grace (Gospel).[30] Faith as a personal decision

---

26. FC SD XII.9; Tappert, 633; *BKS*, 1093–94. Amazing is the infatuation of some Lutherans with prominent Baptist preachers who do not hesitate to show their distaste for Baptism by homiletical ridicule.

27. Hoffmann, "Baptism," 79.

28. Pieper, *Christian Dogmatics* 3:281. For whatever reason, this scriptural support is not cited in the Lutheran Confessions.

29. See Hoenecke, *Ev.-Luth. Dogmatik* 3:67–68.

30. Grane remarks, "Despite the disregard for the sacraments which followed from

and commitment remains at the center of Baptist theology. Baptism is not the only area of Christian life in which for the Reformed the practice does not meet the requirements for the divine ideal. For example, Calvin endorses infant Baptism, but not in cases of emergency, when it would seem most valuable. Though he sees Baptism as a divine pledge, it also serves as an act of the believer's commitment; thus, the Gospel is clouded by the Law.

In the Middle Ages, the church saw the Holy Communion as Christ's body and blood, but it was offered only in one form, and few received it. Still, it was a sacrament, and the church was there. Inconsistencies between divine revelation and human belief and practice are the stuff out of which church history is made. Some failures in practice raise the question of whether the church is present even in a group professing to be Christian. Luther could not concede that the Anabaptists were church, not only because of aberrant beliefs, but particularly because they denied Baptism to infants. He applied a similar judgment to the Zwinglians: "We earnestly believe that the Zwinglians and all sacramentarians who deny that the body and blood of Christ are taken with the bodily mouth in the venerable eucharist are heretics and estranged from the church of God."[31] Our situation may be even more difficult. Some churches with a trinitarian confession have clergy administering Baptism in the name of "the Creator, Redeemer, and Sanctifier," a formula which intends to satisfy feminist aversion to the Father-Son-Spirit terminology. Use of the aberrant formula has suggested to several members of the churches in which it is used that they are already in a state of apostasy. Here the question is not a matter of sacramental validity, but to what extent the church is present where the aberrant formula is deliberately made part of the liturgical formula. Baptism, which the Scriptures and the Confessions see as necessary for salvation, forms and shapes the church. Where the church is not present, what purports to be Baptism really is not a Baptism.[32] Liturgies which closely resemble the ancient heresy of gnos-

---

this, the Anabaptists, because of their biblicism, maintained the necessity of Baptism" (*Augsburg Confession*, 110).

31. WA 54:427.8–10. Translated and quoted in John Stephenson's article "Reflections on the Appropriate Vessels," *Logia* 4 (January 1995): 17, n. 2.

32. See David P. Scaer, "The Validity of the Churchly Acts of Ordained Women," *Concordia Theological Quarterly* 53 (January–April 1989): 3–20. Pastors receiving members from Protestant denominations will inquire carefully under what circumstances Baptism was administered. A person brought up in a Baptist church and transferring to another church may have avoided being baptized. Other cases are simply uncertain. A faithful member and her husband were regular attenders of my congregation in Rockville, Connecticut. A few months before his death he requested to join our church to receive the Lord's Supper. When he claimed that he had been baptized, his wife said that he did not really know whether he had been baptized. Then she pointed out that typically in small towns in New England, one congregation may have been associated with Baptist,

ticism are prevalent in some mainline congregations, and in some cases are clearly the marks of absolute apostasy.[33]

We conclude by making the distinction that Baptism is necessary as the means for salvation, but not absolutely necessary in the sense that its absence automatically excludes one from the redeemed on the Last Day. The granting of exceptions is at the discretion of the church's Lord, not of the church. Rather, the church must work under the command of her Lord, who makes Baptism necessary for salvation. A confessional Lutheran theology today has no reason to be any less adamant than Luther and the other reformers in seeing Baptism as necessary, and it must continue to reject those groups who do not see Baptism as divinely commanded, also for infants. Exceptions may be a fact of church life, but they cannot determine the norm or even be part of a theology of Baptism. No exception can be made for those without faith.[34]

Congregationalist, and Unitarian associations, often at the same time. She clinched the argument for him to be baptized by asking what good an uncertain Baptism was. Not only was there no certain proof of a prior Baptism, but there was no way of ascertaining what had been involved in that Baptism.

33. "Characteristically the gnostic god is a dyad, a harmonious admixture of God the Father and God the Mother" (*Forum Letter* 24 [February 1995]: 1–4).

34. Compare Prenter, who is willing to make exceptions for the heathen and puts them in the same category as unbaptized infants (*Creation and Redemption*, 467).

12

KARL BARTH ON BAPTISM

The Reformation controversy over Baptism was, strictly speaking, a controversy over infant Baptism, because here the concept of an alien righteousness was most obvious.[1] Baptism was central for the Anabaptists, but they did not baptize infants. This controversy, albeit in a different form, reappeared in the deliberate rejection of infant Baptism by Karl Barth, arguably the most significant twentieth-century theologian. His *Church Dogmatics*[2] rightfully deserves to be called the major theological work of the twentieth century. It remains to be seen whether anything approaching it in depth and length will appear for a long time to come. Apart from the question of whether any one theologian has adopted his method and approach *in toto*, Barth has made a significant impression on Protestant and Roman Catholic theologians. In an earlier period he reluctantly allowed for baptizing infants, but acknowledged reasons for omitting the practice. But as he approached the end of his life, he came down squarely against infant Baptism. His was not a complete reversal, because he did not adopt the practice of the sixteenth-century Anabaptists in insisting that Baptism be repeated.[3] Their position should also be distinguished from the practices of modern Baptists, who may re-baptize those who were baptized as infants but who hold that Baptism is ultimately inconsequential for salvation. If "Baptist" implies that Baptism is at the center of their theology, then the term is a misnomer, since in their view salvation and inclusion in the church do not depend on whether or not one has been baptized.

Barth does not simply adopt Baptist positions, though both his theological and exegetical arguments at points correspond with theirs. For Barth, Baptism is a required action of obedience, but it cannot be identified with the moment of salvation. With terminology characteristic of his theology, he says Baptism is "the event in which God in Jesus Christ makes a man His child and a member of His covenant, awakening faith

---

1. It is hard to quarrel with Oberman's observation that a repudiation of infant Baptism is a repudiation of Baptism (*Luther*, 230).
2. References are taken from Karl Barth, *Church Dogmatics*, 5 vols., trans. G. W. Bromiley (Edinburgh: T. & T. Clark, 1969), 4/4. The fourth volume is titled *The Christian Life* and the fourth fragment, printed as a separate volume, is titled *Baptism as the Foundation of the Christian Life*. The original German publication is *Die Kirchliche Dogmatik* (Zürich: EVZ Verlag, 1967), 4/4.
3. Barth, *Church Dogmatics* 4/4:189.

through His grace and calling a man to life in the Christ."[4] Though Barth's language can be sacramental, he is insistent that Baptism is no more than a picture, a witness, a sign or representation (*Abbild*).[5]

Having defined Baptism as a human act, Barth was closer to Zwingli than to any other sixteenth-century Protestant reformer. Zwingli separated faith, the inner Baptism, from the water Baptism about which he was indifferent.[6] With his emphasis on the objectivity of divine action, Barth may have appeared to have parted with Zwingli, for whom the power of Baptism was nothing else but the individual's faith, and to have moved closer to Luther.[7] He makes use of the Small Catechism's explanation that the Word and not the water accomplishes salvation. Barth's citing of Luther is deceptive, however, since he does not hold that God is intimately involved with the water of Baptism. Luther's view, that the water is a water of salvation because of the Word, is unacceptable to him.[8] Barth condemns Lutherans, along with Roman Catholics and Anglicans, for attributing regenerative power to water Baptism.[9] Still, he views Baptism as a pledge of the certainty of salvation. While insisting on the willing assent of the baptized, he sees an objectivity in the act. Baptism without the willingness and readiness of the baptized is a true, effectual, and effective Baptism. But it is not correct Baptism, since it is not done in obedience and administered according to the proper order. Therefore it is necessarily a clouded Baptism, even though it ought not and must not be repeated.[10] Barth's theology of Baptism does not fit into previously existing categories, which is evident in that those with opposing views have cited him to establish their positions. His position on Baptism should be judged within the context of his own theological development.

During the sixteenth and seventeenth centuries, Lutheran, Reformed, and Roman Catholic theologies assumed their characteristic forms. In the eighteenth century their place at the center of the Western religious world was replaced by the Enlightenment's historical critical approach to the Bible and its view that Christianity was one religion among others (*Religionsgeschichte*). Following World War I, Barth, along with others associated with neo-orthodox theology, reacted to ideas popularized during the nineteenth century by Schleiermacher. Neo-orthodox theologians, of whom Barth was the prince, had developed a peculiar understanding of the Scriptures as "the Word of God," an understand-

---

4. Barth, *Teaching of the Church*, 14.
5. Ibid., 9.
6. Trigg, *Baptism*, 213.
7. Barth, *Teaching of the Church*, 20.
8. Ibid., 19–23.
9. Ibid., 26–27.
10. Ibid., 40.

ing which differed from the classical Christian definition. The Bible could be understood as the Word of God not because of the Holy Spirit's inspiration of the writers and their words, but because it was a proclamation. His understanding of the Word of God was an overarching category which embraced the Bible and the sacraments. Central to this proclamation was Jesus Christ, who was the solitary revelation of God. Barth determined to steer away from the kind of syncretism which had developed within the classical liberalism generated by Schleiermacher. Barth's brand of neo-orthodoxy became widespread in the 1950s and 1960s in North America, where his use of traditional theological language may have suggested falsely to some that he really belonged to the classical Christian tradition.

His concept of revelation, which Barth set forth in strict christological terms, would lead him to place the sacraments in a subsidiary role, since according to his definition they have no inherent revelatory significance. Jesus Christ as God's working in history is the only sacrament.[11] He deliberately distanced himself from any traditional definition of the sacraments, and saw them as human actions or even reactions. His views left no doubt that he remained closer to his own Reformed heritage, particularly to Calvin, than to Luther, whose influence he claimed for his theology. For Calvin, Baptism consisted of two parts: God's promise to man and man's testimony to what he believed, *symbolum testandae apud homines religionis*. Luther saw faith as a necessary requirement for and response to Baptism, but never introduced faith into his definition of Baptism as Calvin did.[12] Zwingli saw Baptism purely in terms of individual faith, without any symbolic or sacramental significance.[13] Thus, Calvin tended toward a middle position between Luther and Zwingli, to which Barth also gravitated. Barth was uncomfortable with the first part of Calvin's definition of Baptism as divine promise, but favored the latter part, that Baptism was a human testimony to divine regeneration. Calvin's view was similar to his own view that Baptism was man's response to God. He also correctly observed that infant Baptism, which for him lacked the necessary response, was on that account more difficult for Calvin to justify than for Luther.[14] Barth was hardly ready to part company with Zwingli, who in his opinion rightly rejected a sacramental interpretation of Baptism, yet he found him to be of little use in developing his own ideas that this rite must be

---

11. Barth, *Church Dogmatics* 4/4:102.
12. Trigg summarizes Luther's position: "Faith is essential to the reception of baptism; baptism remains baptism in the absence of faith. Baptism understood as water which is embraced in the divine word of promise demotes all questions about the presence or absence of faith to a secondary level" (*Baptism*, 153).
13. Gäbler, *Zwingli*, 128.
14. Barth, *Church Dogmatics* 4/4:173–74.

seen as a human response. Barth would be happy to be labeled a neo-Zwinglian.[15] Baptism with the Spirit, which is a form of God's reconciliation with the world, does not take place in what he calls water Baptism, nor are the two identical.[16] Here Barth moves from Calvin toward Zwingli and the Radicals in holding that the Baptism with water is an unconnected parallel to the Spirit's Baptism.[17]

A couple of years before Barth's death in 1968, Baptism was one of two questions awaiting resolution in his already massive *Church Dogmatics*. The other was eschatology. A separate section on the Lord's Supper was also lacking, but this rite was not as crucial to his system as were Baptism and eschatology. His volume on eschatology never appeared; its appearance would have forced him to come to terms with the dialectic between judgment and grace, both of which he understood in terms of divine sovereignty. A yawning canyon went right through the middle of his theological system. Judgment without eternal damnation could hardly be called judgment. Absolute sovereignty applied to grace moved his theology toward the very universalism he once opposed in other religions. His abhorrence of the liberal system which stemmed from Schleiermacher was hardly incidental to his own theological development, since his theology was a deliberate reaction against it. It is not unreasonable to conclude that the failure to produce his volume on eschatology was deliberate, and that he determined his volume on Baptism to be his final word. Though in the divine-human encounter he had consistently placed the initiative with God, and not man as the receiving subject, his doctrine of Baptism shows he adopted the subjectivism which his system explicitly rejected.

Barth may be seen to sidestep the question of where the initiative lay in the divine-human encounter by "de-sacramentalizing" Baptism. He thus removed the issue of whether Baptism could be the occasion

---

15. Ibid., 128–30.
16. Ibid., 32–33.
17. In commenting on the Heidelberg Catechism (which was highly influenced by Calvinist theology), Ulrich Asendorf uses the Latin words *cum* and *tum* to describe the parallel and simultaneous but unrelated actions which take place during the administration of the sacraments. The external sacramental act is accompanied by an internal act in the believer in which God works forgiveness; however, the sacraments themselves are not the means of forgiveness. Simultaneously with the water bath of Baptism, the blood of Christ and the Holy Spirit cleanse from sin. So the Heidelberg Catechism describes the Lord's Supper: "As I receive from the hands of the minister the bread and chalice, given to me as certain marks of the body and blood of Christ, so He feeds and gives me drink for eternal life" ("Luther's Small Catechism and the Heidelberg Catechism," in *Luther's Catechisms—450 Years*, ed. Robert D. Preus and David P. Scaer [Fort Wayne, IN: Concordia Theological Seminary Press, 1979], 4–5). Luther recognizes the same position in Duns Scotus: "Nor do we agree with Scotus and the Franciscans who teach that Baptism washes away sin through the assistance of the divine will, as if the washing takes place only through God's will and not at all through the Word and the water" (SA III.v.3; Tappert, 311; *BKS*, 450).

for a real encounter. By denying Baptism to infants because they do not qualify as receiving subjects, he placed the weight on the human response in the encounter between God and man. He judged infants to be incapable of participating in the encounter with God. It is hard to distinguish his anthropology from that of the Anabaptists, who also did not find children fit candidates for Baptism because they lacked faith, except in that he did not endorse rebaptizing as they did.

In his preface to what became the last volume in his *Church Dogmatics*, Barth says that he expects his readers to deduce his position on the Lord's Supper from what he says about Baptism. We are the poorer for not having his logical presentation of his vast knowledge of the sources and his critical analysis of this doctrine, but it is not impossible to determine the outline of what that position might have been. How he thought on any issue could be constructed from the fundamental basis for his theology, that revelation or salvation occurs in the encounter in which God calls man to a decision about Jesus Christ as God's Word, and to obedience. Gospel precedes Law according to this definition. The Lord's Supper is, like Baptism, a human decision, albeit within a community, in which the believer encounters Christ.[18] We will never know for certain how Barth would have handled the different ideas of the presence of Jesus in the Supper. Roman Catholic and Lutheran ideas of Real Presence probably would have been rejected for the same reason that he denied regenerative power to water Baptism: any meaningful identification of the sacramental bread with Christ's body would have had no place in revelation as an encounter between God and man. Calvin's idea of the human nature present through the divine nature may also have been too speculative for him. In discussing Baptism, Barth had to wrestle only with the element of the water. With the Lord's Supper, he would have had to address two elements. While Baptism and the Lord's Supper are indeed separate kinds of rites, they both have subsidiary roles in serving to bring about God's revelation in Jesus Christ, who is the true mystery or sacrament. Since this encounter can take place in other situations, no necessity can be attached to actions considered sacramental in Barth's sense, which can better be described simply as actions eliciting human responses.[19]

Barth's views on Baptism can be anticipated in his views on the Scriptures as the Word of God. God can use Baptism and the Scriptures for His action, but there is no one-to-one correspondence between the divine and human. The Bible is not the Word of God and Baptism is not the Spirit's work, but God can use the Bible and Baptism without identifying with them. These are occasions for divine activity, without being

---

18. Barth, *Church Dogmatics* 4/4:130.
19. Ibid., 108–9.

that activity themselves. Barth approaches what could be called an existential Nestorianism. A thing or a rite can be the occasion for the divine activity, so that the human and divine can exist side by side, but not in a permanent way. Even though he can speak of Baptism as the foundation of the Christian life, Barth's theology is inimical to the traditional understanding of the sacraments as vehicles of the divine grace: "[Baptism] is not, itself, a divine work and word. It is the work and word of men who are obedient to Jesus Christ and who have put their hope in Him."[20] Or again, "Obedience and hope are two terms for the one human action which constitutes the meaning of Baptism."[21] In so many words, Barth can say that "baptism is not a sacrament,"[22] but can subtitle his book "Baptism as the Foundation of Christian Life." He wants to distance himself from Luther, whose views are too close to the Roman Catholic view of *ex opere operato*.[23] Barth's views on Baptism confirmed a basic component of his theology, namely that revelation, or the encounter, is initiated by God as a giving subject requiring man as a receiving subject. In a sense he had to sacrifice his earlier view that Baptism represented the priority of sovereign grace, but this shift is so subtle that it is not as significant as he claims.[24] At his best, Barth saw Baptism first as the representation of man's renewal by the Holy Spirit, and second as the representation of man's association with Christ.[25] It signified that God had done something.

As early as 1948, Barth was aware that his system could not theologically support infant Baptism, though he was reluctant to give it up.[26] Barth's theology of Baptism and how it developed over the years reflected how he struggled with the dialectic of his own theology. It seems that he would have been more comfortable if he had left this volume of his *Church Dogmatics* unwritten. Still, Barth could reverse himself on Baptism without calling his entire system into question. By denying Baptism to infants, he clarified the components of his encounter theology, which depended as much on man as a receiving subject as it did on God's initiative. God's sovereignty was limited by human response. In the end, as already stated, he returned to the anthropocentric theology he had detested in nineteenth-century liberalism and which had provided the negative impetus for his own theological journey. Barth's idea that the divine action depended on a human response was

---

20. Ibid., 102.
21. Ibid., 135.
22. Ibid., 128.
23. Ibid., 172.
24. "The strongest [argument]—I myself used it for some decades—is that infant baptism is so remarkably vivid a depiction of the free and omnipotent grace of God which is independent of all human thought and will, faith and unbelief" (ibid., 189).
25. Barth, *Teaching of the Church*, 9.
26. Ibid., 54.

determinative in the development of his doctrine of Baptism, but not his doctrine of eschatology. Sovereign grace without a human response would embrace all mankind. Barth is going in two opposite directions. Infants are excluded from Baptism, but grace will embrace all at the end.

His rejection of infant Baptism, which was never absolute, was a natural outgrowth of the principle of his theology that revelation occurs in the encounter between God and man, as one subject to another subject. Revelation was impossible without actively-receiving subjects. Infants, not capable of decision and obedience according to his definition, could not be receiving subjects in the encounter with God, and so they were not fit for Baptism.[27] Here Barth was working with an anthropology, with roots in the Renaissance and the Enlightenment, which has rarely been challenged, even by an apparent majority of Lutheran theologians. His definition of revelation as taking place between two subjects involved a cognitive component. Practically all denials of infant Baptism assume but never prove that children are without reason and will and hence cannot believe. Calvin seemingly ascribed faith to baptized infants, but as Barth correctly shows, he had to readjust his ordinary definition of faith, with its emphasis on the cognitive aspect, to accomplish this. Luther ascribed the same kind of faith to infants as to adults.[28] Barth's anti-sacramentalism may not be a repristination of the classical Reformed position, but, again, he did follow its principles to their logical conclusion in denying Baptism to infants. Without a sacramental necessity attached to Baptism, the Reformed arguments for infant Baptism are not convincing even to the Reformed themselves. In spite of differences, Zwingli, Calvin, Barth, and of course the Anabaptists agreed in seeing Baptism as unnecessary for the salvation of infants. Baptism was a rite granting entrance to the church as an external religious community, and not to the church as the Body of Christ and the fellowship of believers. Baptism has as little to do with regeneration as did circumcision, according to the Reformed definition. Theologically, the Reformed have had no real reason to deny fellowship with the Baptists, since for both grace is not dependent on means, including Baptism. From the opposing currents of the sixteenth-century Protestant Reformation Barth attempted to locate a middle position, in denying Baptism to infants but not requiring a second Baptism.[29]

Though Barth's doctrine of Baptism fit logically within the overall parameters of his system, he found biblical support in the scholarly research of his son, Markus Barth, which he incorporated into his *Church*

---

27. Barth, *Church Dogmatics* 4/4:182.
28. Ibid., 172–73.
29. Ibid., 150–51.

Dogmatics.³⁰ He had barely touched upon the exegetical question in his *Teaching of the Church on Baptism*, but already questioned the traditional biblical proofs for baptismal regeneration, including that of infants.³¹ Without underestimating the influence of his son's exegetical conclusions, the logic of his view of revelation as consisting of a subject meeting another subject in the divine-human encounter led to a change of heart. Already in 1943 he opposed Luther's *baptizatus sum* as magical.³²

The locus on Baptism is rarely the engine for any theological system, but more often than not it is the clue to uncovering the system's foundations. While theological differences tend to be focused in the practice of Baptism, similar practices can conceal fundamental differences. Though the differences over the Lord's Supper took center stage, Reformation Protestants first divided themselves over the Baptism of infants, and in their practice of Baptism fundamental theological differences became clear. Lutheran and Anabaptist differences emerged over the question of who could be baptized, but opposing views of man, God, grace, and conversion were the real issues, and these perspectives indicated that each had a fundamentally different view of Christianity. At the same time, Zwingli's demand that infant Baptism be practiced gave the impression that he agreed with Luther on this issue, but just the opposite was so: his views on Baptism were not far removed from those of the Anabaptists, but Zwingli decided to retain this rite only for the sake of the solidarity of the community. In the twentieth century, Barth out-zwinglied Zwingli in suggesting that infants no longer be baptized, but he never adopted the Anabaptist view that it was a useless act. Barth's attempt to overcome Reformation differences was unsuccessful, and only served to reveal that they are still incapable of being reconciled. Attempts have been made among Evangelical Protestants to consider both Baptism and the practice of infant Baptism as non-divisive issues.³³ Here Barth's legacy survives. Since Lutherans have understood Baptism as necessary, a declaration of a truce over these differences would amount to capitulation.

In 1943 Barth set forth his objections to infant Baptism, but was not absolute in demanding its abolition. No Baptism was invalid, even if it was not administered under ideal conditions, and "no abuse of Bap-

---

30. Markus Barth's *Die Taufe ein Sakrament*? ("Is Baptism a sacrament?") appeared in 1951 (Zoolikon-Zürich: Evangelischer Verlag AG, 1951). The lectures which Karl Barth developed into *Die Kirchliche Lehre von der Taufe* (translated into *The Teaching of the Church Regarding Baptism*) were given in 1943. His volume on Baptism in *Die Kirchliche Dogmatik* appeared in 1967. Karl Barth died the following year. Both father and son answered the question "Is Baptism a sacrament?" with a clear "no."
31. Barth, *Teaching of the Church*, 43–45.
32. Ibid., 62.
33. For example, Bridge and Phypers, *The Water That Divides*. Grudem also urges mutual accommodation, suggesting "a common admission that baptism is not a major doctrine of the faith . . . " (*Systematic Theology*, 982–83).

tism can affect in any way its actual efficacy." He even used traditional Roman Catholic language that "it operates irresistibly."[34] Here Barth may have gone beyond even what was allowed in Lutheran and Roman Catholic positions, which hold that not every ritual which claims to be a Baptism is in fact a Baptism. Whatever Unitarians and Mormons do is not Baptism. Yet Barth does not even touch on this issue, and we can only speculate about this omission. Baptism may have been so individualized for him as to make the profession of the community insignificant.

At one time Barth could call Baptism a sacrament, but he later repudiated this view in his dogmatics.[35] He admitted to the previous error, "that infant baptism is so remarkably vivid a depiction of the free and omnipotent grace of God which is independent of all human thought and will, faith and unbelief."[36] But Barth had said already that "the sacrament does not redeem—since under redemption the experience of reconciliation, rebirth and deliverance into faith must be understood."[37] To describe Baptism, he much preferred the Reformed terms *significare, declarare, repraesentare, offere; accipere, obtinere, impetrare* described human participation.[38] Barth set down his doctrine of Baptism within Reformed dimensions, to which he added his characteristic idea of the encounter. At times, Barth could sound sacramental in calling Baptism "the sacrament of *regeneratio*," but he interpreted regeneration as the Christians' self-proclamation of their salvation.[39] Like Calvin, he saw Baptism as he did the Lord's Supper, as a subsidiary form of divine proclamation.[40] This fact should alert Lutherans to the impossibility of exhausting the meaning of Baptism and the Lord's Supper as only subdivisions under the Word, as if one sacrament could be substituted for another or that the content of one is the same as the other. We have been vehement in rejecting such sacramental homogenization that implies one sacrament has the same results as the other. This, however, is Barth's position. Amazingly, he sees his principle that the sacraments are subspecies of the Word at the heart of the Lutheran doctrine, and faults Lutheran theologians for failing to conclude that Baptism is not a sacrament.[41] Each reader will have to conclude whether some Lutheran theologians have clearly kept the sacraments distinct from the preached Word, or whether Barth has falsely read our position. Elsewhere he points out that each of the means of grace has a distinct character and purpose

---

34. Barth, *Teaching of the Church*, 57–58.
35. Barth, *Church Dogmatics* 4/4:x.
36. Ibid., 189.
37. Barth, *Teaching of the Church*, 28.
38. Ibid., 27–29.
39. Ibid., 31–32.
40. Ibid., 34.
41. Barth, *Church Dogmatics* 4/4:103–4.

(though it is hard to see what this is), even if each must be understood in relation to the Gospel, that is, the death and resurrection of Christ. In the end Barth could see in Baptism no more than a human rite, though he carefully nuanced this conclusion with language stressing the primacy of divine action.

Barth's position is not Calvin's, but it fits under the broader dimensions characteristic of Reformed theology in general, since what they call sacraments are by their own definition not sacraments. Lutherans and Roman Catholics agree that the Reformed have Baptism, but this does not mean that the Reformed see it in the sacramental sense that these bodies do. Ironically, Lutherans and Roman Catholics see in the Reformed practice of Baptism a sacramental quality which the Reformed themselves are incapable of seeing or are unwilling to see. Barth is aware that his position aligns him more closely with Calvin, and does not hesitate to dismiss Luther's and Roman Catholic views, which to him are similar. His view of a transcendental God, like Calvin's sovereign Deity, forces Barth into an almost Nestorian Christology and a less than fully developed sacramentalism. Barth has a theology of incarnation, but his theology is not incarnational. So also he has a theology of the sacraments, but his theology is not sacramental. Thus, it is not surprising that in the end Barth denied that anything else besides Jesus Christ, including Baptism, could be sacrament. His theology, like Luther's, is extremely christocentric, but Barth goes beyond Luther to a Christomonism. Barth's Christology is understood within the terms of revelation and not incarnation; Luther's Christology developed from his idea of incarnation and not revelation. Sacraments are for Luther an extension of God's incarnation in Christ, and not an opportunity for the encounter, as they were for Barth. Barth's volume on Baptism, the last in his dogmatics, made it clear that sacraments played no essential role in his theology. Whatever was said about Baptism could be said about the Lord's Supper, and so the need for him to write a separate volume on this sacrament was obviated. Barth went beyond Zwingli and allowed a place for symbolic interpretation of Baptism and the Lord's Supper. On this point Barth was closer to the more radical Zwingli than he was to Calvin. The sacraments are signs of the Spirit's presence and define the dimensions of the church. For Enlightenment Rationalism and Schleiermacher, the sacramental rites served to define the sociological dimensions of the church or community. Barth's views go beyond these, but the similarities are easily recognizable.

In the last analysis, sacraments in the Reformed theological tradition, to which Barth belongs, are not essential in the sense that they are for Lutherans. This much is evident in the role they play in the common liturgical life of the respective churches. Lutherans are aware of the lack of sacramental character in Reformed liturgical practice. While they recognize the Baptism of the Reformed church, they are less generous in regard to the Reformed celebration of the Lord's Supper. By his insistence that Baptism be administered in the church's public worship by authorized ministers and by his failure to allow lay Baptism in cases of imminent death (emergency Baptism), Barth follows the Reformed tradition in not seeing the sacraments as essential vehicles of God's grace.[42] Some Lutherans may find it uncomfortable to speak about Baptism in such absolutist terms, but this is clearly the confessional position: *De baptismo docent, quod sit necessarius ad salutem*.[43] Lutherans allow for exceptions, as has been discussed elsewhere, but these exceptions do not compromise its necessity. For the Reformed, Baptism is optional in the matter of salvation.

By renouncing his earlier position that these church rites are actually sacraments, Barth had gone beyond Calvin, but he was taking the Geneva reformer's ideas to their logical conclusions. Calvin held that the Spirit works *alongside* of the sacraments without an essential involvement in them. Barth separates Baptism with water from Baptism with the Holy Spirit. Strangely, the more important Baptism with the Holy Spirit amounts to no more than one-fifth of his volume on Baptism. Sacraments are an opportunity for the encounter with God, but are not the encounter itself. If they were, Jesus Christ would be deprived of His role as God's only revelation to man. He is *the* sacrament.

Barth has certain similarities to Paul Tillich in that he keeps the action of God independent of the sign itself. This was typical of neo-orthodoxy, of which they both were considered representatives, Barth being the more conservative in theological and biblical expression. Unless Barth is read carefully, he can also mistakenly be regarded as a repristination theologian, which he is not. Both Tillich and Barth fault Roman Catholicism, and perhaps Lutheranism by implication, for their views of the sacraments.[44] Tillich saw all creation as potentially sacramental, with some parts of creation better suited for this purpose than others. Though all creation has sacramental potential for Tillich, the divine action cannot be tied down to things, with the only exception being Jesus as the Christ.[45] Here lies the philosophical flaw in Tillich's theology: the necessity of connecting the divine revelation with the historical Jesus is not established. Tillich's affirmation that the historical Jesus is the conduit of divine revelation is hardly a philosophical judgment, but is rather a conclusion of faith. A similar critique can be made

---

42. Barth, *Teaching of the Church*, 26. Lutherans are condemned along with Roman Catholics and Anglicans in teaching that Baptism regenerates.

43. AC IX.1; Tappert, 33; *BKS*, 63; cf. AC II.

44. Ibid.

45. Paul Tillich, *Systematic Theology*, 3 vols. (Chicago: University of Chicago Press, 1951–63), 1:118–22, 1:135–37, 3:120–25.

of Barth's claim that Jesus Christ is God's only revelation and hence the only true sacrament. In the light of this critique we may then ask whether Barth has any meaningful sacramental doctrine at all. Barth can apply the term "sacraments" to all church rites, since they have the capacity to lead to an encounter between God and the believer. Prayer and works of charity, and not only Baptism, belong to the church's proclamation.[46] Barth does not discern such a wide range of sacramental potential in creation, but like Tillich he refuses to tie down the divine action to any one element. Tying divine grace to the sacraments, regardless of how they are defined, infringes upon God's sovereignty and His free act of grace in Jesus Christ.

Even though Barth explicitly denied that the liturgical rite of Baptism was a sacrament (in a genuine sense), he still granted it sacramental significance. It did point to an activity of God, even if the rite itself was not its cause. Since at the beginning Barth had redefined what was meant by sacraments, his public reversal of his earlier position on Baptism could not have been unexpected. He could clarify himself with regard to Baptism in a way he could not do with eschatology, because less was at stake for him. Changing what one thought about Baptism was not as sensational as changing what one thought about the existence of hell. In his book *Honest to God* John A. T. Robinson rejected his former belief in hell, for which he earned notoriety. Since infant Baptism has been controverted in Protestant circles since the Reformation, Barth's views could hardly qualify as sensational. Baptists constitute a huge portion of the American Protestant population, and to them his discoveries were hardly new. In a sense, Barth satisfied no one. Though he endorsed traditional Baptist arguments, he still found no reason to call infant Baptism invalid.[47] This is hardly the traditional Baptist position, but perhaps it was his political as much as his theological genius to leave such matters in a suspended state.

Barth dismissed as irrelevant any political concerns which could arise from discontinuing infant Baptism.[48] European territorial churches

---

46. "We begin from the fact that baptism is in any case a part of the Church's proclamation and this is plainly a human act. Like the Lord's Supper, preaching, prayer, the whole worship of the Church, pastoral care, works of charity, church order and Christian education, it is part of the Church's proclamation. One is accustomed to distinguish it from the other activities of the Church, as, like the Lord's Supper, a 'sacrament.' But whilst being clear about baptism and the Lord's Supper, it is even more important to realize that all the activities of the Church are in their way sacramental. That is to say, they are activities involving signs and symbols; moreover, they are dependent for their effectiveness on certain signs and symbols" (Barth, *Teaching of the Church*, 16).

47. "This baptism [customarily given in infancy] may have been administered in a way which is highly doubtful and questionable, because irregular. Nevertheless, one cannot say that it is invalid" (Barth, *Church Dogmatics* 4/4:189).

48. Ibid., 168.

were established on the practice of infant Baptism, and without this practice they would have to be continued as voluntary associations, as they are in the United States. Of course, he is right in asserting that infant Baptism should not be maintained to provide national unity, and here we might agree with him. Integration of church and state in Europe has a tradition going back to the emperor Constantine in the fourth century, and hence is more complex than most American theologians can recognize. Culture and religion form one cloth, in which governments have varying degrees of control. Different arrangements are in place from nation to nation throughout Europe, and it would be inappropriate for someone on the other side of the Atlantic to get involved in this question. The Reformation occurred within this context in which church, religion, and government were integrated. Immigrants to North America have maintained infant Baptism within a free church situation; here national unity in no way depends on a widespread practice of infant Baptism. While the disbanding of territorial churches in Europe has often been proposed in the past, it is only now being carried out.[49] Some territorial church ministers, following Barth's lead, left their own children unbaptized.[50] As Barth was questioning the theological basis for infant Baptism, Kurt Aland was questioning the historical grounds for its practice. The furor among theologians over continuing infant Baptism as a foundation for territorial churches has become less significant as the culture of Western Europe has become voluntarily secularized, a route which was involuntarily enforced in the late 1940s in the Soviet-dominated countries. It seems that traditionally Protestant countries have succumbed more thoroughly to this religious malaise than have Catholic ones. No part of Europe has remained immune to this secularization, though. The Napoleonic Code had already weakened

---

49. The Church of Sweden (Lutheran) is in the process of being disestablished as the official state-sponsored religion. While the system of the government collecting taxes for churches within the original boundaries of the Federal Republic of Germany commands a constantly dwindling majority of the population, its reinstitution in the former Democratic Republic of Germany has produced insufficient funds to support the existing clergy in these traditional Lutheran territories. Reasons for breaking church-state ties and for members not using the government as a church tax-collection agency seem more secular than theological. Since payment assured church services, those who opt out might no longer be entitled to have their children baptized and confirmed.

50. Wilhelm Oesch recounts how in 1968 Karl Barth attacked Pastor J. Beckmann, who as president of the Evangelical Church of the Rhineland was determined, so Barth believed, to enforce the legally binding Lutheran and Reformed confessions by removing one hundred pastors in the Rhineland who announced support of adult Baptism. This was the same year in which Barth's volume on Baptism (*Church Dogmatics* 4/4) appeared. Oesch also relates that in a press release issued on September 20, 1969, the Lutheran World Federation reported that in the German Democratic Republic fifty percent of the children, many of whom were pastors' children, were left unbaptized (Oesch, "Abschluss" [see chap. 8, n. 1], 235. This essay was originally published in the *Lutherische Rundblick* 17 [1969]: 175–85).

the church's civil authority in countries where it was instituted. Infant Baptism is not as vital for citizenship as it once was, and it may in the majority of cases be carried on as a custom without any connection to a vital church life at all. Indeed, the formerly widespread practice of nominally Christian Europeans having their infants baptized as a matter of custom may well be disappearing. If Barth saw the end of the once near-universal custom of infant Baptism as the dawn of a great evangelical awakening, he was dead wrong.

Even if in the end Barth rejected infant Baptism out of hand, since he never advocated rebaptizing he could never be called a Baptist. Infant Baptism is "an ancient ecclesiastical error," but not a heresy.[51] The church benefits from listening to the theologians, especially to him, so Barth claimed, but in the final analysis he allowed that the church and not the theologians would have to make the choice.[52]

In the view of some, Europe is returning to its pagan origins. The detachment of the territorial churches from their governments, which was accompanied by the decline in the practice of infant Baptism, is a final step in the secularization of Europe which began in the eighteenth-century Enlightenment. This decline would have occurred without Barth's opposition to the practice, but his influence did provide reasons for those who were intent on looking for theological reasons. With infant Baptism falling into disuse, the church may once again have to think in New Testament terms of baptizing adults and with them their families, until such a time as Christianity may be restored to its former place of influence in Europe.

---

51. Barth, *Church Dogmatics* 4/4:194.
52. For further discussion see Richard Schluter, *Karl Barths Tauflehre* (Paderborn: Verlag Bonifacius, 1973). One year after Barth's death, Wilhelm Oesch published an appraisal of his doctrine of Baptism and noted the significance that the last volume in the series dealt with Baptism. Without hesitation, Oesch says Barth's rejection of any means of grace places him squarely with the fanatics. He stripped Baptism of any sacramental meaning and placed it within the Law as the first ethical step which the Christian takes. Cleverly, Oesch describes Barth's divine-human theology as a contract between senior and junior partners ("Abschluss," 237). His self-proclaimed Christomonism is really a monism of the Holy Spirit (ibid., 238).

13

THE RITUAL OF BAPTISM

The rite and practice of Baptism are important for dogmatic theology, because they serve as the church's confession to all those who are present. At the same time, it must be made clear that Baptism should not be used simply as a visual aid or teaching device for the observers, but should be honored as the sacrament of regeneration for the recipient and conducted with the appropriate solemnity. Carelessness and disrespect have no place, for these call into question our own commitment to this sacrament as the mysterious working of the Triune God.[1] Baptism is first for the candidate, whether adult or child, and then for the members of the congregation, who are reminded of their own Baptism and, as Luther reminds us, are invited by the priest to pray for the child with the words, "Let us pray." In churches practicing infant Baptism, Baptisms of adults are less frequent, but should be conducted with equal solemnity. No impression can be given that Baptism for the catechumen who has been instructed in the faith is unimportant or incidental to his Christian life. Faith for an adult is not a substitute for Baptism. Quite to the contrary, Baptism provides the foundation for the adult's faith just as it does for the child's. This foundation remains in place for the rest of life and can be equated with the Christian life itself, as discussed in chapter 4. It might be good to call attention to the practice of the Eastern Orthodox, who use the same liturgy for the Baptisms of adults and infants.[2]

Until recently infant Baptism was administered in the church shortly after birth, without the congregation or often even the mother present. In apostolic times Baptisms were conducted outside in streams or pools, and then under the churches where water, often flowing, was available. Later, specially constructed baptistries were attached to the church for this purpose. At first baptistries contained pools large enough to accommodate either adults or children, but as the population became Christian these were replaced by fonts large enough to accommodate only the immersion of infants.[3] Baptistries are still found in some

---

1. So also Luther, who also admonishes that "boorish priests" not be permitted to administer Baptism (*AE* 53:101–2, "Order of Baptism, 1523").
2. Meyendorff, *Byzantine Theology*, 192–94.
3. For a selection of pictures and photographs of these baptistries see Brown, *Baptism through the Centuries*, 43–73.

churches. In some cases they remain separate from the church itself, and in others they are in a separate section of the church, away from the nave.

Fonts are more common in Lutheran churches, and are often placed at the entrance to the nave. Thus, in the past, parishioners entering from the narthex into the church passed the baptismal font and were reminded of their own Baptism. Since Baptism is now generally administered during the regular Sunday service, the fonts have been moved to the front of the nave, near the chancel, to allow more easily for congregational participation. Though the congregation contributes to the rite with its prayers, Baptism is God's act and not a congregational rite. A publicly administered Baptism allows the individual believer to make every Baptism his own concern.[4] On the other hand, nothing in the rite should suggest that its significance is no more than a rite of admission to the external community, a view held by the Reformed and perpetuated by the Rationalists.

Our rite of Baptism did not originate during the Reformation, but is derived from Luther's modification of what was already in place in the ancient and medieval churches. Remaining in place in his rites of 1523 and 1526 were the exorcism, the renunciation of Satan, the sign of the cross, and questioning based on the creed before administering the water in the name of the Triune God. Lutheran rites have the same origins as those used by the Roman and Anglican communions, and their similarity is easily detected.

During the eighteenth-century Enlightenment this ancient rite was significantly altered by elimination of the exorcisms, the renunciation of Satan, and sometimes the creed. This development proceeded from the Rationalists' rejection of angels, Satan, and original sin as superstitious remnants of a primitive Christianity. Faith was denied to infants, and so questioning the child on the basis of the creed was not found necessary, and would have given the false impression that he believed. With no need for sponsors, the baptismal rite focused more on the obligations of the parents to provide a moral upbringing for the child than on the child's faith.[5] Nothing was left to suggest that Baptism was the sacrament of regeneration. Baptism as the pouring of water on the child

---

4. For an historical overview of the places for administering Baptism see J. G. Davies, *Architectural Setting of Baptism* (see chap. 5, n. 30).

5. Julius August Wegscheider, *Institutiones Theologiae Christianae Dogmaticae*, 366–67 (see chap. 2, n. 1). This dogmatics appeared in eight editions between 1815 and 1844, the twilight years of German Lutheran Rationalism. In spite of the admitted uncertainty about whether Baptism was intended past the apostolic age, it was maintained as an initiation rite for the child into the Christian community. The Rationalists agreed with sixteenth-century Reformed theology in at least these matters: (1) Baptism did not regenerate, (2) it had to be administered by a lawful minister of the church, and (3) emergency Baptism was not practiced.

in the name of the Father and of the Son and of the Holy Spirit was retained as custom and not as divine mandate. So at the turn of the nineteenth century, rites of Baptism more and more resembled child dedication ceremonies, as still currently used among Baptists, with the exception, of course, that a Baptism actually took place, poorly defined though it was.[6] Enlightenment theology in Germany and England drew from Pietism and Methodism, respectively. These movements did not deny baptismal regeneration, but shifted the emphasis to a personal commitment or a second rebirth by the Spirit later in life. By the end of the eighteenth century, the importance of Baptism even among Lutherans had greatly diminished, and was retained often for no more than cultural, familial, and civil purposes. Some parents had grown so indifferent that at least in one case, the government required that parents have their infant children baptized or incur penalty.[7]

The revival of confessional Lutheranism under such theologians as C. F. W. Walther and Wilhelm Loehe restored the ancient rite of Baptism with the renunciation of Satan, the making of the sign of the cross, and addressing the questions about the creed directly to the child with the sponsors answering them. Francis Pieper lists thirteen ancient customs associated with the rite of Baptism: (1) reminder of original sin; (2) giving of the name; (3) the small exorcism; (4) sign of the cross; (5) the Psalm verse used as a prayer for the preservation of the child, the so-called *devotum Davidicum*; (6) the great exorcism; (7) reading of Mk 10:13–16; (8) the laying on of hands; (9) renunciation of Satan; (10) the Apostles' Creed; (11) use of sponsors; (12) the covering of the child with the white gown; and (13) the final prayer.[8] With the exception of the exorcisms and the placing of the white garment on the child, these customs were made part of the baptismal rite in *The Lutheran Agenda* (195–) used by The Lutheran Church—Missouri Synod.[9] In the rite of *Lutheran Worship Agenda* the use of the white garment and the giving of a candle were reintroduced as options.[10] Still omitted were the small

---

6. For a study of Rationalistic views see David P. Scaer, "The Doctrine of Infant Baptism in the German Protestant Theology of the Nineteenth Century" (Th.D. diss., Concordia Seminary, St. Louis, 1963), 22–52.

7. On February 25, 1802, a royal decree was published in Prussia requiring infants to be baptized within six weeks of birth. Parents failing to comply were threatened with being deprived of these children (Adam Theodor Albert Lehmus, *Über die Taufe* [Heidelberg: Mohr und Zimmer, 1807], 7). It is unknown whether this law was enforced. The government was moved less by religious reasons than by the desire to have an accurate list of males eligible for military service. Within a generation Lutherans would be forced to use an agenda which no longer held to baptismal regeneration.

8. *Christian Dogmatics* 3:282.

9. St. Louis, MO: Concordia Publishing House, 195– (for use with *The Lutheran Hymnal*).

10. St. Louis, MO: Concordia Publishing House, 1984 (for use with *Lutheran Worship*).

The Ritual of Baptism

and greater exorcisms. Dressing the baptized in a white gown after the Baptism was an early church custom. Early Christians went into the water for Baptism to signify death by drowning, and then were clothed with a white garment to symbolize the resurrection of the new man who is clothed in Christ's righteousness.[11] The host arrayed in white in the Book of Revelation (Rv 7:9–17) are presumably martyrs or those who by Baptism have washed their robes in Christ's blood.[12] Traditionally, Lutherans have brought their children to Baptism in white christening gowns, so this placing of a white garment on the baptized is a variation of an ancient Christian custom.

Significant omissions in the current rites are the exorcisms, which have a firm place in church tradition and are biblically and theologically defensible. Luther had two exorcisms in both of his rites. Exorcism, the driving out of Satan, draws a line between the kingdoms of God and of Satan, over which believers cross through Baptism. Though this crossing from one kingdom to another is expressed in the renunciation of Satan ("Do you renounce the devil and all his works and all his ways?"), this is the believer's commitment to what God has already done. We must say emphatically that no one can free himself from Satan's grip. Pelagianism, Arminianism, Socinianism, and Rationalism—that is, any form of synergism with its optimistic understanding of human moral capabilities—have little use for the seriousness of sin and Satan. Exorcism is an answer to synergism, since here God alone acts to release the believer from Satan's grip. Not only is the use of the exorcism in Baptism a statement of the awareness of the supernatural power of Satan and evil, it is also a complete rejection of human righteousness. Only after Jesus has conquered Satan in our lives (exorcism) are we able to renounce the latter and then confess Jesus as Lord. Together the exorcism and the renunciation constitute the prelude to confessing the creed and the act of Baptism itself.[13] After the "unclean spirit" (Satan) is removed, the Holy Spirit, in whose name Baptism is administered, is given. Here we are speaking of a logical sequence of cause and effect, and not of a chronological one. In the one moment the sinner is released from

---

11. Spinks, "Luther's Timely Theology," 30.

12. Massey H. Shepherd, Jr., proposes that the first seven chapters of Revelation describe the initiatory rites of Baptism: "1. The renunciation of Satan 2. The profession of faith 3. The washing 4. The sealing with the Name 5. The investment with the white garments" (*The Paschal Liturgy and the Apocalypse* [Richmond: John Knox Press, 1960], 85–91).

13. Luther's 1526 rite has these exorcisms: "Depart thou unclean spirit and make room for the Holy Spirit." "I adjure thee, thou unclean spirit, by the name of the Father and of the Son and of the Holy Ghost that thou come out of and depart from this servant of Jesus Christ, N. Amen" (*AE* 53:107–8). Luther's three renunciations of Satan are combined into one in our agenda.

Satan's kingdom and believes. The liturgy expresses this as one event happening after another.[14]

Exorcisms were not reintroduced into the current baptismal liturgy, but their place in the rite of Baptism can be defended biblically. By driving out Satan through exorcisms, Jesus brought God's kingdom. Mark's pericope on John's baptizing of Jesus (Mk 1:4–11) was included in several baptismal liturgies. Subsequent pericopes in Mark focus on Jesus and Satan. Satan puts Jesus to the test (Mk 1:12–13). His ministry is described as a preaching of the kingdom (Mk 1:14–15). After the selection of four disciples (Mk 1:16–20) comes a lengthy discourse on an exorcism in a synagogue (Mk 1:21–28). Jesus, who has received the Spirit of God in His Baptism, drives out evil spirits. Unclean spirits flee before the face of God's Holy One (Mk 1:23–27) who is endowed with the Spirit (Mk 1:10, 12). Jesus drives out Satan with the finger of God (Lk 11:20), which is the Spirit of God (Mt 12:28). Though there is no explicit reference to the demon-possessed and exorcized persons being baptized, there is every reason to assume that they were baptized, along with the blind, the lame, and the deaf whom Jesus healed! Following Jesus meant being baptized. Here is the biblical precedent that exorcism should precede Baptism. Baptism forgives original sin, and, just as importantly, delivers from Satan. What Jesus did by exorcism (Mk 1:25), the church still does in every phase of its ministry (Mt 10:1; Mk 16:16–17; Acts 19:12), but especially in Baptism.

A word must be said regarding what specifically is meant by exorcism. In the Bible exorcism is intended for those who are possessed by devils and no longer have control over themselves. Demon possession does not mean that these people are necessarily guilty of more horrible sins than anyone else. They are presented not as malefactors or felons, but as victims (Mk 1:16; Mt 12:22–32; Acts 16:16–18). Damaging to salvation is Satan's exercise of his power through a person's deliberate alliance (Judas [Jn 13:2, 21–27]), unwitting cooperation (Peter [Mt 11:22–32; Lk 22:31]), idolatry (Baal, pagan gods [1 Cor 10:6–22, esp. v. 20]), or vigorous and obstinate unbelief (Jewish opponents of Jesus [Jn 8:44]), and the ignorant unbelief of the sons of disobedience (Eph 2:1–2). These people may be aligned with Satan, but they are not, properly speaking, demon-possessed. In some of these cases Jesus had mercy on them (Mt 9:35–10:1) and healed them as He did the sick (Mt 4:24, 12:22–32; Mk 1:34). Demon possession is a particular illness of the soul, and not deliberate enmity against God. Those who allied themselves with Satan were rebuked (Peter), warned (Peter, Judas), or condemned

---

14. Trigg correctly notes of Luther that, though he attributes regeneration to Baptism, "it is by no means clear that it can be ascribed without qualification to the moment when baptism is administered" (*Baptism*, 154).

(opponents of Jesus), but were not exorcized. In the rite of Baptism Jesus continues to show His mercy on those who have fallen under Satan's power and reestablishes God's kingdom in territory over which Satan illegally rules (Mt 10:1, 12:22–32). We may hesitate to call children morally innocent, but they are victims of sin and Satan, and we agree with Luther that exorcisms in the rite of Baptism are appropriate. Attached to his 1523 rite, Luther says that exorcism makes the devil an enemy of the church: "Remember, therefore, that it is no joke *to take sides against the devil* [the renunciation] and not only *to drive him away from the little child* [the exorcism], but to burden the child with such a mighty and lifelong enemy."[15] A future revision of the baptismal rite might consider reinserting Luther's exorcism, which the Rationalists removed. A secular age requires not only belief in God, but the awareness that the world remains under the sway of the prince of darkness. Certainly we cannot renounce Satan by our own power, but only because Christ by His Word has forced him to flee. Another argument for restoring the renunciation of Satan into the baptismal rite is Jesus' own baptism. In His baptism, he receives the Spirit (πνεῦμα θεοῦ καταβαῖνον ὡσεὶ περιστερὰν καὶ ἐρχόμενον ἐπ' αὐτόν; Mt 3:16) who equips Him to fight against Satan (Τότε ὁ Ἰησοῦς ἀνήχθη εἰς τὴν ἔρημον ὑπὸ τοῦ πνεύματος πειρασθῆναι ὑπὸ τοῦ διαβόλου; Mt 4:1). Similarly, in our Baptism we receive the Spirit who not only takes the place of the Evil Spirit, but arms us to do battle with him. Luther's rites, like the ancient ones, did not have a discourse on original sin and the nature and efficacy of Baptism, as ours does in order to emphasize baptismal regeneration against the Reformed denial of it.

Circumstances may dictate a shortened form of Baptism, but an abridgement of the rite can never suggest that certain items in the service are irrelevant or incidental. Eighteenth-century Rationalist theologians altered the baptismal liturgies because they no longer believed in what these signified. Even with a shortened form, Baptism delivers from death and the devil, forgives sins and grants eternal life, and regenerates the baptized through faith. This does not mean that all parts of the rite are of equal value. Use of the creed is more important than the giving of a candle or the application of salt or oil, which Luther retained in his 1523 rite but omitted in 1526.[16] Oil points to the giving of the

---

15. *AE* 53:102; emphasis added.

16. Luther kept the ancient ceremonies in connection with Baptism, but provided these sage words: "Now remember, too, that in baptism the external things are the least important, such as blowing under the eyes, signing with the cross, putting salt into the mouth, putting spittle and clay into the ears and nose, anointing the breast and shoulders with oil, signing the crown of the head with the chrism, putting on the christening robe, placing a burning candle in the hand, and whatever else has been added by man to embellish baptism. For most assuredly baptism can be performed without all these, and they are not the sort of devices and practices from which the devil shrinks or flees. He

The Ritual of Baptism

Spirit, but it must be clear that the Spirit is given in the water of Baptism as an act of the Triune God.[17]

The baptismal ritual must make clear that the child is being baptized on the basis of his own faith and not the faith of his parents (Reformed), the faith of the church (Roman Catholic), or his own future faith, a view held across denominational boundaries.[18] Our current rites

---

sneers at greater things than these!" (*AE* 53:102).

17. Luther's "Order of Baptism" (1523) contained the ritual of placing salt on the mouth of the child; putting spittle in the right ear during the reading of Mk 7:34, "'Ephphatha,' that is, 'Be opened'"; and the anointing of the child with oil, accompanied by the words, "And I anoint thee with the oil of salvation in Jesus Christ our Lord" (*AE* 53:95–103). The placing of the white garment on the child and the giving of the burning torch (candle) were not retained in the 1526 service, but have been reinstated in the current rite of *Lutheran Worship*. In the use of any of these ceremonies there are two questions: Are they practical, that is, can these comfortably be done? What is their theological significance? Many liturgical practices were instituted for what were once practical reasons and then were given theological explanations. The practice of baptizing in fonts rather than pools developed for practical reasons. In the ancient church, adults who were being baptized could take their children into the pools with them. When parents who had already been baptized had their children baptized, pools became unnecessary. Colder climates may have made pools less attractive. Some pastors may have to be reminded of what follows what, and suddenly a well-informed and efficient assisting deacon becomes necessary. Salt on the mouth signifies the commitment to speak the wisdom of the Gospel. The "Ephphatha" ceremony of touching the ear with spittle makes the point that Jesus acted *through means* in His ministry and continues to do so now through Baptism. Burning torches suggested for Luther the parable of the virgins waiting for the return of Christ, the heavenly Bridegroom (*AE* 53:101). *Lutheran Worship* keeps this thought, and also sees the candle as symbolizing the baptized living by the light of Christ. An iconoclastic spirit, more fitting of the Reformed, often prevents the church from making fuller use of its rich tradition of symbolism; but this is said with the caveat that little be done to detract from the essential act of God's working in the water.

18. An ambiguity exists in the 1944 edition of the *Book of Common Prayer* of the Episcopal Church. "A Catechism," included in this edition, states that children cannot fulfill the requirements for Baptism of repentance and faith (ibid., 581). The Thirty-nine Articles are even more explicit. The liturgy for Baptism in this edition, however, suggests something quite other, and holds that the child really believes (ibid., 276–77). After a prayer that the child may be reborn by the Holy Spirit, a thought which is repeated in the address to the sponsors, follows this question: "Dost thou, therefore, in the name of this Child, renounce the devil and his works . . . ?" The other questions, including one about whether the candidate accepts the Apostles' Creed, are addressed directly to the child. Prayers before and concluding the service affirm that the child believes, is a member of the church, and receives the Holy Spirit. Bishop Philpotts of Exeter refused to install the Reverend George Cornelius as the clergyman for Brampford Speke, because he denied that regeneration occurred during the administration of Baptism (Trigg, *Baptism*, 153). We could hardly do better than to take over the question of renunciation from the *Book of Common Prayer*: "Dost thou, therefore, in the name of this Child, renounce the devil and his works, the vain pomp and glory of the world, with all covetous desires of the same, and the sinful desires of the flesh, so that thou wilt not follow, nor be led by them?" A more recent edition of the *Book of Common Prayer* retains the questions addressed to the child, but a promise made by the parents and godparents sees the full effect of Baptism in the future: "Will you by your prayers and witness help this child to grow into the full stature of Christ?" ([Kingsport, TN: Kingsport Press, 1977], 302). This understanding follows the Reformed tradition on infant Baptism. "An Outline of Faith

assume that the baptized child believes and is regenerated by the Holy Spirit, as shown in this blessing taken from Luther's rite: "Almighty God, the Father of our Lord Jesus Christ, who has given you the new birth of water and of the Spirit and has forgiven you all your sins, strengthen you with his grace to life everlasting."[19] An invitation to the congregation by the officiant to "confess our Christian faith, into which this child is to be baptized: I believe in God the Father Almighty . . ."[20] stresses the objectivity of what the church believes (*fides quae*), but it skirts the issue of whether the child himself is a believer. Hence the questions must be addressed to the child, with the answers provided by the sponsors acting on behalf of the child. This point is important, since the Lutheran church alone is consistent in holding to the *fides infantium*, the faith of infants. A child's inability to articulate does not indicate the absence of faith. Answers given by the sponsors are *the child's own*! In civil law parents, or where parents are absent court-appointed guardians, act on behalf of the child; thus the use of sponsors to confess the child's faith should not be considered an offense against the child's free will or an unusual or unethical practice. Jesus informs us that children (infants) can and do believe, and His words have more truth than the personal confession of any adult! Asking questions of the children and the use of sponsors also shows that there is no difference between the Baptism of adults and infants.

To avoid giving the impression that we are in any sense accepting the Reformed covenant view in which Baptism only ratifies the special relationship the child already has with God through his parents, parents should not be encouraged to serve as sponsors for their own children. Children are not baptized based upon the faith of others, *fides aliena*, whether it is the faith of believing parents, *fides parentium*, the local congregation, or the universal church, *una sancta*.[21] Justification is

---

Commonly Called the Catechism," included in this edition, only supports our assessment: "Parents and sponsors . . . guarantee that the infants will be brought up within the Church, to know Christ and be able to follow him" (859). The explicit denial of baptismal regeneration is missing, however.

19. *Lutheran Worship*, 203. Some nineteenth-century Lutheran theologians, especially those identified with the Erlangen theology, posited regeneration of children in Baptism, but without faith. This idea was based on a peculiar anthropology which allowed Baptism to work on their "spiritual and physical nature," but restricted the working of the Word later on in life to their "spiritual personality." In this way these theologians could assert baptismal regeneration without ascribing faith to the child. Those who held to this or similar views were Johann Hoefling, Hans Lassen Martensen, and Gottfried Thomasius. For a further discussion see Scaer, "Doctrine of Infant Baptism," 73–156. Pieper among others noted the similarity to the Roman position.

20. "The Baptism of Infants (without Sponsors)" under "The Order of Holy Baptism," *The Lutheran Agenda*, 10.

21. In Roman Catholic theology, the child is baptized on the basis of the faith of the believing community and not that of his parents. See Kurt Stasiak, *Return to Grace*

always and only by the faith of the baptized, but we insist that Baptism saves. Placed side by side are these statements by Luther: "For unless faith is present and is conferred in Baptism, Baptism will profit us nothing"[22] and "Baptism, too, is a work of God, not invented by man but commanded by God and witnessed to by the gospel."[23] Limiting Baptism to the children of those parents who convince us that they are truly believers leaves us with the horrible burden of determining the nature, quality, and character of their faith, *fides parentium*.[24] Those not formally associated with the church should not be discouraged from bringing their children to Baptism.

This is not to say that the faith of others, *fides aliena*, *fides parentium*, has no place in Baptism. Luther holds that the faith of the church—who else has faith?—brings our children and those of others to Baptism. This faith helps but does not take the place of the child's. The church's faith is not a vicarious faith (German, *stellvertretender Glaube*), a faith substituting for the child's.[25] In fact, the church prays that God would give the child faith. Luther goes so far as to suggest that many people baptized as children turn out badly because their sponsors have not offered up sufficient prayers for them in their fight against the devil.[26] Baptism and the church's prayer both are the cause of regeneration, but in different senses. Thus even before a child is born he is offered up to God by the prayers of the church, a matter discussed in the section on the salvation of unbaptized children.

The baptismal rite in *Lutheran Worship* has the parents and the congregation join the sponsors in answering the questions about renouncing Satan and affirming the creed: "Because this child cannot answer for *himself/herself*, we shall all, together with sponsors and parents, faithfully speak on *his/her* behalf in testimony of the forgiveness of sins and the birth of the life of faith which God our Father bestows in and through

---

(Collegeville, MN: Liturgical Press, 1996), 22–23. Oberman was mistaken in claiming that Luther held that children were baptized on the vicarious faith of others (*Luther*, 230); however, Luther did hold that the faith of the church, and especially that of the sponsors, was a factor in the child's attaining his own faith. For a review of Luther's writings from 1517 to 1520 in which he articulated his views, see Brinkel, *Die Lehre Luthers von der fides infantium*, 24–36.

22. *AE* 36:59.
23. *AE* 40:239.
24. See Spinks, "Luther's Timely Theology," 41. Spinks is concerned with the intrusion of parental obligations into baptismal liturgies: "Parents take an active part in their children's justification. Zwingli's righteousness of faith based on obligation and sealed by the Spirit, of which baptism is merely an ecclesial sign, seems to have burst in upon us without invitation" (ibid.).
25. Brinkel, *Die Lehre Luthers von der fides infantium*, 85–88.
26. "And I suspect that people turn out so badly after baptism because our concern for them has been so cold and careless; we, at their baptism, interceded for them without zeal" (*AE* 53:102).

Baptism."[27] This language might appear awkward to some. The rite in *The Lutheran Agenda* (195–) is explicit about the questions being addressed to the child, but loses some of its force when it says that the questions "signify thereby what God in and through Baptism works in him."[28] Not only do the questions signify God's activity in Baptism, but with Luther we insist the child is participating in the rite and is *really* answering the questions! In both the 1523 and 1526 rites, these rubrics are found: "Then the priest shall have the child, *through his sponsors*, renounce the devil and say . . ."[29] Answers offered by the sponsors for the child are no more symbolic than the questions asked about the creed.[30] Through the creed, as through the entire rite of Baptism, God is creating and confirming faith!

Also problematic in the *Lutheran Worship* rite is that the parents join the congregation and the sponsors in answering the questions. Reformed churches frequently do not use sponsors, but have the parents bring the child to Baptism. This practice reflects the belief that through the parents the child is *entitled* to salvation. Lutheran rites traditionally have no liturgical role for the parents, and reference to them in the rites is absent. A general invitation in the rite of *Lutheran Worship* for everyone present to answer the questions relieves the pastor of requiring that those carrying the child to Baptism be Lutheran. Here the rite is useful. While it is desirable to have Lutherans carry the child to the font as sponsors, the pastor cannot delay Baptism for a child until this requirement is met. No one needs a reminder that some chosen as sponsors can hardly fulfill the traditional function of articulating the child's faith. *Lutheran Worship* presents an acceptable way of keeping the questions and answers in the rite where the "sponsors" are not really sponsors. Where there were no sponsors, *The Lutheran Agenda* (195–) provided another service which simply eliminated the questions from the rite. As we have said elsewhere, the absence of questions addressed to the child is regrettable, especially in regard to our position on the *fides infantium*. To avoid giving the impression that birth from Christian parents is a guarantee of salvation, they should not ordinarily serve as sponsors. So the rubric that the parents should "faithfully speak" on behalf of their child is as problematic as having less than fully qualified sponsors. Every pastor knows of cases where grandparents insist on the Baptism of their grandchildren. This means that disgruntled parents may be present at the font for the Baptism of their children under an obvious protest. These

---

27. *Lutheran Worship*, 201.
28. 6.
29. *AE* 53:99, 108; emphasis added.
30. If the congregation joins in reciting the creed in answering the questions, then there is no reason to recite the creed again in the service. Repetition will not rid the church of cryptic Arians.

parents can hardly be said to "faithfully speak" on behalf of their child. It may be best to have the congregation answer the questions only when neither parents nor those holding the child are Lutheran. In most cases the grandparents or other friends and relatives who have been instrumental in bringing the children to Baptism are more likely to be qualified. Not every child needs sponsors to answer for him. A child as young as five or six or even younger might easily answer "yes" to the questions of whether he renounces Satan and believes in the articles of the Apostles' Creed. The less than fully articulate confession of a child requires no apology.

One expendable part of the ordinary baptismal rites in the current agendas may be the obligations placed on sponsors and parents before the act of Baptism itself. First of all, this element makes an unhealthy distinction between the rite of Baptism for infants and that for adults, as explained above. Certain medieval rites admonished sponsors to teach children the Lord's Prayer and the creed, but early Reformed rites went further in exacting promises to teach the child Christian order, discipline, and the fear of God. Exacting promises from the sponsors gives the impression that certain conditions must be met before infants can be baptized. Thus it may appear that the sacrament is a bilateral agreement, an idea characteristic of Calvin's covenant theology but foreign to Luther's theology.[31] Granted, Baptism is a covenant, but it is a *unilateral* one God makes with us and not a *bilateral* agreement we make with God in which grace depends on meeting certain conditions.[32] Such admonitions would be more proper after the rite, both for adults and for the sponsors of infant children.[33] Of course, nothing would be lost if these admonitions were omitted altogether.

Lutheran churches might consider adopting Luther's 1526 rite, which is not only shorter but also less didactic than those in current use.[34] While this rite contains the two exorcisms, like the 1523 rite it does not require a promise from the sponsors. Questions about the creed are more brief.

---

31. Spinks, "Luther's Timely Theology," 27.
32. For a fuller discussion of Baptism as a "pact" see ibid., 23–28.
33. Ibid., 42.
34. Spinks says of Luther's rite for Baptism: "Luther was not incompetent. He knew the importance of instruction, of catechesis, of schooling, and parental care. But these were pastoral issues, which were ongoing. The sacrament was not a human ceremony celebrating ecclesiastical pastoral work. Baptism was the place where God had chosen to justify and declare the non-imputation of sin. It was the visible sign of unmerited justification through God's grace. *This was not the place to arrange agreements with God and exchange contracts.* This was the place where one fled from evil, and threw oneself into the mercy of God, trusting that God would be faithful and save in this place in this appointed ceremony. Faith was simply trust, like the woman who touched the cloak of Jesus, trust that here, somehow, for some reason, *even if it is not fully understood or completely comprehended, this God-made-man could save*" (ibid., 41; emphasis added.)

The Ritual of Baptism

The confessional life of believers (the church) is derived from their Baptism. Creed (confession) and Baptism belong together, because the creed expresses the faith which receives Baptism and which is created by Baptism. Of all the churches in Christendom, the Lutheran church is characterized by its subscription and submission to confessions, of which the Apostles' Creed is fundamental and essential. To be a creedal or confessional church means to be a sacramental church, because the creed had its origins in the earliest rites of Baptism.[35] Reciting the creed first at the Baptism and again at the Holy Communion is unnecessary, and really adds nothing. A second recitation may take the focus away from the creed's place in Baptism.

The 1982 rite in *Lutheran Worship* concludes with the congregation saying to the baptized: "We welcome you into the Lord's family. We receive you as a fellow member of the body of Christ, a child of the same heavenly Father, to work with us in his kingdom."[36] This language lacks beauty and dignity, and might be left to an announcement after the service. Also, its inclusion is not without theological problems. Incorporation into the church is done by Christ through the Holy Spirit in Baptism, and not by one or all of the members. Welcoming the baptized "to work with us in his kingdom" detracts from Luther's idea that Baptism is pure grace.[37] It also might be difficult to demonstrate a liturgical precedent for the phrase. After the Baptism Luther had the blessing which remains in our agenda, crediting God for the regeneration (cited above), and ending with "Peace be with thee. Amen."

Dogmatics cannot go into each liturgical detail, but a word should be said about the positioning of the participants around the baptismal font during the rite. Candidates, ministers, assistants, sponsors, and parents should surround the font and not the altar during the entire rite of Baptism, since in this act God is present and acting. Facing the altar with backs toward the font during any part of the rite, *including the prayers*, may give the false impression that God is not present in the water of Baptism and that this sacrament is inferior to the Lord's Sup-

---

35. For a discussion of this issue see Kelly, *Early Christian Creeds*, especially 30–61. The Apostles' Creed is assumed into the Nicene and Athanasian Creeds, and is one of the six parts of the Small Catechism and one of the five parts of the Large Catechism. It is mentioned specifically in the Smalcald Articles and in the Epitome and Solid Declaration of the Formula of Concord. A confessional church is by definition a sacramental one, because the fundamental statement of her faith originates and is given in and confessed at Baptism.

36. 204.

37. Spinks reports that "as early as 1524, Osiander had issued a version of Luther's baptismal rite to which he added, among other things, a pre-baptismal admonition. In 1533 he replaced this rite with that of Luther, perhaps because he realized that even the admonition gave liturgical expression to a *pactum* theology and thereby undermined grace" ("Luther's Timely Theology," 42).

per, which of course it is not. Accordingly, Luther suggests that kneeling (genuflecting) is as appropriate during the rite of Baptism as it is during the Holy Communion. He sees each act of Baptism as a replication of the Baptism of Jesus in which the Triune God is present. The presence and appearance of the Holy Trinity in the Baptism of Jesus occurs in the Baptism of each Christian. *In Baptismo sonat vox Trinitatis.*[38]

---

38. Consider also these words of the Reformer: "Thus it is good that the Sacrament of the Altar is honored with bended knee; for the true body and blood of the Lord are there, likewise the presence of the Holy Spirit and the promise of the Word of God, which should be heard reverently. For God works there, and the Lord shows Himself. In Moses this is sometimes called the face of God. He means God is present and appears to me. Here it is certainly fitting for me to rise or to fall on my knees. And the appearance and faces of God we experience are equal to, yes, superior to, all the appearances in the Law of Moses. When I approach Baptism, I must certainly conclude that nothing human is being done there. But the water is a veil or a means. So is the Word with which God is veiled. Behind these [Eucharist, Baptism, Word] stands our Lord God, and they are faces of God through which He speaks with us and works in every person individually. He baptizes me; He absolves me and gives His body and blood through the tongue and the hand of the minister. *For God works salvation in Baptism. And this is the presence or form and epiphany of God in these means. Therefore we do the right thing when we bow and revere God when He speaks with us. If we do not do so with our bodies, we should at least do so with all our hearts.* And in Baptism, of course, our eyes and hearts should be directed to the manifest appearance in the Jordan, where the voice of the Father is heard from heaven, the flesh of the Son is seen, and the Holy Spirit appears in the form of a dove. Thus also in our Baptism" (*AE* 8:145; emphasis added).

14

BAPTISM AND CATECHESIS

With infant Baptism the most commonly practiced form of this sacrament, our attention must finally be focused on its relationship to catechesis, that is, instruction in Christian doctrine. In recent years both Lutherans and Roman Catholics have given attention to the role of catechesis, which now most commonly follows Baptism.[1] Some Roman Catholic theologians have proposed that the necessity of catechesis presumes that the Baptism of adults is the norm, from which infant Baptism is a deviate though acceptable practice.[2] The Lutheran discussion of Baptism has been shaped largely by the practice of infant Baptism, which it inherited from the ancient church, and subsequently by the Reformation conflict with the Anabaptists. Infant Baptism is now the most commonly practiced, and, as we have argued, the most proper form of this sacrament. Baptism corresponds to circumcision, since both rites or sacraments are now associated most frequently with infancy. Although circumcision was given as a sign of the covenant to the aged Abraham, it became and remained chiefly a rite for infant boys. Not that circumcision was never again performed on adult males (see e.g. Gn 24:34), but the rite was in nearly all cases administered in infancy. Still, we should not lose sight of the fact that Baptisms in the New Testament were administered first to adults and then to children who shared their faith, and who thus were baptized with them. It is also not surprising that therefore the New Testament should preserve the catechesis which preceded the administration of Baptism to adult converts. In churches practicing infant Baptism, the catechesis follows Baptism, an issue which deserves some discussion.

There is no support in the New Testament for the practice of some Protestant churches today in which the only prerequisite for Baptism is a loosely defined profession of faith, for in the apostolic church the prerequisite faith for Baptism was a fully formed faith. This latter faith had no resemblance to what today are called decisions for Christ, which are too often uninformed commitments, frequently made under personal emotional stress or peer pressure. Along with the confession that the crucified and resurrected Jesus was Lord or Christ, a confession of sins was required, an element taken over into Christian Baptism from

---

1. Stasiak, *Return to Grace*, 37–42.
2. Aidan Kavanagh, *The Shape of Baptism* (New York: Pueblo, 1978), 105–8.

the baptism of John. Jews who received Baptism already had a prior knowledge of the promised Messiah, and so the basic structure of Christian doctrine was already in place. This outline was fleshed out by the acceptance of Jesus' claims that by His crucifixion and resurrection he fulfilled the Old Testament, demonstrating that He was the Christ, the Son of God (Lk 24:44). He assumed into Himself such Old Testament institutions as Temple, priest, prophet, and king (Mt 12: 5, 41–42). In Jesus, Israel reached perfection. Describing the faith of the first Jewish converts as "instant recognition" of Jesus as the fulfillment of the entire Old Testament may not be too far off the mark. Several New Testament figures seem knowledgeable about what "Christ" meant before they identified Jesus with Him. Simeon is a clear example (Lk 2:26). The gospel of Matthew assumes that Jesus' enemies identified Him with the Christ, but refused to believe Him in spite of the evidence (Mt 12:21, 31–32, 28:11–15). Before St. Paul became a Christian, he was by his own admission completely knowledgeable in the Old Testament. As a persecutor of the church, he was fully versed in what he considered to be a heresy which he in the name of God intended to eradicate by persecution (Phil 3:5–6).

Stephen's sermon is an example of how the earliest Christian preaching was catechesis built upon the faith of Israel. In proclaiming that Jesus had been put to death, Stephen surveyed the five books of Moses. Likewise, the apostle Paul after his conversion preached that Jesus was the Christ (Acts 9:22).[3] Peter's first sermons to the Jews in the book of Acts are probably condensed catecheses in which he demonstrated that Jesus was the Christ (Acts 2:14–41, 3:12–26, 5:42). Such summary catechesis led these first converts to Baptism (ἐβαπτίσθησαν) and then to participation in church services which centered in the *didache* (τῇ διδαχῇ τῶν ἀποστόλων, catechetical sermons), and then to receiving the Communion, which is called the breaking of the bread (τῇ κοινωνίᾳ, τῇ κλάσει τοῦ ἄρτου).[4] Philip's instruction of the Ethiopian eunuch is another example of how catechesis led to Baptism (Acts 8:26–39).

---

3. Catechesis for confirming children in the Lutheran church has traditionally required intense instruction, generally over a period of two years or more. Instruction of adults for Baptism or confirmation often covers months. The New Testament examples of baptizing some persons immediately after their hearing a sermon seems to be at odds with the ancient church and traditional and current Lutheran practices. A parallel between Paul and Luther can be drawn. Luther was thoroughly versed in the facts of the Bible before his well-known "tower experience." Justification by faith provided him with the key to understanding the biblical data. The same was true of his co-reformers, who were versed in theology before they accepted his reformation. So the Damascus Road appearance of Jesus put what Paul knew about the Old Testament and Jesus in proper perspective. He was baptized immediately (Acts 9:18).

4. "And they devoted themselves to the apostles' teaching and fellowship, to the breaking of bread and the prayers" (Acts 2:42).

From these pericopes it is evident that the Old Testament, which had served as the catechesis for Israel, continued to be used for that purpose in the earliest church. In some cases in the apostolic church, the additional catechesis or instruction of believers may not have been much longer than a few hours, after which Baptism was immediately administered. It is quite arguable that the gospel of Matthew is for the Jews the earliest written form of the catechesis in which the life and death of Jesus are shown to correspond with Old Testament events and persons. Luke's gospel may have been directed to Jews in the diaspora and to Gentiles.[5] The Lutheran insistence that Word and sacrament belong together preserves the early church view that catechesis leads to Baptism, where the catechumen meets Christ in His death and resurrection.

In the New Testament churches which were more thoroughly Gentile—thus consisting of people with virtually no knowledge of the Old Testament—the period of catechetical instruction could take years. Because of the penetrating influence of pagan ideas and Greek philosophies, St. Paul may have remained for a longer time in certain churches, for example at Corinth and Ephesus, to prepare these Christians for Baptism. The catechesis of the first Gentile converts more often than not had to be rigorous. Even monotheism was strange to some.[6] Problems, which St. Paul addressed in his epistles, were often distortions of Christian beliefs, which had been laced with pagan ideas and customs. Though the recipients of these letters appear to be baptized, Paul provides them with additional catechesis to correct their aberrant beliefs.

The catechetical tradition which grew up out of the New Testament reached a classical formulation for Lutherans in the Small Catechism. Instruction in the catechism must be related directly to Baptism by bringing believers to Baptism or confirming the faith given in Baptism.[7]

---

5. For a fuller discussion of the gospels of Matthew and Luke as catechesis, see Arthur A. Just, Jr., *Luke 1:1–9:50*, Concordia Commentary (St. Louis: Concordia Publishing House, 1997), 13–16. Just says, "Matthew's highly semitic perspective assumes that the hearer is familiar with OT and Jewish customs and beliefs. Therefore, Matthew may not have satisfied the increasingly Gentile audience that became a force in the church" (ibid., 15).

6. Acts provides highly condensed versions of the apostolic sermons, which were more like extended dissertations than today's twenty-minute Sunday morning homilies. See Acts 20:9 in regard to the length of Paul's sermon which brought the sleeping Eutychus to his death. In the apostolic period some may have received Baptism after a comparatively brief catechesis, but others required longer instruction. Note can be made of Paul's year-and-a-half stay in Corinth (Acts 18:11) and his two-year stay in Ephesus (Acts 19:10); this suggests that instruction had to be longer for those who were pagan, with no knowledge of the Old Testament. The language of Acts 18:11 suggests that he was presenting the *didache* (διδάσκων ἐν αὐτοῖς τὸν λόγον τοῦ Θεοῦ).

7. The revival of catechesis in The Lutheran Church—Missouri Synod is signaled by the publication of *Catechesis in the Lutheran Congregation* by its president, Dr. A. L. Barry

Luther's Small Catechism follows the apostolic model, namely, that after repentance (the Ten Commandments), the Gospel (the Apostles' Creed) works faith. The catechumen is then taught the Lord's Prayer and receives Baptism, which is the gateway to his participation in the Lord's Supper. Unless catechesis is understood within a sacramental context, faith is in danger of being understood purely in intellectual terms.

Contemporary Christianity is besieged, no less than was the ancient church, by philosophies threatening the true faith. As in the ancient world, some candidates for Baptism will have virtually no prior knowledge of the Christian faith. Others may come with a faith which is already more fully formed. For those baptized as infants, the formal catechesis comes after Baptism. This is not a post-apostolic distortion of a New Testament practice, but continues the Old Testament practice in which boys were instructed in the meaning of the Passover after they had been included in the community of Israel by circumcision (Ex 12:25–27). Girls were included in that community of faith, though no particular rite of initiation was required for them. Since infant Baptism was in place in the apostolic church, as we have argued throughout this book, these baptized children received the catechesis which was given to their parents before their Baptism. Certain sections of the Pauline epistles address them specifically as members of the baptized community with special instructions.[8]

The understanding that catechesis and Baptism belong together as an indissoluble unit has not been without problems. Children of practicing Christians are more likely to receive catechesis than those whose parents are nominal church members or not members at all. This likelihood has led some pastors to refuse Baptism to children who are brought by their grandparents or other relatives, and not by the parents themselves. One reason given for refusing Baptism in such cases is that no assurance can be given that the faith given in Baptism will be nurtured later in life. Such a refusal correctly sees that Baptism and catechesis form one unit, but fails to recognize that Baptism is a complete work of God in and of itself. If Baptism's effects depended on the certainty that catechesis would follow, then there would be no need for emergency Baptism. Administering Baptism or giving catechesis does not mean that the one cannot or should not be administered without the other

---

(St. Louis: The Office of the President of The Lutheran Church—Missouri Synod, 1996). Along with discussing the role of catechesis in the church today, it provides a survey of the historical development of catechesis from Old Testament times through the New Testament, the ancient church, and the Reformation.

8. E.g. Col 3:20: "Children, obey your parents in everything, for this pleases the Lord"; and Ti 1:6: "If any man is blameless, the husband of one wife, and his children are believers and not open to the charge of being profligate or insubordinate . . ."

following as soon as possible. Let us put aside the question of whether Baptism can be administered to those who openly make a mockery of it; this simply cannot be done. However, determining the probability of a future catechesis is not an issue in deciding which children to baptize. The gifts given an infant in his Baptism are not contingent on the promise of future instruction or his parents' faith. To be consistent, a pastor would have to provide catechesis only to those adults who could give evidence that they would finish the course of instruction leading to Baptism.

Of course, the Scriptures (Mt 13:20–22) and our own experience teach otherwise. No certainty exists that any or all of a pastor's adult catechumens will finish the catechesis leading to Baptism or that they will remain believers after Baptism. Still, no pastor would refuse Christian instruction to apparently unpromising adult candidates. Any failure to finish the catechesis and be baptized does not mean that their catechesis, which is nothing else than the proclaimed Word, should have been refused them or was totally ineffective. The Parable of the Seeds (or of the Sower) carries the message that there is no guarantee that every preaching of the Word will have positive results (Mt 13:1–23). On the other hand, most pastors know of children who were brought to Baptism by those other than their parents and who have been instrumental in bringing their parents into the church. Baptism is a self-contained Word of God, and though connected necessarily with catechesis, its efficacy does not depend upon catechesis. Consider also that Jesus did not make His blessing of the children contingent on the probability that their parents would assure they would receive catechesis later. Like the others who heard Jesus, these parents were very likely also beset with misconstrued ideas about His person and mission. Though it is highly likely that their parents brought these children, there is no explicit reference to them. Considering the structure of the ancient world household, it is equally probable that some children were brought by relatives or other members of the household. Let no one argue that the episodes of Jesus blessing the children have no applicability to Baptism. Surely Jesus receiving the children through blessing them is as effective as His working on them through Baptism.[9]

---

9. Karl Brinkel's *Die Lehre Luthers von der fides infantium bei der Kindertaufe* arose partially in response to the question of the role of Baptism in connection with the catechetical work of the church (6). Churches practicing infant Baptism must have a principle of following up this practice with later instruction in the faith. Since the Reformed and the Roman Catholics are strangely aligned in disagreeing with Lutherans that infants at their Baptism do not have faith, the issue is less problematic for them. The Reformed see infant Baptism only as a symbol of their hope that the child may be among the elect and may believe in the future. Baptism is not fundamentally *sacramental*, in the sense that God is working salvation in the rite itself. Schleiermacher, who would gladly have dropped infant Baptism, could only endorse its continued practice in connection

with confirmation which followed catechesis (*The Christian Faith* 2:634–38, esp. 637).

Roman Catholics hold that Baptism works *ex opere operato* in obliterating original sin apart from faith, but it does not serve as an instrument in forgiving actual sins committed after Baptism. In attempting to maintain the necessary connection between Baptism and catechesis, some of their theologians have urged that adult Baptism be seen as the norm. Making adult Baptism the normative form of Baptism is an unacceptable capitulation to the Baptist position and must be repudiated. The view of these Roman Catholic theologians that infant Baptisms should not be administered where subsequent catechesis is less than fully certain is also common among some Lutherans who favor stringent requirements before baptizing the children of non-members. Catholics who oppose the view that adult Baptism is normative agree with the Lutherans who insist that catechesis follow for those who have been baptized as infants, but at the same time recognize that the validity and efficacy of Baptism does not depend on a formal catechesis. In seeing infant Baptism as a complete salvific act, one Catholic theologian can also speak for Lutherans: "For in infant baptism, as in the celebration of all our sacraments, it is God's word that effects, transforms, reconciles, consecrates, and comforts" (Stasiak, *Return to Grace*, 212).

Bryan Spinks quotes Heiko Oberman that "'an age that thrives on concepts like self-determination and credibility demands adult baptism'" ("Luther's Timely Theology," 40). He goes on with his own observations: "It is no accident that the most recent activity on baptism rites has been concerned with adult baptism—thus the Rite of Christian Initiation of Adults, and the move to make the adult initiation rite the norm in service books" (ibid., 40). What Spinks sees as a positive benefit has led some baptized as infants to request and receive re-baptism from pastors of paedobaptist churches. He notes, "And infant baptism has been under attack. Thus for example in Colin Buchanan's *Infant Baptism and The Gospel*, it is urged that only infants of committed Christians should be baptized. The problem is, what is meant here by 'committed'?" (ibid., 40–41).

CONCLUSION

Nearly all churches practice some form of Baptism, but differences between them come to the surface in the sacrament in which the church's unity has its foundation. Baptism is administered for different reasons, and from it different results are expected. For the Reformed churches which find their origins in Zwingli, Calvin, and Arminius, Baptism is law. Those who practice infant Baptism see it as a regulation necessary to provide cohesion to the Christian community. Others who advocate baptizing only those who have reached the age of reason insist it be administered by immersion. Though these two groups differ on who may be baptized and its form, they agree that salvation cannot be found in or attached to the water. Roman Catholics see Baptism as necessary for salvation and have preserved the ancient baptismal liturgies and practices. In doctrine and practice, Lutherans share a common heritage with them which they do not share with the Reformed. While Roman Catholics see the necessity and importance of Baptism as foundational for Christian life, they see it only as the first of the other necessary church rituals of Confirmation, Penance, and Last Rites which supplement Baptism. To them, the Eucharist is the sum and summary of faith, an honor which Lutherans give to Baptism. In comparison with other churches practicing Baptism, Lutherans have the most comprehensive understanding of what this sacrament is and what it does. Roman Catholics see Baptism in terms of the past tense: it forgives original sin and sins already committed. In contrast, the Reformed see Baptism in terms of the future; that is, it anticipates faith which in the case of an infant is not present at the time the rite is administered, but which they hope will arise at the time of reason and maturity. For Lutherans, Baptism embraces past and future sin and continually creates the faith which it requires. At every stage of life, from infancy to death, Baptism is the constant divine reality for believers.

Current concerns for Lutherans are the place of Holy Communion in the regular Sunday worship and the frequency of its celebration. Confirmation does not have the sacramental implications for Lutherans which it has for Roman Catholics, but Lutherans continue to debate its role in church life and the age for its administration. Private confession and absolution have the support of the Augsburg Confession and the Apology, but continued attempts to reinstitute its practice have not met with much success. The ordination of women has raised many issues in the vast majority of Lutheran churches, especially the issue of the ministry itself. Ironically, Baptism has been used to provide a basis for ordaining women ministers, an argument which raises the question of how then ordination is different from Baptism.

For Lutherans, Baptism should permeate all of Christian life and so stand at the foundation of our sacramental theology and practice, but this has hardly been the case. The majority of Lutheran theologians who have discussed the issue seriously adopt Reformed and even Baptist arguments, the most blatant of which is that infants cannot believe. Current Lutheran baptismal liturgies follow a Reformed practice in placing the emphasis on the promises made by the sponsors, and so detract from the understanding of Baptism as the sacrament of regeneration. Lutherans baptized as infants later as adults make "decisions for Christ," and thus show they do not really believe or at least fully understand that Baptism works the forgiveness of sins and gives eternal life. Sadly, proposed elaborate rites for baptizing adults may carry the message that those baptized as adults have benefits which those baptized as infants failed to experience.

Such pioneer American Lutheran church leaders as Henry Melchior Muhlenberg and C. F. W. Walther were aware that this country's Reformed theological climate was inherently hostile to the success and survival of the Lutheran faith. Their predictions continue to come true all too often. In examining the recent plethora of English translations of the Bible, one scholar concludes that American religious life has its root in the sixteenth- and seventeenth-century sects, including the Anabaptists.[1] This influence, to which Lutherans have not been immune, also accounts for the low esteem in which Baptism is held among Americans.

The only solution in restoring to Baptism the place of importance it has in the New Testament and in the early church is understanding Baptism as a totally christological act—an act or ritual in which Christ baptizes and in which the baptized Christian is joined to Christ's death and resurrection. By His being baptized by John, Jesus was committed by God to death and resurrection, and now in our Baptism he makes us participants in that same death and resurrection. Jesus is at the same time both object and subject of Baptism, the baptized and the baptizer.

---

1. Theodore P. Letis, *The Ecclesiastical Text* (Philadelphia: The Institute for Renaissance and Reformation Biblical Studies, 1997), 168–74. Chapter 8, "The Revival of the Ecclesiastical Text and the Claims of the Anabaptists," 153–204, was originally published in *Calvinism Today* (July 1992). Letis borrows from other scholars, including Nathan Hatch, in making his assessment. America has been the home for Unitarianism, Pentecostalism, and Mormonism, a situation Letis calls "a cocktail of cults." Without adding to his list, we might safely say that none of these sects has a truly sacramental view of Baptism. They also do not baptize infants, with the exception of the Unitarians, who use this as a naming rite and rarely baptize adults. Letis, who rightly sees Calvin as an opponent of sects, fails to mention the Geneva reformer's unfortunate bequest of an unsacramental view of Baptism to American religion.

Conclusion

The One who commands His church to baptize is Himself baptized into death, and baptizes all Christians into that same death. What is confessed in the Apostles' Creed actually takes place concretely in Baptism. Baptism is the summary of the Christian faith and the history of salvation. The waters out of which the world arose, which lifted the ark of Noah, which were separated at the Red Sea, and which at Jordan flowed from the hands of John the Baptist over Jesus to lead Him to His cross—these same waters are found in every font, and embrace all Christendom. When we confess *unum baptisma in remissionem peccatorum*, "one Baptism for the remission of sins," we are only confidently confessing our faith in Jesus Christ, and we and all His church are joined to Him.

BIBLIOGRAPHY

Aland, Kurt. *Did the Early Church Baptize Infants?* Translated by G. R. Beasley-Murray. Philadelphia: Westminster Press, 1963.

———. *Taufe und Kindertaufe.* Gütersloh: Gerhard Mohn, 1971.

Althaus, Paul, Jr. "Martin Luther über die Kindertaufe." *Theologische Literaturzeitung* 12 (1948): 19–31.

Althaus, Paul, Sr. *Die Heilsbedeutung der Taufe im Neuen Testament.* Gütersloh: C. Bertelsmann, 1897.

Asendorf, Ulrich. "Luther's Small Catechism and the Heidelberg Catechism." In *Luther's Small Catechism: 450 Years,* edited by Robert D. Preus and David P. Scaer. Fort Wayne, IN: Concordia Theological Seminary Press, 1979.

Atkinson, James. *Martin Luther and the Birth of Protestantism.* Baltimore: Penguin Books, 1968.

Aulen, Gustaf. *Christus Victor.* Translated by A. G. Hebert. London: SPCK, 1953.

———. *The Faith of the Christian Church.* Translated by Erich H. Wahlstrom and G. Everett Arden. Philadelphia: Muhlenberg Press, 1948.

Bagnall, Ronald B., ed. "Should Babies Be Communed?" *Lutheran Forum* 30 (Winter 1996): 16–35.

Baier, John William. *Compendium Theologicae Positivae,* edited by Carl Ferdinand Wilhelm Walther. St. Louis: Lutheran Concordia Verlag, 1879.

Ballard, Ruth H., Pamela J. Carnes-Chapman, Carol E. A. Fryer, et al. "Open Letter: Turning Down 'Stirring Up.'" *Lutheran Forum* 24 (May 1990): 8–9.

Balthasar, Hans Urs von. "The Holy Church and the Eucharistic Sacrifice," *Communion* 12 (Summer 1985): 139–45.

Barry, A. L. *Catechesis in the Lutheran Congregation.* St. Louis: The Office of the President of The Lutheran Church—Missouri Synod, 1996.

Barth, Karl. *Church Dogmatics.* Translated by G. W. Bromiley. 5 vols. Edinburgh: T. & T. Clark, 1969.

———. *The Teaching of the Church Regarding Baptism.* Translated by Ernest A. Payne. London: SCM Press, 1948.

Barth, Markus. *Die Taufe ein Sakrament?* Zoolikon-Zürich: Evangelischer Verlag AG, 1951.

———. *Ephesians.* The Anchor Bible, vol. 34, nos. 1–2. Garden City, NY: Doubleday, 1974.

Bartlett, David L. *Ministry in the New Testament.* Minneapolis: Augsburg, 1993.

Beasley-Murray, G. R. *Baptism in the New Testament.* Grand Rapids, MI: William B. Eerdmans, 1962.

Die Bekenntnisschriften der evangelisch-lutherischen Kirche. Edited by the Deutscher Evangelischer Kirchenausschuss. 10th ed. Göttingen: Vandenhoeck & Ruprecht, 1986.

Book of Common Prayer and the Administration of the Sacraments and Other Rites and Ceremonies of the Church According to the Use of the Protestant Episcopal

Bibliography

Church in the United States of America. New York: Thomas Nelson & Sons, 1944.
The Book of Concord: The Confessions of the Evangelical Lutheran Church. Translated and edited by Theodore G. Tappert. Philadelphia: Fortress Press, 1959.
Bridge, Donald and David Phypers. *The Water That Divides.* Downers Grove, IL: InterVarsity Press, 1977.
Brinkel, Karl. *Die Lehre Luthers von der fides infantium bei der Kindertaufe.* Berlin: Evangelische Verlagsanstalt, 1958.
Broderick, Robert C. *The Catholic Encyclopedia.* Nashville: Thomas Nelson Publishers, 1976.
Bromiley, Geoffrey W. *Children of the Promise.* Grand Rapids, MI: William B. Eerdmans, 1979.
Brown, Henry F. *Baptism through the Centuries.* Mountain View, CA: Pacific Press Publishing Association, 1965.
Brown, Raymond E. *The Gospel According to John XIII–XXI.* The Anchor Bible, vol. 29, nos. 1–2. Garden City, NY: Doubleday, 1987.
Brunner, Frederick Dale. *The Christ Book.* Waco, TX: Word Publishing, 1987.
———. *Matthew: A Commentary.* Dallas: Word Publishing, 1990.
Bultmann, Rudolf. *The Gospel of John: A Commentary.* Translated by G. R. Beasley-Murray. Philadelphia: Westminster Press, 1971.
Calvin, John. *Institutes of the Christian Religion* (1536 edition). Translated by Ford Lewis Battles. Grand Rapids, MI: William B. Eerdmans, 1975.
———. *Institutes of the Christian Religion* (1559 edition). Translated by Henry Beveridge. 4 vols. in 2. Grand Rapids, MI: William B. Eerdmans, 1994.
Carson, D. A. "Current Issues in Biblical Theology: A New Testament Perspective." *Bulletin for Biblical Research* 5 (1995): 17–41.
———. "Did Paul Baptize for the Dead?" *Christianity Today* 42 (August 10, 1998): 63.
Catechism of the Catholic Church. Mahwah, NJ: Paulist Press, 1994.
Chase, Eugene C., Jr. "The Translation of the Greek Words Τηρέω and Φυλάσσω in the New International Version, and Its Implications for Theology Today." *Lutheran Theological Review* 6 (Spring/Summer 1994): 21–36.
Childs, Brevard S. "Toward Recovering Theological Exegesis." *Pro Ecclesia* 6 (Winter 1997): 16–26.
Collins, John N. *Are All Christians Ministers?* Collegeville, MN: Liturgical Press, 1992.
———. *Diakonia: Reinterpreting the Ancient Sources.* New York: Oxford University Press, 1990.
Cullman, Oscar. *Christian Baptism in the New Testament.* Translated by J. K. S. Reid. Studies in Biblical Theology, no. 1. London: SCM Press, 1950.
———. *Early Christian Worship.* Philadelphia: Westminster Press; Bristol, IN: Wyndham Hall Press, 1953.
Danielou, Jean. *The Theology of Jewish Christianity.* Translated and edited by John A. Baker. London: Darton, Longman, & Todd, 1964.
Davies, J. G. *The Architectural Setting of Baptism.* London: Barrie & Rockliff, 1962.
Davies, William David and Dale C. Allison. *Matthew: International Critical Com-*

mentary. 3 vols. Edinburgh: T. & T. Clark, 1988–97.

DeMaris, Richard E. "Corinthian Religion and Baptism for the Dead (1 Corinthians 15:29): Insights from Archaeology and Anthropology." *Journal of Biblical Literature* 114 (Winter 1995): 661–82.

"Didache." In *The Apostolic Fathers*. Translated by Kirsopp Lake. Loeb Classical Library. 2 vols. Cambridge, MA: Harvard University Press, 1985.

Dodd, C. H. *Historical Tradition in the Fourth Gospel*. Cambridge and New York: Cambridge University Press, 1963.

Ebeling, Gerhard. *Word and Faith*. Translated by James W. Leitch. Philadelphia: Fortress Press, 1963.

Eichrodt, Walter. *Theology of the Old Testament*. Translated by J. Baker. 2 vols. London: SCM Press, 1967.

Elert, Werner. *Der Christliche Glaube*. 5th ed., revised by Ernst Kinder. Hamburg: Furche-Verlag, 1960.

Farmer, William R. *The Last Twelve Verses of Mark*. London and New York: Cambridge University Press, 1974.

Foschini, Bernard Marie. "Those Who Are Baptized for the Dead." *Catholic Biblical Quarterly* 12 (July 1950): 260–76, (October 1950): 379–88; 13 (January 1951): 46–78, (April 1951): 172–98, (July 1951): 276–83.

Gäbler, Ulrich. *Huldrych Zwingli: His Life and Work*. Translated by Ruth C. L. Gritsch. Philadelphia: Fortress Press, 1986.

Gear, Felix B. *Our Presbyterian Belief*. Atlanta: John Knox Press, 1980.

Gerhard, Johann. *A Comprehensive Explanation of Holy Baptism and the Lord's Supper*. Translated by Elmer Hohle. Decatur, IL: The Johann Gerhard Institute, 1996.

———. *Loci Theologici*. 9 vols. 1770. Reprint (9 vols. in 3) edited by Eduard Preuss. Berlin: Gustaf Schlawitz, 1866.

Gieschen, Charles. *Angelomorphic Christology: Antecedents and Early Evidence*. Leiden: E. J. Brill, 1998.

Grane, Leif. *The Augsburg Confession*. Translated by John H. Rasmussen. Minneapolis: Augsburg Publishing House, 1987.

Grenz, Stanley J. *Theology for the Community of God*. Nashville: Broadman & Holman, 1994.

Grudem, Wayne. *Systematic Theology*. Grand Rapids, MI: Zondervan Publishing House, 1997.

Gutmann, Joseph, ed. *Ancient Synagogues: The State of Research*. Chico, CA: Scholars Press, 1981.

Hachlile, Rachel. "Synagogue." In *Anchor Bible Dictionary*, vol. 6. Garden City, NY: Doubleday, 1992.

Hampson, Daphne. *Theology and Feminism*. Cambridge, MA: Basil Blackwell, 1990.

Higgins, A. J. B. *The Lord's Supper in the New Testament*. Reprint. Chicago: Henry Regnery, 1952.

Hodge, Charles. *Systematic Theology*. 3 vols. London: Thomas Nelson, 1873.

Hoekema, Anthony. *Holy Spirit Baptism*. Grand Rapids, MI: William B. Eerdmans, 1972.

Hoenecke, Adolf. *Ev.-luth. Dogmatik*. 5 vols. Milwaukee: Northwestern

Publishing House, 1909–17.

Hoffmann, Gottfried. "Baptism and the Faith of Children." In *A Lively Legacy: Essays in Honor of Robert Preus*, edited by Kurt E. Marquart, John R. Stephenson, and Bjarne W. Teigen. Fort Wayne, IN: Concordia Theological Seminary Press, 1985.

Huovinen, Eero. "*Fides Infantium—Fides Infusa*?: A Contribution to the Understanding of the Faith of Children in Luther." *Lutheran Forum* 30 (Winter 1996): 37–42.

Jenson, Robert W. "Part Two: The Two Sacraments." In *Christian Dogmatics*, edited by Carl E. Braaten and Robert W. Jenson. 2 vols. Philadelphia: Fortress Press, 1984.

Jeremias, Joachim. *Hat die älteste Christenheit die Kindertaufe geübt?* Göttingen: Vandenhoeck & Ruprecht, 1938.

———. *Hat die Urkirche die Kindertaufe geübt?* Göttingen: Vandenhoeck & Ruprecht, 1949.

———. *Infant Baptism in the First Four Centuries*. Translated by David Cairns. Philadelphia: Westminster Press, 1958.

———. *Nochmals: Die Anfänge der Kindertaufe*. Munich: Chr. Kaiser, 1962.

———. *The Origins of Infant Baptism: A Further Study in Reply to Kurt Aland*. Translated by Dorothea M. Barton. London: SCM Press; Naperville, IL: Allensons, 1963.

Johnson, William Stacy and John Leith, eds. *Reformed Reader: A Sourcebook in Christian Theology*. 2 vols. Louisville, KY: Westminster Press/John Knox Press, 1993.

Jungkuntz, Theodore R. *Confirmation and the Charismata*. Lanham, MD: University Press, 1983.

Just, Arthur A. *Luke 1:1–9:50*. Concordia Commentary. St. Louis: Concordia Publishing House, 1997.

Karmiloff-Smith, Annette. "Annotation: The Extraordinary Cognitive Journey from Foetus through Infancy." *Journal of Child Psychology and Psychiatry and Allied Disciplines* 6/8 (1995): 1293–1313.

Kavanagh, Aidan. *The Shape of Baptism*. New York: Pueblo, 1978.

Kelly, J. N. D. *A Commentary on the Epistles of Peter and Jude*. New York and Evanston, IL: Harper & Row, 1969.

———. *Early Christian Creeds*. 2d ed. New York: David McKay, 1960.

Kettner, Edward. "The Practice of Infant Communion." *Lutheran Theological Review* 1 (Fall/Winter 1988–89): 5–17.

Kingsbury, Jack. "The Composition and Christology of Matthew 28:16–20." *Journal of Biblical Literature* 93 (December 1974): 573–84.

Klein, Leonard. "Catholics in Exile." *First Things* 73 (May 1997): 9–10.

Koester, Craig R. "Infant Communion in the Light of the New Testament." *Lutheran Quarterly* 10 (Autumn 1996): 233–39.

Kolden, Marc. "Infant Communion in the Light of Theological and Pastoral Perspectives." *Lutheran Quarterly* 10 (Autumn 1996): 249–57.

Lehmus, Adam Theodor Albert. *Über die Taufe*. Heidelberg: Mohr und Zimmer, 1807.

Leith, John H., ed. *Creeds of the Churches: A Reader in Christian Doctrine from the*

Bible to the Present. 3d ed. Atlanta: John Knox Press, 1982.
Letis, Theodore P. *The Ecclesiastical Text.* Philadelphia: The Institute for Renaissance and Reformation Biblical Studies, 1997.
Lieu, Judith M. "The Mother of the Son." *Journal of Biblical Literature* 117 (Spring 1998): 75–76.
Longenecker, Richard N. *The Christology of Early Christianity.* Grand Rapids, MI: Baker Book House, 1970.
Louw, Johannes P. and Eugene A. Nida. *Greek-English Lexicon of the New Testament.* 2 vols. New York: United Bible Societies, 1988.
Lutheran Church—Missouri Synod. *The Lutheran Agenda.* St. Louis: Concordia Publishing House, 195–.
———. *Lutheran Worship.* St. Louis: Concordia Publishing House, 1982.
———. *Lutheran Worship Agenda.* St. Louis: Concordia Publishing House, 1984.
———. *Small Catechism.* St. Louis: Concordia Publishing House, 1943.
Luther, Martin. *Luther's Works.* Edited by Abdel Ross Wentz. Philadelphia: Fortress Press, 1959.
———. *Luther's Works: The American Edition.* 55 vols. Edited by Jaroslav Pelikan and Helmut T. Lehmann. St. Louis: Concordia Publishing House; Philadelphia: Fortress Press, 1955–72.
———. *The Martin Luther Christmas Book.* Translated and arranged by Roland H. Bainton. Philadelphia: Muhlenberg Press, 1968.
Mann, C. S. *Mark.* The Anchor Bible, vol. 27. Garden City, NY: Doubleday, 1986.
Meuser, Fred. *The Ordination of Women.* Minneapolis: Augsburg Publishing House, 1970.
Meyendorff, John. *Byzantine Theology.* New York: Fordam University Press, 1987.
Moody, Dale. *Baptism: Foundation for Christian Unity.* Philadelphia: Westminster Press, 1968.
Neyrey, Jerome H. "The Footwashing in John 13:6–11: Transformation Ritual or Ceremony?" In *The Social Word of the First Christians: Essays in Honor of Wayne A. Meeks,* edited by L. Michael White and O. Larry Yarborough. Minneapolis: Fortress Press, 1995.
Nichol, Todd W. "Infant Communion in the Light of the Lutheran Confessions." *Lutheran Quarterly* 10 (Autumn 1996): 241–47.
Nuechterlein, James. "Catholics at Home." *First Things* 73 (May 1997): 9–10.
Oberman, Heiko. *Luther: Man Between God and the Devil.* Translated by Eileen Walliser-Schwarzbart. New Haven and London: Yale University Press, 1989.
Oesch, Wilhelm. "Abschluss des Barthischen Lebenswerk." In *Solus Christus Sola Scriptura,* edited by Dieter Oesch. Gr. Oesingen: Lutherische Buchhandlung, 1996.
Pfitzner, Victor. "'General Priesthood' and Ministry." *Lutheran Journal of Theology* 5 (November 1971): 107–8.
Philippi, Adolf. *Kirchliche Glaubenslehre.* 5 vols. Stuttgart: Samuel Gottlieb Liesching, 1864.
Pieper, Francis. *Christian Dogmatics.* Translated and edited by Theodore Engelder, John Theodore Mueller, and Walter Albrecht. 3 vols. St. Louis: Concordia Publishing House, 1950–53.

Bibliography

Prenter, Regin. *Creation and Redemption*. Translated by Theodore I. Jensen. Philadelphia: Fortress Press, 1967.

Preus, J. Samuel. *From Shadow to Promise: Old Testament Interpretation from Augustine to Luther*. Cambridge, MA: Harvard University Press, 1969.

Preus, Robert D. *The Theology of Post-Reformation Lutheranism*. Vol. 1, *A Study of Theological Prolegomena*. St. Louis: Concordia Publishing House, 1970.

Preus, Robert D. and David P. Scaer, eds. *Luther's Catechisms—450 Years*. Fort Wayne, IN: Concordia Theological Seminary Press, 1979.

Reicke, Bo. *The Roots of the Synoptic Gospels*. Philadelphia: Fortress Press, 1986.

Robinson, Armitage. *The Historical Character of John's Gospel*. London and New York: Longman's Green, 1929.

Robinson, John A. T. "The One Baptism." *Scottish Journal of Theology* 6 (1953): 257–74.

———. *The Priority of John*. Edited by J. F. Coackley. Oak Park, IL: Meyer-Stone Books, 1987.

———. "The Significance of the Foot-Washing." In *Neotestamentica et Patristica: Eine Freundesgabe Herrn Professor Dr. Oscar Cullmann zu seinem 60. Geburtstag überreicht*. Supplements to the New Testament, vol. 6. Leiden: E. J. Brill, 1962.

Saarnivaara, Uuras. *Scriptural Baptism: A Dialog between John Bapstead and Martin Childfont*. New York: Vantage Press, 1953.

Sasse, Hermann. *We Confess the Sacraments*. Translated by Norman Nagel. St. Louis: Concordia Publishing House, 1985.

Scaer, David P. "Augustana V and the Doctrine of the Ministry." *Lutheran Quarterly* 6 (Winter 1992): 403–24.

———. "The Doctrine of Infant Baptism in the German Protestant Theology of the Nineteenth Century." Th.D. diss., Concordia Seminary, St. Louis, 1963.

———. "An Essay for Lutheran Pastors on the Charismatic Movement." *The Springfielder* 37 (March 1974): 210–23.

———. *James, the Apostle of Faith*. St. Louis: Concordia Publishing House, 1984.

———. "May Women Be Ordained as 'Pastors'?" *The Springfielder* 36 (September 1972): 89–109.

———. "The Relation of Matthew 28:16–20 to the Rest of the Gospel." *Concordia Theological Quarterly* 55 (October 1991): 245–67.

———. "Sacraments as an Affirmation of Creation." *Concordia Theological Quarterly* 54 (October 1993): 241–64.

———. "The Validity of the Churchly Acts of Ordained Women." *Concordia Theological Quarterly* 53 (January–April 1989): 3–20.

Schaff, Philip, ed. *Nicene and Post-Nicene Fathers*. First series [NPNF]. 1886. Reprint. Peabody, MA: Hendrickson, 1995.

Schleiermacher, Friedrich Daniel Ernst. *The Christian Faith*. Edited by H. R. Macintosh and J. S. Stewart. 2 vols. New York: Harper & Row, 1963.

Schlink, Edmund. *The Doctrine of Baptism*. Translated by Herbert J. A. Bouman. St. Louis: Concordia Publishing House, 1972.

———. *Ökumenische Dogmatik*. 2d ed. Göttingen: Vandenhoeck & Ruprecht, 1985.

Schluter, Richard. *Karl Barths Tauflehre*. Paderborn: Verlag Bonifacius, 1973.

Bibliography

Seizer, Claudia J. "Rulers of the Synagogue." In *Anchor Bible Dictionary*, vol. 6. Garden City, NY: Doubleday, 1992.

Shepherd, Massey H., Jr. *The Paschal Liturgy and the Apocalypse*. Richmond: John Knox Press, 1960.

Spinks, Bryan D. "Luther's Timely Theology of Unilateral Baptism." *Lutheran Quarterly* 9 (Spring 1995): 23–45.

Spiritual Gifts. A Report of the Commission on Theology and Church Relations of The Lutheran Church—Missouri Synod, September 1994, 29–30.

Stasiak, Kurt. *Return to Grace: A Theology for Infant Baptism*. Collegeville, MN: The Liturgical Press, 1996.

Stephenson, John. *Eschatology*. Confessional Lutheran Dogmatics, vol. 13, edited by Robert D. Preus. Fort Wayne, IN: Luther Academy, 1993.

———. "Reflections on the Appropriate Vessels," *Logia* 4 (January 1995): 11–19.

Strong, Augustus Hopkins. *Systematic Theology*. 3 vols. 1907. Reprint (3 vols. in 1). Boston: Griffith & Rowland Press, 1912.

Thielicke, Helmut. *The Evangelical Faith*. Translated by Geoffrey W. Bromiley. Grand Rapids, MI: William B. Eerdmans, 1982.

Thiessen, Henry C. *Lectures in Systematic Theology*. Revised by Vernon D. Doerksen. Grand Rapids, MI: William B. Eerdmans, 1979.

Thomas, John Christopher. *Footwashing in John 13 and the Johannine Community*. Sheffield: Sheffield Academic Press, 1991.

Tillich, Paul. *Systematic Theology*. 3 vols. Chicago: University of Chicago Press, 1951–63.

Toon, Peter. *Born Again*. Grand Rapids, MI: Baker Book House, 1987.

Trigg, Jonathan D. *Baptism in the Theology of Martin Luther*. Leiden: E. J. Brill, 1994.

Vatican Council II: The Conciliar and Post-Conciliar Documents. Edited by Austin Flannery. Wilmington, DE: Scholarly Resources, 1975.

Walch, Johann Georg. *Faith of Unborn Children*. Edited with annotations by Adam Lebrecht Mueller, translated by Otto Stahlke, and edited by David R. Liefeld. St. Paul, MN: Lutherans for Life, 1988.

Walther, C. F. W. *Americanische-lutherische Pastoraltheologie*. 2d ed. St. Louis: Druckerei der Synode von Missouri, 1875.

Wegscheider, Julius August Ludwig. *Institutiones Theologiae Christianae Dogmaticae*. 3d rev. ed. Halle: Gebauer, 1817.

Wenham, John. *Redating Matthew, Mark and Luke*. Downers Grove, IL: InterVarsity Press, 1992.

Werblowsky, R. J. Zwi and Geoffrey Wigoder, eds. *The Oxford Dictionary of the Jewish Religion*. New York: Oxford University Press, 1997.

World Council of Churches. *Baptism, Eucharist, and Ministry*. Geneva: World Council of Churches, 1982.

Yeago, David S. "The New Testament and the Nicene Dogma: A Contribution to the Recovery of Theological Exegesis." *Pro Ecclesia* 3 (Spring 1994): 152–64.

SACRED SCRIPTURE INDEX

Genesis
1:2   60, 116
17:4–8   21
17:19–21   21
24:34   194

Exodus
20:7   161n

1 Samuel
22:16   129n

Psalms
1:1   11
22:1   155n
22:8   155n
54:1   79

Isaiah
Is 12:3   117

Jonah
2:1–10   95

Matthew
1:15   75
1:18   75
1:20–25   75
2:15   75
2:16   138
3:1   36
3:1–6   137
3:1–17   75, 75n
3:2   37, 81, 140
3:5–6   141
3:9   14
3:13–17   105n
3:15   39, 75
3:16   75, 104, 138, 186
3:16–17   46

3:16–4:1   104n
4:1   47, 75, 104, 186
4:17   37, 137, 140
4:24   185
8:5–13   136
9:35   127
9:35–10:1   185, 186
10:1–2   81, 137
10:2   114
10:32–33   82n
11:11–12   36
11:22–32   185
11:27   75, 102, 103, 144
12:5   195
12:21   195
12:22–32   185, 186
12:28   138, 185
12:31–32   195
12:41–42   195
13:1–23   198
13:11   74n, 77n, 103
13:20–22   198
14:19   86
16:17   103
16:18   27, 130
17:22, 23   135
18:1–5   135–37
18:1–14   139
18:1–35   137
18:2–4   136–38
18:5   139, 148
18:5–9   138–40
18:6   136, 138, 140
18:10–14   140
18:20   82, 82n
19:1–30   136
19:13–15   135, 136, 138, 139
19:28   60n
20:17–28   135

20:21   137
20:22–23   40n
20:26–28   135, 137
21:1–45   135
21:9   139
21:14–16   140
21:25   37
25:32   141
26:28   37
27:43   129, 155n
27:46   155n
27:50   104, 105, 138
27:51–54   136
28:1–20   30n, 36, 74, 75, 75n
28:11–15   195
28:16–20   75, 118, 137
28:19   24, 25, 27, 30, 31, 37, 39, 42, 74–76, 79, 86, 91n, 105, 133, 135, 136, 139, 141, 141n
28:19–20   27, 80, 82n
28:20   24, 24n, 28, 28n, 47, 82

Mark
1:4   37, 44, 45, 81
1:4–11   105, 185
1:8   30, 77
1:10–12   104, 185
1:12–28   185
1:34   185
3:14–18   81
7:3–4   94
7:34   187
9:37   139
9:38   88
10:13–16   104n, 136, 138, 139, 149n, 183

211

Sacred Scripture Index

10:38–39   39, 39n, 40, 40n
10:39   44, 110
13:10   80n
14:22   139
16:8   30n
16:9–20   30n, 80n, 81
16:15   80
16:16–17   30, 30n, 42, 80, 81, 155, 162, 185
16:20   131

Luke
1:1–9:50   196n
1:2   86
1:15   103
1:41   148
2:3   44
2:26   195
3:3   81
3:12–16   81
3:15   105n
3:16   77n
3:21–23   104n, 105n
4:16   127
4:44   127
7:33   36
9:48   139
11:20   185
11:38   94
12:50   39, 40n, 44, 110
18:15–17   138–39
22:31   185
23:42–43   161
24:44   195
24:47–49   80, 81
24:49   106

John
1:1–3   74
1:1–14   143
1:6–8   62
1:12   79
1:13   61, 79, 143
1:14   74
1:19–34   62
1:32   39, 104
1:32–36   44
1:33   77n, 103, 104n, 105n
1:35   99
1:35–42   62
1:35–51   37
1:41–42   99
2:1   143
2:12   143
2:28   143
3:1–15   61, 141, 143
3:1–36   36, 53
3:3–5   38n
3:5   53, 60, 61n, 62, 96, 116, 142, 143, 162, 164
3:7   143
3:8   111
3:22   77n, 86
3:22–30   62
3:26   126
3:31   61
4:1   77n, 126
4:1–2   140
4:1–3   37
4:2   77n, 86, 99
4:4–15   117
4:10–14   117
5:2   96
6:11–13   86
7:2   117
7:38–39   116, 116n
8:44   185
9:7   96
13:1–11   97
13:2   185
13:5–11   98
13:21–27   185
13:27   98
15:3   97
17:1   116
18:37   143
19:30   105, 116
19:34   116
19:35   117
20:22   107
20:30   30n
20:30–31   118
20:34   96
21:15   116
21:24   117
21:25   30n

Acts
1:1–26   38
1:4   81
1:5   103, 104, 106
1:15   127
2:1–47   38
2:4   106
2:14–41   195
2:32   103
2:33   78, 81
2:36   46
2:38   41, 44, 45, 74, 77, 78, 91n, 104, 108
2:39   130
2:41   96
2:42   195n
2:47   103
3:12–26   195
4:4   96
5:31   45
5:38–39   46
5:42   195
8:14–18   89
8:17   138
8:26–39   195
8:27   128
8:27–39   126
8:36   138
8:38   85
9:18   195n
9:22   195

212

Sacred Scripture Index

10:1–48   126
10:38   78
10:43–48   45
10:45   108
10:47   108, 139
10:48   74, 77
12:17   131
13:5   127
13:14   127
13:15   128
14:1   127
15:8   131
16:1   128
16:13–15   97
16:15   126
16:16–18   185
16:27–34   126
16:33   97
17:1   127
17:10   127
18:4   127
18:7–8   126, 127n
18:11   196n
18:18   127
19:1–7   37
19:3   97n
19:5–6   108
19:8   127
19:8–9   128
19:10   196n
19:12   185
20:9   196n
22:11   8n
22:16   77n, 96, 99n

Romans
1:4   78
6:1–11   58
6:1–23   95
6:3–4   95
6:4   30, 47, 59, 142, 143
6:10–11   65
8:2   11
8:33   77n

10:4   11
10:9   112
10:10   154
15:16   77n

1 Corinthians
1:1–16:21   76, 131
1:10–16   76
1:10–17   94
1:13   76
1:14   126, 131
1:14–17   86
1:15   126
1:16   126
1:16–17   76
4:15   145
5:6–8   34
6:1–6   54
6:1–11   53
6:3   53
6:10   53
6:11   53, 59, 77–79, 79n, 99n, 108, 145, 154
6:11–20   53, 54
7:14   145, 154, 160n
8:1–9   55
8:6   103
10:1   34
10:1–2   35, 54, 146
10:2   76
10:6–22   185
10:16   139
11:20–22   54
11:24   55
11:26   66
12:3   55, 83, 103, 112
14:1–40   108
14:5   109
14:16   54
14:18   109
14:19   109
14:20–25   109
14:26–28   109
15:1–58   34, 55, 57

15:3–4   113
15:6   38
15:29   34, 54, 56, 58, 58n, 76
16:15   132
16:19   132

2 Corinthians
12:1–10   113
12:11   109
13:14   77

Galatians
1:1–6:18   32, 73
3:27–28   71–73
3:28   132
4:5   64
4:16   77n
6:2   11

Ephesians
1:1–6:24   76, 145
2:1–2   185
2:20   114
4:4–6   105
4:8   113
4:16   68n
5:21–6:9   65, 132, 145
5:25   65
5:25–27   59, 145
5:26   62, 77n, 96, 99n

Philippians
2:9–10   79n
2:11   83
3:5–6   195

Colossians
1:1–4:18   32, 141
2:1–23   32n
2:11   145
2:11–12   31, 32, 141n
2:13   145
3:20   197n

213

Sacred Scripture Index

1 Thessalonians
2:13   77n
5:23   77n

1 Timothy
4:13   128, 129

2 Timothy
1:4–5   129
3:15   128, 129

Titus
1:6   197n
3:5   30, 34, 52, 59–61, 99n
3:5–6   96

Hebrews
9:14   105
9:19   96
10:22   96, 99n

James
2:7   82
2:22   127

1 Peter
1:1–5:14   34, 71
1:2   77n
1:21   156n
2:4–10   68n
2:9   71
3:18–22   33, 47
3:20–21   34, 45, 52
5:1–5   72n

2 Peter
3:5   34

1 John
2:1   144
2:12–14   132, 144, 144n
2:18   144
4:5–6   63
5:1   144
5:4   144
5:5–6   144
5:6   37
5:6–8   96, 144

2 John
1   144
13   144

3 John
1   144

Revelation
1:1–7:17   184n
1:1–22:21   82, 184
3:1   82n
3:5   82, 82n
3:12   79n
7:9–17   184
11:18   82n
14:1   82
20:12   159
21:1   60
22:4   82n

LUTHERAN CONFESSIONS INDEX

Apostles' Creed
25, 33, 45, 47, 48n,
103, 183, 187n,
191, 192, 197, 202

Nicene Creed
39, 45, 47, 48n,
103, 192n

Athanasian Creed
106, 192n

Augsburg Confession
6, 12, 14, 16, 18,
29, 51, 133, 161,
163, 200
AC II 12, 15–19, 59,
112, 119, 125, 133,
161, 177
AC II.1 13, 132
AC II.2 107, 132, 142,
161
AC III 133
AC III.2 133
AC III.3 133
AC III.4 133
AC IV 15, 133
AC IV.1 133
AC V 72, 133
AC V.1 69
AC V.2 113
AC VIII.2 88
AC IX 5, 12, 19, 133
AC IX.1 177
AC IX.2 133
AC XII.6 29
AC XIII 51
AC XVI 16

Apology of the
Augsburg Confession
6, 163, 200
Ap. II.2 24
Ap. II.35–37 14, 15
Ap. IX 5, 6, 14
Ap. IX.2 23, 133, 135,
160, 163
Ap. IX.3 114, 135
Ap. XII.46 32
Ap. XIII 51
Ap. XIII.4 29

Smalcald Articles
192n
SA III 5
SA III.v.1 121
SA III.v.3 170n
SA III.viii.7 155
SA III.viii.7–12 155
SA III.viii.8 155
SA III.viii.10 155,
156n
SA III.viii.12 155
SA III.viii.13 155
SA V 5

Small Catechism
24, 29, 30, 52, 59,
60, 62, 80, 92n,
106, 148n, 168,
192n, 196, 197
SC II.3 102
SC IV 5, 24, 81
SC IV.2 41, 84
SC IV.6 63
SC IV.10 96
SC IV.12 50, 95

SC V 29
SC V.8 63

Large Catechism
25, 29, 41, 163,
192
LC II.39 103, 110
LC II.54 103
LC IV 5
LC IV.3–9 24
LC IV.4 10
LC IV.6 14, 17, 25, 42,
162
LC IV.6–9 164
LC IV.8 10
LC IV.21 36
LC IV.27 60
LC IV.28 162
LC IV.28–29 52
LC IV.31 10, 13, 25, 83
LC IV.34 26, 43, 115,
162
LC IV.35 10, 13, 43
LC IV.38–40 11
LC IV.41 12, 41, 49,
50, 86, 113, 114,
162
LC IV.42 64, 69
LC IV.44 49, 52
LC IV.49–51 148
LC IV.54 115
LC IV.55 26, 115, 147
LC IV.56 113
LC IV.58 7, 113
LC IV.60 10
LC IV.65 13, 60
LC IV.71 29
LC IV.76 111

Lutheran Confessions Index

LC IV.77   11, 14, 29, 112, 163
LC IV.77–79   113
LC IV.77–82   114
LC IV.78   163
LC IV.79–82   43
LC IV.82   15

Formula of Concord   15, 163, 164, 192
FC Ep. and SD XII   92
FC Ep. III.15   14
FC SD II.2–5   16
FC SD III.18–19   34
FC SD III.47–49   14

FC SD XII.2   163
FC SD XII.4   20, 163
FC SD XII.9   164
FC SD XII.11   19, 155
FC SD XII.13   155

NAME INDEX

Abelard, Peter 13
Aland, Kurt 119n, 125, 126, 129, 179
Allison, Dale C. 74n, 75n, 82n, 141n, 159n
Althaus, Paul, Jr. 149n, 150
Althaus, Paul, Sr. 148n
Arminius, Joseph 5n, 200
Asendorf, Ulrich 170n
Atkinson, James 2n, 156n
Augustine 97, 119, 121
Aulen, Gustaf 13n, 150
Baier, John William 154, 154n
Balthasar, Hans Urs von 98n
Barth, Karl 3n, 9n, 31, 32, 42, 53n, 55, 59n, 61n, 62, 63n, 68–70, 72, 95, 114, 124, 125, 167–80
Barth, Markus 68n, 124, 173, 174n
Bartlett, David 68n, 69, 70, 70n, 72, 73n, 89
Beasley-Murray, G. R. 35n, 40n, 55, 56n, 57n, 58, 61n, 62n, 77n, 79n, 103n, 125, 136n, 144n, 160n, 162n
Bellarmine, Robert 33n
Bridge, Donald 91n, 174n
Brinkel, Karl 147n, 148n, 156n, 161n, 189n, 198n
Bromiley, Geoffrey W. 163n
Brown, Henry F. 99n, 104n, 181n
Brown, Raymond E. 86, 97, 142n, 143
Brunner, Frederick Dale 36n, 150, 155n
Buchanan, Colin 199n
Bultmann, Rudolf 57n, 58, 58n, 97n
Cabasilas, Nicholas 92n
Calov, Abraham 34n
Calvin, John 5–10, 12, 16–18, 20–22, 25n, 31, 32, 43, 50n, 51n, 53n, 61, 62, 64n, 67, 86, 87, 89n, 102, 103n, 104n, 107, 112–14, 120, 142, 150, 160, 162–65, 169–71, 173, 175–77, 191, 200n, 201n
Carlstadt, Andreas 5, 8
Carson, Donald A. 3n, 56
Childs, Brevard S. 3n
Clemens, Aurelius Prudentius 159n
Collins, John N. 68n
Cullmann, Oscar 98n, 138
Cyprian 97
Cyril of Jerusalem 97
Danielou, Jean 82n
Davies, J. G. 75n, 82n, 85n, 141n, 159n
Davies, William D. 74n, 75n
DeMaris, Richard E. 58
Dodd, C. H. 86, 144n
Ebeling, Gerhard 3n
Eichrodt, Walter 79
Elert, Werner 30n, 150
Eusebius 47n
Farmer, William R. 30n, 162n
Findlay, J. A. 144n
Foschini, Bernard Marie 56
Gerhard, Johann 5, 6n, 32, 32n, 33n, 54, 58n, 118, 154
Gieschen, Charles 78, 79n, 82n
Grane, Leif 14n, 22n, 29, 88n, 114n, 164n
Grenz, Stanley J. 7n, 45n, 61n, 91n, 92n, 103n, 108n, 111n, 136n, 149n, 153n, 162n, 163n
Grotius, Hugo 5n
Grudem, Wayne 9n, 17n, 91n, 92n, 132n, 147n, 151, 151n, 174n

Name Index

Hampson, Daphne 71n, 72n, 73n
Harnack, Adolph von 47n
Hatch, Nathan 201n
Hippolytus 119
Hodge, Charles 50n, 51n
Hoefling, Johann 188n
Hoekema, Anthony A. 102n, 107n
Hoenecke, Adolf 35n, 36, 164n
Hoffmann, Gottfried 124n, 150n, 164n
Hopko, Thomas 121n
Hort, F. J. A. 47n
Hunnius, Nicholas 157n
Huovinen, Eero 148n
Jenson, Robert W. 42n, 74n
Jeremias, Joachim 119, 119n, 125, 129, 138
Jerome 15n, 43
Jungkuntz, Theodore R. 108n
Just, Arthur A., Jr. 196n
Karmiloff-Smith, Annette 151n
Kavanagh, Aidan 194n
Kelly, J. N. D. 47n, 71n, 103n, 192n
Kettner, Edward 48n
Kingsbury, Jack 75n
Klein, Leonard 159n
Koester, Craig R. 48n
Kolden, Marc 48n
Lee, E. K. 144n
Lehmus, Adam Theodor Albert 183n
Letis, Theodore P. 201n
Lieu, Judith M. 143n
Loehe, Wilhelm 183
Longenecker, Richard N. 82n
Louw, Johannes P. 93n, 100n, 101n
Luther, Martin 1, 2, 3n, 4n, 5–8, 10, 11, 13, 15n, 19–21, 24–27, 29–36, 39–43, 46, 49–52, 53n, 57, 59, 60, 63–67, 69, 73, 75, 77n, 79–81, 83, 85–87, 92n, 95, 96, 100, 102, 103, 104n, 105, 106, 107n, 110–15, 120–22, 123n, 124, 133n, 137, 140, 141, 147, 148, 149n, 150, 152–55, 156n, 157, 159, 160, 161n, 162–66, 168, 169, 170n, 172–74, 176, 181, 182, 184, 185n, 186, 187n, 188–93, 195n, 197
Mann, C. S. 40n, 56n, 58n
Marcion 11
Marcus, Joel 116, 117
Martensen, Hans Lassen 188n
Melanchthon, Philipp 3n, 6, 20, 24, 29, 51, 114, 160
Meuser, Fred 73n
Meyendorff, John 4n, 50n, 92n, 120n, 153n, 181n
Moody, Dale 125n, 129n, 132n, 137n, 144n, 149n, 150n, 159n
Muhlenberg, Henry Melchior 201
Müntzer, Thomas 8
Neyrey, Jerome H. 99n
Nichol, Todd W. 48n
Nida, Eugene A. 93n, 100n, 101n
Nuechterlein, James 83n, 159n
Oberman, Heiko 2n, 6n, 8n, 24n, 133n, 167n, 188n, 199n
Oesch, Wilhelm 124n, 179n, 180n
Osiander, Andreas 14, 192n
Pelagius 13, 16n
Pfitzner, Victor 73n
Philippi, Adolf 64n
Phypers, David 91n, 174n
Pieper, Francis 36, 67n, 83, 87, 94, 96n, 131, 136, 148, 149n, 150, 153, 154, 157n, 159, 160, 164n, 183, 188n
Prenter, Regin 39n, 60n, 78, 136, 150, 166n
Preus, J. Samuel 20n
Preus, Robert D. 157n
Quenstedt, John Andrew 148
Reicke, Bo 75n
Rietschel, Georg 156n
Robinson, Armitage 38n
Robinson, John A. T. 38, 38n, 86, 86n, 98n, 178
Saarnivaara, Uuras 147n

Name Index

Sasse, Hermann 125n
Scaer, David P. 33n, 71n, 72n, 75n, 82n, 109n, 165n, 183n, 188n
Schleiermacher, Friedrich Daniel Ernst 64n, 67, 121, 124, 149, 150n, 168–70, 176, 198n
Schlink, Edmund 24n, 74n, 149n
Schluter, Richard 180n
Scotus, Duns 170n
Seizer, Claudia J. 128n
Shepherd, Massey H., Jr. 82, 184n
Spener, Philip Jacob 3n
Spinks, Bryan D. 104n, 184n, 189n, 191n, 192n, 199n
Stasiak, Kurt 188n, 194n, 199n
Stephenson, John R. 14n, 165n
Strong, Augustus Hopkins 7n, 92n, 95n
Tappert, Theodore G. 162n
Tertullian 15n, 97, 119
Theodoret of Cyprus 123n
Thiessen, Henry C. 41n, 91n
Thomas, John Christopher 98n
Thomasius, Gottfried 188n
Tillich, Paul 177, 178
Toon, Peter 7n
Trigg, Jonathan 1n, 2n, 15, 32n, 33n, 43, 46n, 49n, 50n, 51, 52n, 63n, 66n, 107n, 112n, 121n, 152n, 163n, 169n, 185n, 187n
Walch, Johann Georg 156n
Walther, Carl Ferdinand Wilhelm 83, 84n, 148, 154, 154n, 183, 201
Wegscheider, Julius August Ludwig 24n, 64n, 182n
Wenham, John 131n
Wesley, John 111
Westcott, B. F. 144n
Windisch, H. 144n
Yeago, David S. 3n
Zwingli, Ulrich 3, 5, 6, 8, 9, 17, 20–22, 31, 32, 107, 121, 162, 163, 168–70, 173, 174, 176, 189, 200

SUBJECT INDEX

Abortion 120, 151, 156n, 158, 159n
Abraham 120, 141n
Absolution 29, 49, 200
Adam 4n, 13, 16, 18, 54n, 60, 61, 95, 122, 133, 158
Adiaphora 9n
Adult Baptism 95n, 124n, 150n, 179n, 180, 199n
Anabaptist 3, 5–10, 17, 19–22, 25, 27, 28, 91, 92, 107, 114n, 120, 140, 147, 148n, 149, 155, 156n 161–65, 165n, 167, 171, 173, 174, 194, 201
Anglicanism 10n, 108, 168, 182
  See also Church of England
Apostles' Creed 25, 33, 45, 47, 48n, 103, 183, 187n, 191, 192, 202
Arianism 92
Arminianism 5, 5n, 6, 184
Atonement 13, 17, 135
  limited 17n
Baptism 48n
  adult 124n, 150n, 179n, 180, 199n
  believers' 91, 115
  by blood 161
  conditional 66
  emergency 164, 177, 182n
  in the Holy Spirit 93, 105, 107, 108, 110, 112, 114
  in the name of Jesus 74, 77, 106, 110
  inner 102, 107, 112, 114, 168, 193n
  internal 112
  of the Holy Spirit 42, 102, 104–7, 110–14
  outer 107
  second 3
  water 41n, 107, 112, 168, 170

Baptism of John. *See* John the Baptist, baptism of
Baptismal
  grace 4
  necessity 120
  regeneration 94, 108, 151n, 174, 183, 186, 188n
Baptists 2, 3, 6, 8, 19, 21, 35, 66, 91–95, 101, 102, 103n, 113, 114n, 115, 129, 137, 147, 150n, 151, 152, 153n, 154, 158, 161, 163–65, 167, 173, 178, 180, 183, 199n, 201
Brefe 138, 139
Calvinism 6, 20
Catechesis 194–96, 197n, 198, 199n
Catechumens 119
Catholic. *See* Roman Catholic
Catholic Church, Catechism of the 4n, 15n, 22, 28n
Catholic Encyclopedia 22n
Charismatic 102n, 107, 108, 111, 113, 114
Children, unbaptized 158, 159, 163
Chrismation 48n, 153n
Church of England
  Thirty-nine Articles of the 10n
  See also Anglicanism
Circumcision 1n, 6n, 31–33, 35, 104n, 120–22, 132, 140, 141n, 145, 147n, 149, 159, 173, 194, 197
Coming One 37, 38, 46
Confession 29, 49
  private 200
Confirmation 3, 15, 42, 48, 69n, 70, 111, 112, 114, 153n, 199n, 200
Conversion 31, 59, 103, 111n, 137, 174
Corpus Christianum 19n

Subject Index

Covenant 1, 31, 33, 63, 112, 160, 167, 188, 191, 194
Decision theology 22, 61, 94, 171, 201
Depravity 14, 17
  universal 18, 24
Didache 46, 99, 100, 195, 196n
Divine name 105
Doctrines
  fundamental 157, 157n
  non-fundamental 157n
  primary 157n
  secondary 157n
Eastern Orthodoxy 3, 4, 48, 50, 92, 93, 95, 100, 111, 112, 119, 120n, 121n, 153n, 181
Election 16, 107, 107n, 160
Enlightenment 3n, 13, 16, 64, 84, 111n, 121, 137n, 149, 168, 173, 176, 180, 182, 183
Epiklesis 111
Eucharist 2, 4n
Exorcisms 111, 152, 153, 182–86, 184n, 191
Extreme Unction 42
Faith 2, 31
Father-Son–Holy Spirit 13, 46, 74–76, 79, 110, 152
Fides aliena 188, 189
Fides infantium 124, 133, 138, 156n, 188, 190
  See also Infant faith
Fides parentium 188, 189
Fides qua 137
Fides quae 137, 188
Flood 31, 33, 35
Flood Prayer 35, 36, 95, 104n, 105
Footwashing 97, 98n
Future faith 160, 161n
Gospel 10, 11, 26, 28
Gratia infusa 14, 22
Habitus 14
Heidelberg Catechism 170n
Holy Spirit 12, 37, 38, 75, 77, 102–18, 130, 134, 138, 144, 151n, 153, 172, 187n, 188, 192
Household 126–29, 131, 132, 141, 147n
Illumination 67
Immersion 7, 91–101, 113, 163, 181, 200
Infant communion 48n, 159n
Infant faith 120, 133, 147–54, 155n, 156, 156n
  See also Fides infantium
Jehovah's Witnesses 109
John the Baptist 35, 37–39, 62, 96, 97, 99, 103, 104n, 148, 154, 155, 160, 202
  baptism of 40, 44, 97n, 103, 104n, 105, 106, 136, 137, 140, 195
Jordan River 36, 96, 97, 104n, 105, 126, 141, 193n, 203
Justification 2, 12, 15, 18, 100, 120, 148, 154, 195n
Koluein 138
Last Rites 200
Law 10, 11, 26, 28
Limbus infantium 22, 23, 161, 161n
Liturgy 46, 47, 52
Living Bible 45n
Methodism 5n, 111, 183
Ministry 68, 68n, 69, 71–73, 88, 114
Mormonism 109, 201
Neo-Evangelical 41
Neo-orthodox 168
Neo-Pentecostal 107
Nicene Creed 39, 45, 47, 103
Oikos 126, 135
Old Testament 31, 32, 35, 39
  rites 31
  sacraments 32n, 33n
Opus alienum 17
Ordination 68–70, 73, 88
  of women 69, 71, 73, 200
Original sin 3–5, 12, 14, 16, 18, 94, 119, 120, 122, 133, 159, 163, 182, 183, 185, 186, 199n, 200
Paidia 138, 144

Subject Index

Palingenesia 34
Papacy 9
Pelagianism 18, 22, 119, 137, 163n, 184
Penance 3, 4n, 15, 29, 42, 48, 60, 64, 69n, 112, 114, 200
Pentecostalism 93, 108, 111, 158, 201
Pietism 3n, 128, 183
Predestination 5n
Priesthood
 royal 68n
 universal 71
Purgatory 28
Rationalism 3n, 176, 182n, 184
Rationalists 24, 64, 149, 182, 186
Reformation 91, 92n, 94, 100, 107, 111, 132, 150n, 162, 167, 174, 178, 182, 194
Reformed 2–5, 6n, 7n, 8–12, 17n, 21, 22, 32, 33n, 41–44, 51, 64, 64n, 67, 79, 92, 93, 102, 107, 108, 112–14, 120, 150, 151n, 155, 157n, 158, 160, 161, 163n, 164, 165, 169, 173, 175–77, 182, 187, 188, 190, 191, 198n, 200, 201
Regeneration 2n, 59, 60, 96, 103, 107n, 112, 113, 143, 148n, 149n, 151n, 164, 169, 173–75, 181–83, 185n, 186, 188n, 189, 192, 201
 baptismal 94, 108
Renaissance 16
Renunciation 182–84, 184n, 186
Repentance 43, 81, 95, 136, 137, 150, 187n

Righteousness 167
Rites of Christian Initiation for Adults 95n
Roman Catholicism 3, 4n, 14, 15, 17, 22n, 28, 33n, 42, 43, 48n, 50, 51, 60, 66, 66n, 68n, 71, 94, 95n, 108, 111, 111n, 112, 120, 161–64, 167, 168, 171, 175–77, 182, 187, 188n, 194, 198n, 199n, 200
Sacraments 1n, 6, 6n, 8, 10, 19, 24, 31, 32–33n, 42, 44, 48n, 51, 52, 53n, 63, 85, 118, 157, 157n, 169, 170n, 172, 176–78
Sanctification 68, 73, 100, 103, 110
Schleiermacher 149
Schwärmer 111
"Second blessing" 111, 111n
Sign of the cross 100, 183
Socinianism 184
Speaking
 in foreign languages 108
 in tongues 108
Spirit of Christ 106
Stellvertretender Glaube 189
Submersion 96
Synagogue 126–29, 127n
Teknia 143, 144
Tongue-speaking 108, 109, 113
Trinitarian formula 74–80, 83, 84
Unitarianism 201
Universalism 137
Vicarious faith 189
Washing 93n, 96–98, 100, 145, 146
World Council of Churches 114
Zwinglians 162, 165

www.ingramcontent.com/pod-product-compliance
Lightning Source LLC
Chambersburg PA
CBHW060950230426
43665CB00015B/2142